THE HUMAN TRADITION IN MODERN LATIN AMERICA

This Mexican lottery card from the 1920s identifies the "new woman" as a threat to social order.

THE HUMAN TRADITION

IN MODERN LATIN AMERICA

EDITED BY

WILLIAM H. BEEZLEY

AND

JUDITH EWELL

A Scholarly Resources Inc. Imprint
Wilmington, Delaware

Scholarly Resources Inc.
104 Greenhill Avenue
Wilmington, DE 19805-1897

Library of Congress Cataloging-in-Publication Data

The human tradition in modern Latin America / edited by
   William H. Beezley and Judith Ewell.
      p.   cm. — (Latin American silhouettes)
   Includes bibliographical references and index.
   ISBN 0-8420-2612-6 (cloth : alk. paper). —
ISBN 0-8420-2613-4 (pbk. : alk. paper)
      1. Latin America—History—19th century. 2. Latin
America—History—20th century. 3. Latin America—
Biography. 4. Social change—Latin America—History.
I. Beezley, William H. II. Ewell, Judith, 1943–   .
III. Series.
F1413.H87   1997
980.03—dc21   97-20943
                                                            CIP

⊗ The paper used in this publication meets the minimum
requirements of the American National Standard for per-
manence of paper for printed library materials, Z39.48, 1984.

To our parents,

Lorene A. and Howard "Red" Beezley,

Claude and Betsy Ewell, and Ruth Ewell,

vital parts of the Human Tradition

I believe in aristocracy, though—if that is the right word, and if a democrat may use it. Not an aristocracy of power, based upon rank and influence, but an aristocracy of the sensitive, the considerate, and the plucky. Its members are to be found in all nations and classes, and all through the ages; and there is a secret understanding between them when they meet. They represent the true human tradition, the one permanent victory of our queer race over cruelty and chaos. Thousands of them perish in obscurity, a few are great names. They are sensitive for others as well as for themselves, they are considerate without being fussy, their pluck is not swankiness but the power to endure, and they can take a joke.

—E. M. Forster, *Two Cheers for Democracy*

About the Editors

WILLIAM H. BEEZLEY, the Neville G. Penrose Chair of Latin American History at Texas Christian University, has focused his research in recent years on the cultural history of Mexico. This interest has resulted in the publication of *Judas at the Jockey Club* (1987); and *Rituals of Rule, Rituals of Resistance* (1994), with Cheryl Martin and William French. With Linda Curio-Nagy, he is working on a book on Latin American culture and history. He edits Scholarly Resources's Latin American Silhouettes series with Judy Ewell and the Jaguar Books on Latin America with Colin MacLachlan. He also authored, with Colin MacLachlan, *El Gran Pueblo: A History of Greater Mexico* (1994).

JUDITH EWELL is Newton Family Professor of History and chair of the History Department at the College of William and Mary. Most of her research and publications have been in the field of Venezuelan history, including her most recent book, *Venezuela and the United States: From Monroe's Hemisphere to Petroleum's Empire* (1996). She regularly teaches both semesters of the survey of Latin American history, in addition to specialized courses on Brazil, Mexico, the Caribbean, and inter-American relations. As a senior Fulbright lecturer, she also has taught at universities in Venezuela and Ecuador.

Acknowledgments

T he authors of the biographies in *The Human Tradition in Latin America* for the nineteenth and twentieth centuries realized our goal of making the region's history have meaning in terms of individual lives. These life histories gave texture, example, humor, and sorrow to the great events of the past two centuries. In sum, the authors used vignettes to put a human face on the past. In this new, combined volume, our selections reflect a need to give general coverage to the era since independence, to the diversity of nation-states, and to the human dimensions of gender, generations, ethnicity, class, and rural-urban origins. Our choices have been difficult indeed, and we urge readers unfamiliar with the two volumes from which this collection is drawn to consult them and to read the biographies not included here. We have thanked personally all of the authors, but we want to express in print our appreciation for their helping us make the history of Latin America come alive.

Additional background has been provided by the editors in an effort to expand and clarify the political, economic, and social context of the lives of the individuals whose biographies are recounted. Our decision to offer these enlarged discussions of historical circumstances results from the recommendations of teachers who have used *The Human Tradition* in their classes. Of the many instructors who have sent us suggestions and criticism, we single out as representative José Moya of UCLA and Darrell E. Levi of Florida State University for their comments and revisions. The changes in this volume reflect their experience and comments to us. Of course, in addition to thanking these instructors, we extend our appreciation to the students who used the volumes as texts and who made clear their opinions about them, either commenting or complaining to their professors about the strengths and weaknesses. We hope that the books persuaded them to see history as the experiences of a multitude of individuals.

Finally, we extend our gratitude to the editorial staff at Scholarly Resources, who over the years have become not simply our colleagues but also our friends. To Richard M. Hopper and his "team"—Carolyn J. Travers, Ann M. Aydelotte, Sharon L. Beck, and Eileen M. Schultz—we offer E. M. Forster's "two cheers"!

William H. Beezley
Judith Ewell

Contents

Introduction

Westerners have assumed until recently that the traditional societies that encountered modern values and technology were "people without history," passive vessels into which the liquid of Western culture was poured.[1] The persons in this book, on the contrary, have met head-on the changes that uprooted the traditional certainties of their lives. These disruptions, often labeled as progress, sometimes shattered lives, and sometimes inspired creative adjustments to new circumstances. Their adaptations in turn have contributed, in small ways, to a changing social environment. These personal and individual responses are valuable for what they reveal about the durability of the human spirit. They also suggest the many levels on which the dissemination and acceptance of modernization have occurred.

Within Western culture, there has long been a prevailing belief that change—any change—not only is good but also is an improvement that will fit, tongue in groove, with other improvements and within other cultures. Western-style change, so the notion runs, will slowly construct as near perfect a world as humanity can achieve: Western values, especially those liberal tenets that emerged in the eighteenth century, are touted as both universal and modern; Western social science (economics, law, politics, sociology) can guide the reshaping of traditional societies; and Western science will provide a value-free framework for modernization.

Latin American voices have been raised since the late colonial period in challenges to some of the premises of Westernization. In the eighteenth century, Spanish economic and administrative reforms often spurred prosperity for the port cities along South America's east coast, while for the hinterlands they began the process of isolation and abandonment. These reforms from within the Spanish and Portuguese empires, had they continued, might have gradually found ways to reconcile the European-style urban, liberal sectors of the colonies with the rural, traditional elites and their peasant allies. But in 1808, Napoleon's troops occupied the Iberian Peninsula, ending these reform efforts. Latin American colonials suddenly faced new opportunities and new challenges. Urban elites, who had had a head start in adjusting to the enlightened trends, seized the opportunities that political independence offered. Even for these elites, however, independence from Spain and Portugal did not mean autonomy from foreigners, either economically or culturally. Further, for many of the Latin Americans in rural areas, the nineteenth century meant the overwhelming or distortion of traditional culture and relationships as they endured what E. Bradford Burns has called the "poverty of progress."[2]

After 1900, the pressures on individuals and communities became more pervasive. Technology and capital provided roads, bridges, cars, telegraph lines, and radio and television signals, reaching into even the most remote regions of Latin America. In most cases, political rule, still in the hands of the urban elite, assumed a more modern form, using technology and the military to strengthen the dominance of principal cities over rural areas. In most cases, the major city—Mexico City in Mexico, São Paulo in Brazil, Buenos Aires in Argentina, Caracas in Venezuela, Lima in Peru, Santiago in Chile—in effect became the nation and either reshaped or ignored the hinterlands. The modern emphasis on individualism, secularism, and capitalism discounted or destroyed the organized protection offered to ordinary people by village, religion, or family. Some rural individuals chose to remain in the countryside where urban, liberal values had penetrated to a lesser extent. Even there, however, they were often driven by necessity to experience a measure of "modern life," to cross the divide from penurious self-sufficiency to earning pay for work in another man's field. For others the perils of progress appeared when they left their village and moved to the city, when they gave up their ancestral land to work in a factory or go into domestic service.

Political movements, sometimes inspired by foreign pressures or ideologies, have also contributed to changing the social landscape of Latin America. For individuals, joining or refusing to join with guerrillas or government soldiers, aiding combatants or resisting their demands for the produce from their corn patches, altered the humdrum pace of everyday life. For much of the last two centuries, the majority of Latin Americans, whether they live in the cities or the country, have inhabited a kind of borderland between the old and the new. They have been neither Luddites intent on resisting all change nor passive sponges ready to soak up all change. They have made decisions based on their best judgment as to their own interests, limits, and possibilities.

These biographies form a balance wheel, a necessary corrective to the great themes used to organize the history of the past—liberation, urbanization, industrialization, modernization, unionization, male chauvinism, political mobilization, capitalism, and Marxism. These grand-sounding words are poor collective nouns for the lives they purport to represent. Social historians, using census and other statistical data, have sometimes identified the everyday people beneath these terms. Generally, however, flesh-and-blood people have seldom squirmed out of the maze of charts and graphs.

Revitalizing our understanding of the lives of ordinary people must begin by breaking up the dreary high seriousness about their history. Humor leaks out of the past despite historians' best efforts to ignore it. Through the centuries, life, for all its travails, has had its moments of laughter, of pleasure, and of satisfaction. To watch one's children at play, to pick a pocket with a feather-light touch, to joke with friends, to dance until dawn, to win a fight, to exult at one's skill in weaving a blanket or in patting out perfectly round tortillas—these moments cannot be neglected in any account of everyday life. In fact, those individuals who wrestled with progress did so in order to preserve these good parts of life, to protect them from change and from those who would diminish them. Anguish, hunger, misery, and death form a labyrinth without escape. Humor, pride in accomplishment, and human warmth afford consolation in the midst of despair.

The Human Tradition in Modern Latin America tells a story of courage, not only to get up and face another day but also to start out with hope, determination, and, sometimes, a smile. These women and men lived their lives with pluck and stubbornness. They were not blank tablets on which progress wrote with impunity.

II

"The past is a foreign country," writes novelist L. P. Hartley; "they do things differently there."[3] Indeed, the last two centuries of Latin American history constitute for us one of the most foreign of "countries," with cities and pampas, mountains and rivers that must be traversed in our imagination in order for us to meet a host of exotic people. On these journeys, we are occasionally explorers, sometimes travelers, or even tourists. Paul Fussell, author and literary critic, says that "the explorer seeks the undiscovered, the traveller that which has been discovered by the mind working in history, the tourist that which has been discovered by entrepreneurship and prepared for him by the arts of mass publicity."[4] The traveler's mind has more trouble "working in history" if it has never experienced the physical landscape in the present. Can the Rockies prepare us for the Andes, or the Mississippi for the Amazon? When Argentine writer and president (1868–1874) Domingo Faustino Sarmiento explains the difference between the civilized city and the barbaric countryside, do we see in our mind's eye Kansas City and the Nebraska plains? Do we understand "civilization" in the way that he meant it? Contemporary analogies can erect barriers between us and the reality of the past. The word "city" applied to Buenos Aires in 1820 or to Lima in 1870 may conjure up mental snapshots of New York or Miami or Raleigh in the 1990s. The space, the terrain, the language, and the people are foreign to us even as we travel through time and space to try to penetrate the history of Latin America.

Although the people whose stories appear here seem far removed from our lives, most have the qualities that E. M. Forster admires as part of the "true human tradition." We may cringe at the suffering that some of them endured or contributed to, or at the violence that pervaded their lives. Still, we can empathize with the courage and ability that gave most of them the "power to endure" through the "cruelty and chaos" of the distant and recent past.

We might reflect, as historian Lucien Febvre does about life during the French Renaissance, on the effect on people of their physical surroundings. A late twentieth-century individual—urban, sedentary (or sweaty after jogging), and literate—must exercise great imagination to understand people who were none of those. "What a large place the word 'comfort' has come to occupy in our language, modern comfort in which we take such pride," Febvre muses. "What implications the word has, of convenience and material ease: a light turned on or off at the flick of a finger, an indoor temperature independent of the seasons, water ready to flow hot or cold, as we wish, anytime, anywhere."[5] We take these things for granted, and yet surely they affect the assumptions we make about the past.

How, then, to understand those people who lived in a less comfortable past? In addition to different physical and material environments, there are different moral and intellectual ones. What does "freedom" mean to a sneaker-shod California teenager? What did it mean to a bandit in early nineteenth-century Mexico, a Peruvian tenant farmer in 1920, or a Sandinista sympathizer in 1970s Nicaragua? How would they define "liberalism," "conservatism," "federalism," "progress," "selfishness," and "community"? For that matter, did the abstraction "liberalism" have any more meaning to the average person in nineteenth-century Latin America than the abstraction "existentialism" has to most twentieth-century North Americans? Perhaps their operative meanings are similar to what historian Eric Hobsbawm suggests for his social bandits—that is, a bandit can play out a gut-level meaning of freedom or justice without being able to write a treatise on these concepts.

Febvre also has an answer. "Renaissance, Humanism, Reformation are not mere abstractions, personifications wandering over the heavens where the Chimera chases Transcendent Ideals. To understand these great changes we must re-create for ourselves the habits of mind of the people who brought them about."[6] Yet reconstructing "habits of mind" probably is more of a challenge than that which confronts the contemporary archaeologist who must reconstruct an eighteenth-century brick, ceramic jug, or building. Although it is impossible, Febvre concedes, to recreate the people of the Renaissance, we must "evoke them, projecting onto the screen of our imaginations some typical silhouettes."[7] By studying these silhouettes we should be able to comprehend the texture of a society, its ambience, and how it differed from our own. The essays in this volume constitute a guide to an understanding of the inhabitants of that foreign country of Latin America over the last two hundred years.

III

If abstractions like "Humanism" can lead us astray, so too can general terms such as "Latin America" or even "nineteenth century." To suggest that there was a common Latin American experience from 1800 to 1900 is patently absurd. Arguably, Agustín Marroquín in Mexico in 1810 may have had less in common with Emilio Coni of 1890s Argentina than he did with Billy the Kid of New Mexico.

Traditional histories of nineteenth-century Latin America
have subdivided the period and imposed an intellectual or
thematic order to disparate people and places. The most common subperiods have been the age of independence, dominated by the arrogant profile of Simón Bolívar, the tragic
figure of Father Miguel Hidalgo, and the self-deprecating
General José de San Martín; the age of the caudillos, where
Juan Manuel de Rosas forever rides his horse across the
pampas, the scourge of *unitarios*, foreigners, and indigenous
peoples alike; and the age of positivism or modernization,
where we discern the shape of railroad cars, barbed wire,
European immigrants, and cities replete with Parisian-style
boulevards and gracious parks. Each of these "ages" has become an abstraction, a stereotyped silhouette if you will, to
represent the long nineteenth century. Narrative textbooks
leave us with sharp images of the period, but their stereotypes may foster easy generalizations and misunderstandings. They also omit much of the detail in the rich historical
tapestry of the period.

Other historians reject the narrative textbook imagery
in favor of more analytical treatment. Speaking of the century as a whole, Burns refers to a "poverty of progress," in
which liberal urban values that measure progress by production slowly overtake the communal traditions of the folk,
to their detriment. Stanley and Barbara Stein write of the
expansion of capitalism that gradually draws Latin America
more securely into the world system.[8] Still others see a real
modernization and improvement in the political, social, and
economic institutions of the region with the appearance of
technology, education, trade, and improved ports and transportation. Each of these intellectual models helps us to understand the century as a whole—as, too, the notion of the
age of the caudillo does—and offers a good basis for comparative world history. But the people often remain encased,
frozen and nonhuman, in the reified categories of class, community, region, or modes of production.

We know that "in real life," people can play many different roles and that different people, even different historians, might describe the same behavior in different ways.
Louis Pérez, Jr., writing of vagrants and social bandits in
Cuba in the 1890s, observes that "in 1895 the bandits became patriots."[9] Richard Slatta similarly notes that the mere
passage of a law turned gauchos from free men into vagrants,
hounded by the police.[10] Rebecca Scott points out that

Cuban slaves were actors in their own drama in addition to being extras in the plays written by the white elite.[11] Frank Safford warns us that even when we generalize about the upper class, "the use of such categories as landowner, merchant and professional as ways of dividing social interest groups is implausible, because the upper classes in nineteenth-century Spanish America lacked the specificity of function that this description implies."[12] Thus, some examination of individual biographies, although inadequate alone as "history," can help to reveal the complexities beneath historical narrative and analysis.

Both the narrative approach and the grand constructs tend to leave out the people. The followers of Juan Manuel de Rosas remain as shadowy background figures, mere extras in the epic drama. Nor do the folk, or the *jornaleros* or proletariat, stand out any more clearly in most of the analytical studies. There are several reasons for the absence of people in nineteenth-century Latin America. Most obviously, the civil conflicts occupied more attention than did official record-keeping. It is a painstaking job to research the lives of nonfamous individuals for the nineteenth century. Even the more distant colonial period has much richer sources, fed by the Iberian mania for documents. As important as the relative lack of sources, however, has been the way that historians have seen the nineteenth century in the region. After the drama of the Independence Wars, historians have tended to scurry through the century, treating the period as a transition, a necessary but boring link between an Iberian colonial past and the contemporary nation-states in an international setting. Thus, people, the actors on this grand stage, are not seen as individuals in themselves, at least in part because the whole period marks only a parenthesis between two more dramatic epochs. When historians do examine the period more carefully, they tend to look for surviving colonial institutions and traditions or for precursors of subsequent conditions. The nineteenth century becomes part of a purposeful unfolding of history in which "each link in the genealogy, each runner in the race, is only a precursor of the final apotheosis and not a manifold of social and cultural processes at work in their own time and place."[13]

Historians often assume a unilinear transition, the infamous "seamless web" of history. As Florencia Mallon argues, those who have written about political revolutions and the development of national ideologies in the nineteenth century have a "positivist unilinear view of historical development that by definition assigns no creative role to nonbourgeois classes, pre-Enlightenment politics, or non-Western regions in the genesis of nationalism."[14] It matters not whether the direction of the line is a rising one hailing modernity and progress, or a falling one lamenting the distance from a more generous and humane past: it is the direction on which we focus rather than the plots on the line along the way.

Some historians recently have begun to examine more carefully the nineteenth century, to question our assumptions about this transitional period. Most agree that the late colonial crisis, or the wars for independence, did indeed cause a shock to the colonial synthesis. And the dramatic upheavals and conflicts of the century also highlight important changes and continuities. Yet a closer study of the social history of the period can test our assumptions about change, its direction, and its meaning. For example, Steve Stern argues that examination of political action during abnormal times may lead us to assumptions that people passed through intermittent waves of passivity and reaction. With regard to peasants or country people, we only see them as victims, as those who react to the changes forced upon them by others or by the dynamism of the capitalist system. Looking at people's daily adaptations and resistance to change can give us a fuller appreciation of how change occurs. People, after all, are "continuously involved in the shaping of their societies."[15] This shaping covers not only political values but economic and social ones as well.

IV

There is a natural divide in Latin American history that falls roughly in the early twentieth century, with World War I and the Mexican Revolution serving as vital signposts. After about eight decades dedicated to a struggle for progress, events began to undermine confidence in it. Western art, literature, and scholarship became imbued with the despondency of unfulfilled expectations. As historian Barbara Tuchman comments, "We suffered the loss of two fundamental beliefs—in God and in Progress; two major disillusionments—in socialism and nationalism; one painful revelation —the Freudian uncovering of the subconscious; and one unhappy discovery—that the fairy godmother Science turns out to have brought as much harm as good."[16]

Tuchman's first crisis, the loss of faith in religion and in progress, had a different history in Latin America. For most of the nineteenth century, the two competed as opposites. Because Roman Catholicism formed the backbone of the Iberian heritage, those who wanted to preserve this legacy took up arms to support the Church; opponents who wanted progress through secularization proposed to knock down what they perceived as the major obstacle, the Church and its clerical bureaucracy. In most nations, the liberal, anticlerical forces like those of Benito Juárez in Mexico had won by the beginning of the twentieth century, and the Catholic Church surrendered, for a while, much of its wealth and its political power. Yet as people accepted the weakening of the temporal power of the Church, they also saw flaws in the Western ideologies of progress, principally liberal positivism. Could the positive values of the traditional order be incorporated into a more humanistic progress?

The elites had seen, or claimed to see, irreconcilable dichotomies in the struggle between the Church and positivism. Largely unnoted by the elites, many people continued to blend Catholicism with folk and popular beliefs in much the same way as had the indigenous population from the moment of the Iberian spiritual conquest. Catholic traditions mixed with indigenous ones, *macumba* and *voudoun* existed alongside the formal Church, Jews and Mennonites added a different viewpoint in some regions, popular nature cults such as the María Lionza one took on new life as country people brought them to the urban centers. The wisest of the spokesmen for the Catholic Church saw the vitality of popular religion, even as had some of the first missionaries in the sixteenth century, and joined that spiritual energy to the formal Church in base Christian communities and liberation theology. The wisest of political leaders tried to work with folk religion instead of against it.

Do Latin Americans share Tuchman's asserted loss of faith in socialism? Or, though Tuchman does not add this, with capitalism? Some of the 1920s and 1930s experiments with socialism in Latin America—Argentina, Chile, Bolivia—failed, but ideals of socialism continue to be alive: in base communities, in the rhetoric of Mexico's PRI or Venezuela's AD, in the influence of the Socialist International in Latin

America in the 1970s and 1980s, in the "military socialism" of Juan Velasco Alvarado in Peru, in Sandinista Nicaragua, or in the functioning of some agrarian communities. Some may be disillusioned with socialism or communism in Cuba or Nicaragua or with the rigidity of Communist parties or the violent wastefulness of guerrilla warfare. Others find the expression of a communal value more compatible with the Iberian tradition than is liberal capitalism. Few Latin Americans espouse a pure, "ideal" socialism, while most echo the words of Juan Perón and other political leaders in asserting that their models are "neither capitalist or Communist." The invention of "state capitalism" further attests to creativity in adapting ideologies to Latin American conditions. Popular ideas, individual and community choices, have contributed to eclectic political programs. The ideas could be as disparate as Emiliano Zapata's demand to have the community land of Anenecuilco returned to the villagers or UNAG's (National Union of Small Farmers) pressure on Sandinista Nicaragua to retain individual ownership of small properties.

Latin Americans may never have had the same faith in the infallibility of science that many Anglo-Americans have had. Since the sixteenth century modern science and technology have usually come from outside the Iberian tradition. As relative outsiders for so many years, Latin Americans more freely could see that science was the source of both good and evil: it may eliminate malaria with chloroquine or DDT or entire populations with napalm or nuclear holocaust. Railroads allow easier access to foreign markets but bring foreign imports that destroy the livelihood of local artisans. Improved agricultural technology and transportation give a reason to seize peasant lands and produce strawberries for export rather than beans for domestic subsistence. Modern machinery improves production but eliminates jobs. Helicopters carry the sick to hospitals but transport soldiers to intimidate rural communities. Many Latin Americans find their imagination as captured by the U.S. astronauts walking on the moon as they were in the 1920s with Charles Lindbergh's flight across the Atlantic. But they are hardly so naive as to believe that they can receive the benefits of modern science without paying a price.

The malaise and disillusion that afflict the largely middle-class, literate societies of Europe and the United States have not touched Latin America in the same way. Latin Americans have tested and tried both material and intellectual culture coming from abroad. The changes produced by this onslaught of foreign values and technology have often caused distress and discontentment. They have often altered or even destroyed traditional communal and family patterns. Yet the examination of responses to these changes says much for the resiliency of individuals and of societies. Perhaps 1990s intellectuals and philosophers from the so-called developed world might do well to emulate their predecessors of the 1920s and 1930s who looked to non-Western societies for inspiration.

Throughout the years of travail that followed World War I, there survived what E. M. Forster called the representatives of the "true human tradition." These ordinary people won what he declared as humanity's only victory over cruelty and chaos because "they are sensitive for others as well as for themselves, they are considerate without being fussy, their pluck is not swankiness but the power to endure, and they can take a joke."[17]

V

The biographies of such people fill this volume. One or two, Forster's "few great names," might have left enough records for a complete biography, but most lived in such obscurity that they cannot be considered alone. Nevertheless, together they make a collective statement about the dogged determination to take the measure of circumstances and make a life despite all obstacles.

Each of these persons actually lived; several are still alive today. Some have chosen pseudonyms, and those instances are noted in the introduction to the essay. Whether these persons bear real or assumed names, their stories illustrate many of the constraints that face Latin Americans as well as the ways in which individuals can nonetheless give meaning to and achieve satisfaction in their lives. What emerges as limiting circumstances will surprise few: nationality, gender, ethnic or racial heritage, illiteracy, and economic class represent real obstacles. What also emerges as the common disregard of these obstacles will encourage many. Several individuals in this anthology ignored the boundaries imposed on them by the circumstances of their birth and chose to make a different destiny for themselves. With little alternative but to straighten the backbone and stiffen the upper lip, they made the best of life and even on occasion enjoyed it. Their decisions rarely had the hoped-for results, but these actions did change their lives.[18] Few individuals here would oppose changes that they initiate themselves, but progress to most people means change imposed from the outside, a great force that overwhelms any opposition.

Revolution has sometimes been described as progress in that the ordinary person has a say in the changes that occur once the revolution succeeds. Yet, while they are being fought, revolutions mean many things to many people. The Independence Wars, sometimes called revolutions, carried different views of freedom to Simón Bolívar and Marroquín. During the Mexican and Cuban revolutions, some people fought for agrarian reform, some for industrialization, some for women's rights, some for personal power or wealth, some to be free of foreign control, some for new constitutions and laws, some for implementation of old laws and constitutions, some for individual freedom, and some for collective cooperation. Not all of those who were on the winning side won their revolution. For many, especially for women, the elderly, young people, and country people, revolution often appeared to be more changes imposed from without in the name of revolutionary progress.

Surviving in the crucible of change has forced individuals to develop thick hides, tough attitudes, and innovative behavior. Strategies of survival in Latin America demonstrate the diversity of individual responses to modernization and offer suggestive examples for students of other Third World nations.

Latin Americans have been able to draw on a long history of individual and collective responses to change. In the continent the process of European expansion and colonization extended over a long period of time. Thus, during the colonial era it is possible to see the indigenous and later mestizo (mixed ethnic) groups respond to Iberian culture, adjust to it, survive it, and alter it.[19] Then, beginning in the mideighteenth century, these same groups faced a more subtle but more pervasive effort to modernize them, to draw them into the economic and intellectual world of non-Iberian Europe. The pace of scientific and technological change accelerated rapidly in the twentieth century. From the days of the Conquest many Latin Americans have lived in a series of frontiers where values and cultures have clashed and where people have, consciously or not, found ways to combine change and tradition.

It has been easier to plot the interactions between indigenous cultures and conquering cultures in collective terms than in individual ones.[20] An exception to that rule is David Sweet and Gary Nash's compilation of twenty-one biographies of individuals in the Anglo and Iberian New World during the colonial period. Entitled *Struggle and Survival in Colonial America*, the volume includes life histories that reveal both successful and unsuccessful efforts to meet the challenges posed by cultural ambiguity. These people chose strategies of accommodation or of confrontation to survive and even prosper. Most of them, as we all do, influenced their families, friends, and neighbors. Some of them found that their individual actions of accommodation or of defiance also affected the wider community in which they lived.[21]

For the nineteenth and twentieth centuries, the scale of the societies under study has encouraged anthropologists and ethnohistorians to drop down to the village, community, or regional level to study the adaptation to change. Anthropologists have done the pioneer work, often in studies which allow the reader to examine the effects of change at a given time; names like Robert Redfield in Mexico, Charles Wagley in Brazil, Lisa Redfield Peattie in Venezuela, and Oscar Lewis in Puerto Rico and Mexico come to mind. An understanding of the slow process of cultural change can be facilitated if records allow for the study of a longer time period. In *San José de Gracia: Mexican Village in Transition*, Luis González lovingly traces the history of the village for nearly two hundred years as roads, trade, and an expansive federal government intrude more and more.[22] Several other recent works have followed the pace of change in areas which, until relatively recently, have been the hinterlands.[23] These studies highlight community strategies to accommodate the "second conquest" of modernization, much as Charles Gibson, Nancy Farriss, and Karen Spalding chronicled the reactions to the "first conquest" of the sixteenth century.[24]

In the twentieth century, Latin Americans have used the same strategies that ethnohistorians, anthropologists, and the authors of the Sweet and Nash essays describe—that is, some persons have simply fled to more remote areas of the countryside or even to another nation to find a more desirable existence. A few have escaped through drugs, alcohol, or insanity. Other rural people have exchanged one kind of cultural frontier for another by moving to the cities. Many have modified their lives in outward ways to satisfy the authorities that represent the state, or the labor boss, or some cultural agent (such as soldiers carrying out civic action, Peace Corps personnel, or priests). Still others have survived because in the process of modernization, the traditional population has engulfed the modern society and imposed enough trappings of the old way that it looks like home.

These techniques for creating a little room for independent maneuvers within the maelstrom of modern life reveal the toughness of the human spirit in Latin America. They offer points of comparison with other parts of the world that have faced modernization or Westernization and show how resourceful are everyday people. In colonial times, the Spanish viceroys had the privilege of responding to a royal order with the litany of *Obedezco pero no cumplo* (I obey, but I do not carry [it] out). Everyday people, or the "aristocracy of the plucky," as E. M. Forster would describe them, have often taken the same approach to the changes that modernization represents to them.

As we embark on our journey to meet some city and country folk in Latin America, a doubt arises. What do the people whom we shall meet along the way have in common? Febvre argues that projecting their lives in some detail upon the screen of our imagination can help us to understand a period and its prevailing attitude. But how do we know that these people are typical? Or in what ways are they typical? Or atypical? Can we tell the difference?

Emilio Coni in the Buenos Aires of the 1890s will tell us a different story from that of Agustín Marroquín of Mexico in 1810 or from that of Leticia in Nicaragua in the 1970s. For that matter, the neighbors of Coni and Marroquín and Leticia might rip up our pages of notes and insist that we listen to them in order to get the story right. Unfortunately, we do not have the luxury of interviewing all the people who knew our subjects. Few were important enough to merit more than a mention in the "regular" history books. When the liberal, urban historians did grant them a line or two, they shaped their stories to fit their own views of national progress and civilization. Mandeponay no doubt appeared to some as a savage. Carlota Lucia de Brito would have been a *sinvergüenza* (shameless one) or *pobre mujer* (poor woman), and Patrícia Galvão was a crazy woman who scribbled.

These silhouettes do not constitute a random sample of all possible types we might encounter. Rather, they may provide a cross section, both vertical and horizontal, of social types in time and space. They differ greatly from each other, but each is prominent enough or deviant enough to have left sources, or "tracks," as French historian Marc Bloc would have it. In that, we have to recognize that perhaps none of them is entirely "average." Still, we can learn both from the nearly average and from the deviant and from combinations of the two.

Indeed, how can someone who is clearly a deviant—a sociopath, for example, or a camp follower—reveal anything about "normal" society? Historians Robert Forster and Orest Ranum argue that "the moral and social values of a society, especially on the level of collective mentalities and community behavior, are clarified by the study of those who reject those values and are cast out of society."[25] In fact, a silhouette is a profile that can only be comprehended by looking at the background—like the ones in children's books which reveal two different faces according to whether the observer focuses on the black space or on the white space. We can see something from the way their contemporaries treat deviants, from the way the laws and institutions see them. The psychopath Marroquín was lauded when he assisted the "right" side. Nicolás Zúñiga y Miranda represented both a fool and a savant to Mexicans who lived under the Porfirian dictatorship. We see what the Brazilian empire considered deviant, and what it considered appropriate punishment, when we study the life of Carlota Lucia de Brito. If our silhouettes are sharply defined, we can reach some conclusions about the typical and the deviant.

In our magic lantern show—the projection of individual silhouettes over the history of Latin America—we will meet each person as an individual. Yet the profile that he or she casts might be common enough so that hundreds, or even thousands, of people could cast roughly the same shadow. For some of our people, we are fortunate enough to have some inklings of their internal lives as well as the external shape of their behaviors and the reactions of their contemporaries. Can a silhouette, then, be three-dimensional?

These essays will not explicitly discuss the rather fleshless abstractions of aggregate terms such as class, ethnic group, and gender. Again, however, we may employ our own historical imagination to ask the question, To what extent is Ofelia Domínguez Navarro representative of her gender and class? Does Mandeponay tell us anything about Indians overall? Can we understand the role of the Church in Brazil better from knowing something of the concerns of Maria Ferreira dos Santos? Our answers will vary with the specific individual and the depth of the portrait.

We must be alert to the possibility of committing an ecological fallacy when we consider the individuals. No one truly can "stand for" his or her group. Noting that Juan Esquivel behaved in a certain way or believed certain things does not enable us to assert that all Peruvian tenant farmers thought the same way. Yet we must also comment that any aggregate portrait of a group—Indians, for example, or the bourgeoisie—similarly cannot allow us to make any assumptions about the behaviors or beliefs of an individual who is a member of that group. If we concede that it is as fallacious to argue from the particular to the general as it is to argue from the general to the particular, then we may conclude that a full understanding of a historical period may require us to study both the particular and the general. A textbook generalization or a theoretical model of "modernization" needs to be looked at as a general context against which we may place both the murderer Ligia Parra Jahn and the bricklayer Miguel Rostaing as part of Latin America's human tradition.

NOTES

1. Eric Wolf, *Europe and the People without History* (Berkeley: University of California Press, 1982).

2. See E. Bradford Burns, *The Poverty of Progress: Latin America in the Nineteenth Century* (Berkeley: University of California Press, 1980).

3. Quoted in David Lowenthal, *The Past Is a Foreign Country* (New York: Cambridge University Press, 1986), xvi.

4. Paul Fussell, *Abroad: British Literary Traveling between the Wars* (New York: Oxford University Press, 1980), 39.

5. Lucien Febvre, *Life in Renaissance France*, ed. and trans. Marian Rothstein (Cambridge, MA: Harvard University Press, 1977), 3.

6. Ibid., 2.

7. Ibid.

8. Stanley J. and Barbara H. Stein, *The Colonial Heritage of Latin America: Essays of Economic Dependence in Perspective* (New York: Oxford University Press, 1970).

9. Louis A. Pérez, Jr., "Vagrants, Beggars, and Bandits: Social Origins of Cuban Separatism, 1878–1895," *American Historical Review* 90 (December 1985): 1121.

10. Richard W. Slatta, "Rural Criminality and Social Conflict in Nineteenth-Century Buenos Aires Province," *Hispanic American Historical Review* 60 (August 1980): 450–75.

11. Rebecca J. Scott, *Slave Emancipation in Cuba: The Transition to Free Labor, 1860–1899* (Princeton, NJ: Princeton University Press, 1985).

12. Frank Safford, "Politics, Ideology, and Society in Post-Independence Spanish America," in *The Cambridge History of Latin America* (New York: Cambridge University Press, 1985), 3:405.

13. Wolf, *People without History*, 5.

14. Florencia Mallon, "Nationalist and Antistate Coalitions in the War of the Pacific: Junin and Cajamarca, 1879–1902," in *Resistance, Rebellion, and Consciousness in the Andean Peasant World, 18th to 20th Centuries*, ed. Steve J. Stern (Madison: University of Wisconsin Press, 1987), 233–34.

15. Steve J. Stern, "New Approaches to the Study of Peasant Rebellion and Consciousness: Implications of the Andean Experience," in ibid., 10.

16. Barbara W. Tuchman, *Practicing History: Selected Essays* (New York: Alfred A. Knopf, 1981), 269.

17. E. M. Forster, *Two Cheers for Democracy* (New York: Harcourt, Brace and Company, 1951), 26.

18. Novelist Ken Follett discusses briefly this question of individual actions versus great forces controlling the lives of people in the introduction to *The Modigliani Scandal* (New York: New American Library, 1985), a thriller in which he attempted to illustrate his conclusions.

19. William B. Taylor in *Drinking, Homicide, and Rebellion in Colonial Mexico* (Stanford, CA: Stanford University Press, 1979) argues, for example, that the principal characteristic of Spanish colonial rule was its relative lightness. Indigenous peoples who survived the shattering military conquest of the first fifty years often found that they were left relatively alone as long as they did not reject Spanish rule and as long as they supplied whatever tribute was required of them. The Spanish had no interest in, and indeed not the resources for, cultural annihilation.

20. Several excellent volumes examine the ways in which indigenous cultures survived the Spanish and Portuguese efforts to impose European culture, especially its economic and religious forms. Charles Gibson in *The Aztecs under Spanish Rule* (1964) showed the way, and Nancy M. Farriss's prize-winning *Maya Society under Colonial Rule: The Collective Enterprise of Survival* (1984) explores the strategies of flight, outward acculturation, and accommodation to the conquerors that enabled the Mayas in Yucatán to adjust and survive during the colonial period. Farriss correctly points out that the Mayan strategies also modified the Iberian culture that was developing in Yucatán. For the Peruvian colonial period, two other prize-winning works have analyzed the arduous and complex process of cultural interaction: Karen Spalding's *Huarochiri: An Andean Society under Inca and Spanish Rule* (1984) and Steve J. Stern's *Peru's Indian Peoples and the Challenge of the Spanish Conquest: Huamanga to 1640* (1986).

21. David G. Sweet and Gary B. Nash, eds., *Struggle and Survival in Colonial America* (Berkeley: University of California Press, 1981).

22. Luis González, *San José de Gracia: Mexican Village in Transition* (Austin: University of Texas Press, 1972).

23. Florencia Mallon, *The Defense of Community in Peru's Central Highlands: Peasant Struggle and Capitalist Transition, 1860–1940* (Princeton, NJ: Princeton University Press, 1983); Robert Wasserstrom, *Class and Society in Central Chiapas* (Berkeley: University of California Press, 1983).

24. See note 20.

25. Robert Forster and Orest Ranum, eds., *Deviants and the Abandoned in French Society* (Baltimore: Johns Hopkins University Press, 1978), viii.

I

The Independence
Generations: Between Colony
and Republic, 1780–1830

Most Latin Americans had been content to be part of the great Iberian empires, even as those empires were in decline. They did have a number of specific grievances against the colonial administrations, but only a few individuals, such as Simón Bolívar and Francisco Miranda of Venezuela, advocated independence for Latin America before 1808. European events provided the shock that allowed republican ideology to spread. When Napoleon I invaded the Iberian Peninsula in 1807, he drove the Portuguese and Spanish kings into exile. Napoleon's brother, Joseph Bonaparte, ruled Spain until 1814. Six years of a French king, whose reign was considered illegitimate by Spanish Americans, sufficed to allow the seed of independence to grow in America. Dom João VI, the Portuguese king, fled to Brazil and ruled his empire from there between 1808 and 1820. He raised the status of Brazil to that of co-kingdom with Portugal, and when he reluctantly returned to Portugal in 1820, he left behind his oldest son, Pedro I, as regent of Brazil. In 1822, Pedro I declared the nation's independence from Portugal almost without any bloodshed.

The wars for independence in Mexico and Central America were long and drawn out (1808–1821) and were tinged with social and ethnic tensions. Thousands of Indians and mestizos followed two priests, Miguel Hidalgo and José María Morelos, between 1810 and 1815 in a campaign for independence and social justice. The threat of class warfare scared the white creole elite and generally turned them against independence. In the essays that follow, we see that the bandit Agustín Marroquín (a Creole) joined Hidalgo's forces (Chapter 1). Marroquín's earlier life, however, suggests that Hidalgo's ideals attracted him less than did the opportunity to pillage and to get even with his enemies. After the uprising of the lower classes had been quelled, the white creole elite more readily embraced independence. The career of

1

Marroquín also tells us much about the life of early nineteenth-century Mexicans and how the Spanish system of justice worked.

In South America the year 1810 marked the beginning of the white Creoles' movement toward separation from Spain. Conventional history highlights the activities of Bolívar or of Mariano Moreno and José de San Martín of Argentina as well as the constitutions and grand military campaigns of the era. Beneath the surface of the South American march to republicanism existed some of the same ambiguities, albeit muted, of the Mexican wars. Argentines and Brazilians fought each other over the flat grasslands between southern Brazil and the Plata River. Yet patriotic zeal appeared to drive the combatants less than did the desire to build up and protect personal empires of land and cattle. The essay on Maria Antônia Muniz (Chapter 2), who lived for over one hundred years on that harsh frontier, suggests that life there was much the same before, during, and after the Independence Wars. Muniz's family history further reminds us that not all Latin American extended families helped and supported each other.

Clearly, the Independence Wars (1810–1825) did not provide the sharp break between a colonial past and a republican future that idealists hoped for and loyalists feared. Creole society, values, institutions, patterns, and habits persisted. Still, independence did soften the rigidity of colonial class and ethnic divisions, thereby providing greater opportunities for talented individuals, if not for the majority. Some of those who worked hard, moved quickly, and avoided political conflicts could begin to acquire wealth, just as Maria Antônia did. The quickest route to success was through military prowess and forceful leadership. Marroquín met a fate common to leaders of colonial rebellions. The experiences of these two Latin Americans can help us to imagine better their complex world while also inviting us to reconsider the meaning of abstractions such as patriot, royalist, and independence.

1

Agustín Marroquín:
The Sociopath as Rebel

Eric Van Young

The Mexican struggle for independence was especially complex. As Prussian scientist and traveler Alexander von Humboldt pointed out in the early nineteenth century, Mexico enjoyed the richest and most diversified economy of all the Spanish possessions. Its population in 1814—at 6,122,000 the largest in Latin America—consisted of Spaniards, Creoles (American-born Spaniards), mestizos, mulattoes, blacks, and Indians. Mexico City was the second largest in the Spanish empire, after Madrid, and there were also other major cities in the colony, such as Guadalajara, Puebla, Guanajuato, and Valladolid (Morelia). The majority of the Mexican population, especially the Indians, lived in the countryside. Law and order in the countryside and small towns frequently was erratic at best. The Spanish simply did not have the resources to police adequately all of their extensive domain, although some would argue that the relative lightness of administration was a calculated imperial policy to defuse resistance. In fact, rebellions had been few and those usually directed at specific abuses, but ethnic tensions smoldered beneath the surface of this dynamic society.

Father Miguel Hidalgo's "Grito de Dolores" of September 16, 1810, ignited the Independence Wars and attracted "patriots" who responded for many reasons, personal as well as political. For example, Agustín Marroquín began his career as an outlaw in the 1790s, landed in jail several times, and finally was executed in 1811 as one of Hidalgo's patriotic followers. Marroquín forces us to question again what independence meant to the soldiers who fought for it (or against it). Ironically, he was a Creole and not part of the colored masses generally thought of as Hidalgo's followers. As he examines Marroquín's life, author Eric Van Young keeps in mind historian Eric Hobsbawm's theory of social banditry. Van Young concludes, however, that Marroquín committed his crimes for his own satisfaction and wealth and not because he was playing the role of a Robin Hood pleasing the poor with crimes against the rich.

This essay also allows us to examine Spanish administration and criminal justice in the last days of the empire. From what we find we might characterize colonial justice as either ineffective or surprisingly

3

generous to common criminals. Retribution came more swiftly—and with fatal results—to Marroquín for his role as a patriot (or traitor, as the royalists would have it) than it did for his crimes as a robber and murderer.

Eric Van Young, professor of history and associate director of the Center for U.S.-Mexican Studies at the University of California at San Diego, is one of the most accomplished historians of late colonial and independence-period Mexico. His forthcoming revised second edition of *Hacienda and Market in Eighteenth-Century Mexico: The Rural Economy of the Guadalajara Region, 1675–1810* will be followed by his major study of the era of Mexican independence. Professor Van Young received his Ph.D. from the University of California at Berkeley.

A SHOOT-OUT IN GUADALAJARA

On Monday morning, November 11, 1805, the chief magistrate of Guadalajara, don Tomás Ignacio Villaseñor, one of the most important citizens of one of New Spain's most important provincial capitals—a major landowner and the scion of an illustrious family of ancient, conquistador lineage—sat down to write an account of a police action the previous night and to initiate formal criminal proceedings against the bandit Agustín Marroquín and several accomplices. Informed that a highly suspicious group of men were living in a house in the city's *barrio* (quarter) of the Colegio de San Diego, and that the men never ventured out of the house during the daytime but only at night, Villaseñor had resolved to investigate the matter, as was his duty. Around midnight of Sunday, November 10, he had gone to the house with a large detachment of armed soldiers and constables, whom he prudently placed around it. After repeated knockings on the door and injunctions to open in the name of the king, all of which failed to produce any response from the darkened house, Villaseñor ordered the soldiers to break down the door with their rifle butts. Forcing their way into the house, they were greeted with a hail of bullets, and in the ensuing shoot-out two of the soldiers were wounded. Marroquín and an associate, half dressed, were pursued into the patio of the house by several soldiers. Urged by one of these to give himself up to the king's justice, Marroquín replied, "I'll give myself up, you bastard!" and shot the man at point-blank range, although not fatally. Throwing down their pistols, Marroquín and his confederate were arrested along with five unarmed men encountered hiding in various parts of the house and stable, and three women and the landlord found cowering in one of the bedrooms of the house. A number of witnesses to the incident attested that Marroquín had said openly that if he had stayed at his original post in the living room when the soldiers invaded the house, he would have been able to kill six or seven of them. The bandit also inquired ominously of one young officer the name of the magistrate who had commanded the party "in case some day we meet again."

Agustín Marroquín was to remain imprisoned in Guadalajara almost exactly five years to the day of his capture. He was freed in November 1810 by Father Miguel Hidalgo's talented and loyal lieutenant José Antonio ("El Amo") Torres when Torres took the city for the rebel cause and almost immediately emptied the local jails. Hidalgo made Marroquín a captain in the rebel army within a matter of days, and he apparently held the priest's confidence until both were captured by royalist forces the following winter and executed in the early summer of 1811. Marroquín's name is that most commonly associated, besides Hidalgo's own, with the mass executions of European Spaniards that took place in Guadalajara during December and January 1810–11. How had Marroquín come to be in Guadalajara, and what were the outlines of his career prior to 1810? In attempting to answer these questions, we can gain insight into the nature of late colonial Mexican society—a sense of its color and texture—as well as into the nature of the social space created by rebellion, and of at least one of the types of men who erupted into that space. While the social matrix of Marroquín's life is less clear than that of some other secondary leaders, and his short revolutionary career in some ways less representative of the era of rebellion as a whole, his personal story is nonetheless a kind of metaphor for an entire aspect of the period and worth the retelling in and of itself.

A LIFE OF CRIME

Marroquín's life is largely a blank until we encounter him at the age of about twenty, under prosecution for a number of serious offenses and already with a full-blown criminal career of some years behind him. An American Spaniard (Creole), he was born in about 1774 in the provincial city of Tulancingo, to the northeast of Mexico City, the center of an extended rural jurisdiction embracing a population of about thirty-five thousand.[1]

Although nothing is known of his parentage or early life, there are strong cumulative indications that he came from much the same type of middling rural background as many other provincial revolutionary chieftains, or perhaps even a cut above. For one thing, he was literate. For another, what we know of his family, his marriage, at least some of his personal associations, and possibly his wider social connections tends to indicate a middling status in provincial society. His uncle, don Francisco Marroquín, was a priest in the Tulancingo area who enjoyed good relations with local land-owning Creoles and sheltered his errant nephew on at least one occasion, when Agustín was recuperating from an illness. Marroquín's wife, doña Dolores Saldierna, was the daughter of a local estate administrator. One of Marroquín's best friends was a local schoolteacher from a small village in the Zempoala district, a Spaniard named Joseph Diosdado. At one point Agustín worked as a mule driver for a Mexican nobleman resident in Mexico City, a post it is unlikely he would have obtained without some personal connection, however minimal. Furthermore, the fact that Marroquín held the position of sergeant in the provincial militia of Tulancingo, and was by virtue of his position immune from civil prosecution because of the military *fuero*, also indicates a certain social cachet.[2]

As far as Marroquín's personal characteristics are concerned, one has the impression of a man at once devious and ingenuous, charming but inconstant and, on occasion, sadistic, capable of being ingratiating with authorities but prone to challenge authority figures, personally fearless and even reckless, generous and acquisitive, petulant, intelligent, and given over entirely and without conscience to a life of idleness when he could manage it and of undiscriminating crime against individuals and the state whenever his resources dwindled. In short, Agustín Marroquín probably can reasonably be described as a sociopathic personality.[3] He had at least two mistresses recorded in the documents relating to him, and he was strongly implicated in the alleged murder of one of their husbands. He was a notoriously good judge of horseflesh, enjoyed some fame as a bullfighter, and obviously liked to live well. Marroquín was openhanded with his confederates and others; he enjoyed the reputation in his bandit days of being "generous" and of having an easy, intimate manner. He was an object of not unsympathetic curiosity among people whom he had not victimized, and one witness in an 1805 robbery case involving Marroquín attested that he and a local woman had wanted very much to meet the famous highwayman in person.

We first pick up Marroquín's criminal trail in 1795, by which time he was already a robber of considerable notoriety in his hometown of Tulancingo. At the age of twenty he was known as an habitué of *pulquerías* (pulque shops),[4] games of chance, and cockfights. He was a well-known figure on the streets of Tulancingo and was obviously the central member of a little group of criminal associates. He made himself persona non grata among the decent citizens of Tulancingo not only by his swaggering wantonness but also by his preying upon businesses in the town through extortion and robbery, a pattern he was to maintain, as circumstances allowed, over the next decade. Given his obvious intelligence and the equally obvious counterproductiveness of thus fouling his own nest, his local criminal activity suggests a studied defiance and insouciance, a provocative "catch-me-if-you-can" attitude borne out in the impression conveyed by his own statements and later activities.

Marroquín apparently had served at least one term in jail by the age of twenty, probably for tobacco smuggling. In this same year of 1795 he was brought up on charges (the nature of which are vague) and, after briefly attempting to claim sanctuary in a church, was sent to jail in Mexico City and then in Tulancingo. After serving more than two years he escaped in December 1797, smashing through the half-open door of the town jail while several Indian laborers were cleaning out the night soil of the inmates. He was not reapprehended until February 1799. In the meantime, he went to the Gulf Coast, near Veracruz, where he was taken on as an employee by a prominent local hacendado on the recommendation of Marroquín's uncle, the priest. Here Marroquín contracted a serious fever and was forced, after only a short time, to return to the upland area of his hometown in order to recuperate in its more salubrious climate. He remained in his uncle's house in Tulancingo for several months. His health recovered, Marroquín went to the nearby pueblo of Santo Tomás, where he occasionally stayed with his schoolmaster friend Diosdado, a bachelor about forty

years old. It was in this man's company that Marroquín was
arrested by members of the Acordada (New Spain's rural
constabulary) at the beginning of 1799.

Marroquín's movements, apart from his sojourn near the
coast and his return to the Tulancingo area, are somewhat
difficult to trace during the thirteen months between his
escape and recapture. During this time he was accused of a
number of crimes and of different criminal associations, and
the incomplete record of his trials is typically vague on which
charges were resolved in his favor and which against him.
Then, too, he was married by now and probably had children, but his wife remains a shadow playing across the background of his career. She was to continue so for the rest of
his official, documented life, her place usurped by Marroquín's mistresses and criminal accomplices.

What is clear from the records is that, at the very least,
Marroquín and Diosdado had stolen about one dozen oxen
from a hacienda in the area of Zempoala, a small town near
Tulancingo, sometime shortly after the former's escape from
jail in 1797. These oxen Marroquín had hidden for a time on
the estate administered by his father-in-law (without the
man's knowledge), selling some of the butchered meat locally and the rest of the animals to some Indians on the road
to Texcoco and in the town of Texcoco itself. Marroquín was
accused of a variety of crimes putatively committed over the
course of the next year or so, including a number of robber-
ies, a murder, several assaults, and cattle rustling. During
the course of the investigation in 1799, several crimes for
which Marroquín had been under indictment during his imprisonment from 1795 to late 1797 surfaced again, including the robbery of some silver at the mining town of Zimapan,
a house robbery in Zempoala (on which occasion, when a little
girl laughed at him, he swaggeringly told her that "he was a
man capable of even bigger things"), the theft of some horses
that he attempted to sell to the district magistrate of
Zempoala, and unspecified crimes in and around Puebla.

Three features of Marroquín's style as a criminal emerge
clearly during this 1795–1799 period. First, there was his
strong tendency to associate with groups of criminal confederates rather than act alone. At one point his cohorts included several men of "ill fame," and later still, upon his
arrest in Guadalajara in 1805, he headed a large group of
people. While group banditry was by no means unusual, given
the necessity of substantial armed force in such encounters,

Marroquín's clear leadership role among his confederates indicates a certain gregariousness (perhaps even charisma?) and a first-among-equals status, which he took with him, as we shall see, even into the prison environment. Second, there was about Marroquín's doings a certain self-conscious panache, alluded to earlier and emphasized by his tendency to engage in criminal acts in his own hometown as well as by his attempt to sell stolen horses to one of the local magistrates. Although many small-time local criminals and village incorrigibles preyed on their neighbors, Marroquín's geographic range (across most of central Mexico) and his general predilection for assault and robbery on the highways and in rural areas tend to indicate that his crimes in and around Tulancingo were not committed out of a lack of alternatives or professional imagination but were an active choice. Third, and related, Marroquín insisted on violently resisting arrest on at least three occasions, thus putting himself at considerable risk of injury or death and aggravating the crimes for which he was being apprehended.

Marroquín had demonstrated his tendency to resist arrest first in 1795, when he was captured by armed Acordada constables. Upon his reapprehension in early 1799, he led the constables a chase on horseback, and when his horse fell under him he grabbed his own two carbines (one of which was found to be heavily charged), planted himself squarely in the road, and faced his pursuers defiantly, although no shots were actually exchanged. As we have seen, his capture in Guadalajara six years later involved a Bonnie-and-Clyde-style shoot-out that miraculously cost no lives. Furthermore, on all three occasions Marroquín insisted on using threats and provocative language against his captors after he was in custody. In 1795 he threatened that his confederates would free him on the road or break him out of jail; in 1799 he called his captors *cabras* (she-goats); and in 1805 he made fairly explicit threats of vengeance against the arresting magistrate, Villaseñor.

These latter two characteristics particularly—the criminal panache and the defiant provocativeness—suggest that Marroquín's style was, in part at least, a public statement, a conscious stance of some kind. While it is true that Marroquín's career gives absolutely no sign of what we have come to think of, following the work of the English historian Eric Hobsbawm, as social banditry—that is, of Robin Hood-style crime: of any sense of a social inequity to which Marroquín saw his actions as a corrective, or of any shred of a notion of redistributive justice—his criminal activities as theater probably had a wide audience. No less a personage than the viceroy himself once referred to Marroquín as "el famoso reo" (the famous criminal). It seems likely, therefore, that Marroquín's activities were widely known, although what those actions may have meant to people other than his victims (who apparently never included the very poor, it should be noted) is a matter of speculation. Nonetheless, it is difficult to believe that the highly visible clashes of Agustín Marroquín and other such men with the police, the state, and the comfortable citizens of provincial society had no impact on popular awareness or lacked any resonation with popular discontent. What had a highly personal tone and significance to the criminal, then, may have had quite another kind of meaning for a society under stress as a whole.

Marroquín's own declaration, made in Mexico City shortly after his arrest in early February 1799, betrays a certain ingenuous quality beneath an understandable effort to exculpate himself from the various crimes of which he stood accused. He was, he stated, a native of Tulancingo, twenty-six years of age, and a rural laborer; he made no mention of his wife or of his position in the Tulancingo militia. He acknowledged that he was under suspicion for a robbery and murder but denied complicity in the crimes (he was shortly vindicated), saying he was at the home of his ecclesiastical uncle recuperating from fever and praying with his wife when the murder was committed. He admitted the jailbreak in 1797 and the theft of the oxen in company with Diosdado but denied guilt in any of the other crimes ascribed to him or involvement with his alleged band of accomplices. The jail escape he justified by claiming he had grown desperate over the delays in his case (not implausible given the slowness with which the machine of royal justice ground), and his bearing of arms as a necessity for one making his living in the countryside. In general he portrayed himself with some skill as a simple rustic, guilty at worst of poverty and a few mistakes in judgment.

In the meantime, during the years of his imprisonment and illicit freedom, something of a legal controversy had erupted among the viceregal authorities in Mexico City, officials of the Acordada and the militia, and local authorities over which jurisdiction had the right to try Marroquín, whose membership in the militia regiment of Tulancingo presumably entitled him to certain legal immunities and protections. Because of the political delicacy of the question, Viceroy Branciforte summoned an extraordinary commission some-time in 1797, which advised that despite Marroquín's mili-tary status, he should be tried by the civil authorities. The case was thus kicked back to the latter at just about the time Marroquín was escaping from the Tulancingo jail, his fatigue at the protractedness of his case undoubtedly relat-ing to just this question.

After his reapprehension at the beginning of 1799, Marroquín was jailed in Mexico City, where he remained until early 1802, presumably on charges of escaping jail and of rustling and, possibly, on the basis of one or another of the outstanding indictments against him. When the case was reviewed sometime in 1801, the crown attorneys of Mexico City's chancellery court pointed out that Marroquín had served about five years during his two imprisonments, had been completely absolved of the murder charge, the most serious accusation, and had "established in the service of the jail distinguished merit." In a sanguine tone the pros-ecutors asserted that Marroquín, "finding himself chastened in this way, it is prudently hoped will mend his ways be-cause of what he himself, his wife, and his children have suffered over more than six years, and with his separation from those companions who corrupted him." In early Janu-ary 1802 he was freed from jail by order of Viceroy Marquina.

The sanguine, pious hopes of the crown prosecutors and judges were not to be fulfilled. Although Marroquín's move-ments during early 1802 are not known, by the summer he was living in the provincial town of Apam, to the northeast of Mexico City, about midway between the capital and Tulancingo, working in some capacity on a local hacienda. During 1802 and the first months of 1803, Marroquín man-aged to establish a kind of reign of terror in Apam, engage in theft and extortion (or so it was alleged), and carry on an affair with the wife of a local innkeeper.

Specifically, the royal magistrate of the district, report-ing to the viceroy, asserted that Marroquín was well known to the principal citizens of the town for his "violent resolu-tion and daring" in crime. The official continued: "This man has made himself so feared, and has the town so terrorized, that the more comfortable citizens are forced to render as tribute whatever he asks of them as loans, since were they not to do so they would be the victims of his violence." In other words, he was shaking people down. He habitually rode through the town streets heavily armed and openly defiant of local officials and the Acordada, and he said of the latter that it would require an army of constables to capture him. More than one merchant of the town claimed that Marroquín extorted money from him in his store at night. In addition to these incidents of strong-arm extortion, Marroquín was accused by the local tithe collector of having stolen a number of horses and mules from him. Finally, Marroquín had become amorously involved with María Nava, the wife of an Apam innkeeper. Marroquín eventually took her with him on the crime spree that ended in Guadalajara, where she was arrested with him. Nava, witnesses testified, was much given to putting noxious herbs in people's food and drink (an inauspicious habit, one would think, for her husband's establishment). Induced by her involvement with the famous highwayman, she did the same thing with her husband's chocolate, it was generally believed, thus driving him insane, into brief residence in the asylum of San Hipólito in Mexico City, and to a premature death.

Aware of the impending move to arrest him (his apprehension having been the subject of a "very secret" correspondence between the Acordada administrator and the viceroy in Mexico City), Marroquín, in one of his disarmingly ingenuous actions with an apparently disingenuous motive, brought the matter into the public domain, as it were, by writing directly to Viceroy Iturrigaray in an attempt to exculpate himself. "This is not the first time I have been slandered in this way," he wrote, and then detailed his tranquil life in Apam and his innocence. Realizing that protestations of injured innocence would probably not suffice, Marroquín voluntarily presented himself before the viceregal authorities and was jailed on May 7, 1803. From prison he again wrote directly to the new viceroy, protesting his innocence and demanding that his alleged crimes be proved against him:

> There will perhaps be some accusation against me, because in this world no-one is without enemies; but if I am a perverse and delinquent man, let it be specified what crimes I have been accused of in which I am culpable, and what people I have harmed, because it is not enough to say vaguely that a man is bad: the facts and occasions of that badness must be specified and proved. What, then, are the facts that make me feared, bold, and delinquent? I have provoked no-one, nor injured or mistreated anyone; I have

not committed kidnapping or robbery; so that, if I am bad, there should have been proof of my excesses.

The crown prosecutor once more found compelling reasons to urge Marroquín's release and substantial exoneration. He believed that the crimes that could be proved against Marroquín were not of any gravity; that María Nava was (only temporarily, as it turned out) happily back with her husband; and that Marroquín's voluntary surrender argued strongly in his favor. Furthermore, his long-suffering wife and her father testified to his innocence, and Marroquín was able to obtain a bondsman in Mexico City. Then, too, the admittedly exaggerated, nearly hysterical notoriety attaching by this time to Marroquín's doings (apparently every highway robbery in the Valley of Mexico was ascribed to him) may have had, paradoxically, a deflationary effect on his criminal stature in the eyes of the central authorities. In any case, in June 1803, Agustín Marroquín was released on bond by the viceroy but admonished to keep away from Apam and carry no dangerous weapons.

By the end of the year Marroquín, probably through some personal connection, had secured a position as a mule driver for the marquis of Jaral de Berrio, one of the wealthiest of Mexico's titled aristocrats. The employment provided an occasion for yet another scrape with the law. Returning from the marquis's estates in the interior of the country in February 1804, Marroquín was driving a mule train on the road ahead of his master's coach and other entourage. Upon reaching the pass of Barrientos on the way into Mexico City, Marroquín had an encounter with a group of mule drivers and their animals heading in the opposite direction. Heated words were exchanged, tempers flared, and a fight ensued in the road (the marquis, from his coach, was a witness). The strangers pelted Marroquín with rocks, and he drew a long knife and attacked the group, severely wounding one of their number, Juan José Mendoza. The wounded man brought a complaint before the royal authorities, who jailed his assailant. Marroquín was again out of jail shortly, his bond posted by a merchant of Mexico City and influence exerted in his behalf by his powerful employer. But the following spring (April 1805) Mendoza died, apparently due to complications (an infection, one imagines), from the wound inflicted by Marroquín. This mischance resulted in Marroquín's being jailed once again by the Mexico City authorities.

A small monetary settlement with the victim's family (possibly underwritten by the marquis) secured Marroquín's release from jail within a short time.

Marroquín was to remain free only until his capture at Guadalajara the following winter. What impelled him to embark on the crime spree that eventually took him west to the capital of New Galicia and into his (in every sense) fatal encounter with insurrection—whether lack of means, boredom, disillusion with his chances in Mexico City, or some change in personal circumstances—can only be guessed at, but by the summer of 1805 he apparently had left the viceregal capital (although not, for the moment, others of his old haunts) behind forever, and, *sans famille,* had begun to make his way across central Mexico.

Most of what can be pieced together about Marroquín's activities between June and November 1805 is based on testimony and accusations that surfaced after his capture at Guadalajara, so that although some of it is very credible and vivid, much of the material in the record is at worst apocryphal or garbled, and at best lacks immediacy and specificity. His first move had been north and west, into the Bajío region, where he was the major suspect in a highway robbery that netted some ten thousand pesos, committed near the Villa of San Felipe, in the district of San Miguel el Grande (later San Miguel Allende), on June 29, 1805. By this time he was the leader of a group of brigands estimated at twenty men. The royal treasurer of Sombrerete also accused Marroquín and his band of having stolen about seven thousand pesos of royal funds on their way to the mining town in late June 1805 and of having robbed a local merchant of a lesser amount. Although Marroquín denied any knowledge of or complicity in either crime, the evidence for his having masterminded the San Felipe robbery brought a conviction. A crime to which he did confess, although he minimized his role in it, was the theft of some three thousand pesos from a house in the village of Acaxochitlan, near Tulancingo (he had doubled back on his own trail), in September 1805. The victim of the robbery, don Nicolás Pastrana, clearly identified Marroquín, stating that the highwayman "attempted only to disguise his voice by trying to talk like a [European] Spaniard." Other witnesses also placed Marroquín at the scene of this robbery. During the incident two men were nearly killed, and a gunfight ensued in the town cemetery between several armed locals and the fleeing robbers, one of whom was later captured and implicated Marroquín as the leader of the bandits. At this same time other witnesses came forward with the accusation that Marroquín had been involved in large-scale tobacco smuggling, the crime for which he had first been sent to jail a decade previously.

Apparently at this point Marroquín, in the company of at least some of his habitual accomplices, returned to the Bajío area and made stops in Salamanca, León, and other towns on his way to San Juan de los Lagos. With him in the party were María Nava and another young creole woman, María Vicenta Partida, who testified later that Marroquín had bought her a house in Apam and that she had been his mistress for two years or more. Arriving at San Juan de los Lagos in early October 1805, the party of seven to ten people stayed at first in an inn and then rented a house for a month. María Nava posed as Marroquín's wife and prayed daily (perhaps for the elimination of her amorous rival) to the local manifestation of the Virgin, while Agustín posed as don Francisco Villaseñor, a buyer of horses and mules from Cuernavaca. In the rented house in Lagos the highwayman set up an illegal card game, which he kept going at all hours of the day and night. His continual winning of large amounts in cash and jewels (the sum of ten thousand pesos was later mentioned, but it is not clear whether this was recovered when he was arrested) became the talk of the town. Although one witness in Lagos asserted that no "distinguished" citizens of the town gambled with the new arrival, apparently a priest and several local estate owners did play. Wanting to avoid being recognized by anyone at the huge annual livestock and trading fair that was to begin in Lagos on November 1, Marroquín and his party moved on via Jalostotitlan and Tepatitlan to Guadalajara, where, as we have seen, they were shortly captured and jailed.

DE PROFUNDIS[5]

The lengthy parenthesis in Agustín Marroquín's criminal career constituted by his five-year imprisonment in Guadalajara was filled with complex legal argument and controversy, further accusations, and development by the protagonist of an unusual but, one imagines, for him characteristic modus vivendi to ease the rigors of his captivity. Immediately upon the news of his capture becoming generally known, a flood of accusations came to the attention of the Guadalajara authorities, ascribing to Marroquín numerous unsolved crimes in several different towns. Prosecution of Marroquín's case and of that of his associates was entrusted to don José Pérez de Acal, a veteran sergeant major of the provincial militia of Guadalajara, and *alcalde ordinario* (magistrate) of the city in 1805. Pérez de Acal, much given to public questioning of his own competence in legal affairs and to lamenting the complexity of the charges at the same time as he expressed moral and civic outrage at Marroquín's criminality, stated his position strongly, if rather extravagantly, from the beginning:

> All these excesses, judged juridically, give unequivocal proof of the crimes committed by Marroquín and his accomplices, and of the notoriously disorderly life of this man, always with the object of oppressing humanity, of scandalizing and terrorizing all these towns to the point of plunging them into mourning . . . and gaining by these impious means not only the money to support himself, but also making his name famous, as he has accomplished by these reprehensible means, so noxious to public society.

The thicket of jurisdictional and legal complications, the necessity of having local officials and witnesses from distant towns make depositions, and the strictly observed rights of the accused in reviewing and responding to those depositions in various ways led to interminable delays in the case and generated an enormous pile of documentation that had to be reviewed by prosecutors and judges at every stage of deliberation. Notwithstanding the general scrupulosity with which Pérez de Acal and other royal officials handled the case, Marroquín's previous notoriety established in the minds of such functionaries a strong prima facie case for his guilt and that of his associates. Added to this was the perceived need to make of the famous highwayman an example in order to discourage the wave of brigandage prevalent in central New Spain in general, and in the Guadalajara region in particular, at the end of the eighteenth and the beginning of the nineteenth centuries, characterized by one high judicial official in Mexico City as a "flood of evildoers."

In finally summarizing his case, in a statement dated the last day of 1808, Pérez de Acal referred to Marroquín as "famous and singular in the present epoch for his boldness and temerity, and for the wantonness with which he has thrown himself into the commission of many very execrable evils." Reviewing Marroquín's criminal career, Pérez de Acal pointed to the brigand's own admission that by the age of twenty-two he had already committed so many crimes as to win for himself "renown for his wickedness," and that even when he was behaving well he gained his livelihood from gambling and smuggling. Having committed any number of crimes all punishable by death, Marroquín should be so punished, concluded the prosecutor: he should be hanged, and then his severed head displayed publicly in Acaxochitlan for two weeks and his right hand in Guadalajara. For the accomplices, Pérez de Acal recommended long sentences at hard labor and public floggings. A trained lawyer in Guadalajara, asked independently to review the prosecutor's findings and proposed sentence, suggested reducing Marroquín's punishment to public flogging and ten years at hard labor in a *presidio* (military prison). The intendant of Guadalajara agreed in April 1809, and the Mexico City military tribunal confirmed the sentence in September. The sentence for the bandit leader finally came down to ten years' hard labor at a military fortress in Havana, and two hundred lashes, but this punishment only applied to the charge of resisting the king's troops, since this was the only crime the military jurisdiction was competent to try. The crimes of a nonmilitary nature—comprising the bulk of the outstanding charges— were left to the Audiencia of Guadalajara for sentencing, but owing to the necessity of gathering more testimony in these cases, the actions were still pending before the court in September 1810 when Marroquín was freed from prison by the rebels. The two hundred lashes were administered publicly to Marroquín, as to his chief accomplice, Felipe Rodríguez, on Wednesday, October 4, 1809. One has no difficulty at all in imagining that a *gachupín* (European Spaniard) later died for each lash.

In the meantime, while his judicial fate was being decided, Marroquín was not idle in prison but managed to build a small empire and alleviate for himself the discomforts of prison life. In October 1809, after Marroquín's sentence had been confirmed and the lashes administered, Intendant Roque Abarca, who had taken an interest in Marroquín's case because of the involvement of the viceregal authorities and the notoriety of the defendant, noted that the famous highwayman had done quite well for himself within a few days of his capture in late 1805. "The prisoner Agustín Marroquín entered jail with ordinary clothing and with no money; and within a few days it was noticed that he had purchased new clothing, that he was managing business interests [*que manejaba intereses*], that he was loaning money, and trading." Abarca further noted that during the past few years several employees of the prison had petitioned the intendant to release Marroquín, prompting him to comment that the prisoner had a "party" of supporters in jail. More recently, Abarca said, Marroquín, the conditions of whose confinement required him to be chained in a cell, was encountered by the intendant "free in the prison yard, dressed magnificently, and what drew my attention even more was that his baggage gave signs that he was ready to mount a horse." Apparently some prison employee, presumably having been bribed by the bandit, had forged an order with the signature of the royal prosecutor for the release of Marroquín. Abarca's chance arrival at the jail ruined the plot, but he was never able to determine who the accomplice had been.

An even more circumstantial description of jail life at the time gives a hint of Marroquín's position in the social hierarchy of the Guadalajara prison. In April 1810 a prison guard accused an inmate, Gabriel Mesa, before a city magistrate of having had homosexual relations with several other prisoners, an accusation of *pecado nefando* (unnatural crimes), which brought an immediate investigation by the authorities. Mesa, a young Indian (seventeen years old) from a nearby village, was an army deserter. In response to the serious charges against him, he said he had been the passive victim of yet another prisoner, Máximo Rivera, an older Spaniard, who was the only man with whom he had committed any *torpezas* (indecencies). Mesa testified that he had awakened one November night to find himself with an erection and Rivera on top of him "moving up and down upon the witness, thus penetrated." Mesa managed to withdraw himself before ejaculation (an important point in the judges' minds), struck Rivera several times, and told the older man to go back to his own bed in the communal dormitory. During the following weeks Rivera importuned Mesa nearly every night to repeat this performance, once or twice coming to Mesa while he slept and fondling him "with the object of putting [him] in a state so that penetration would be possible." Mesa consistently refused these overtures and acts, at one point reminding Rivera that he and several fellow inmates were in the midst of a course of spiritual exercises being conducted by a priest.

Rivera, in jail for stealing livestock, denied the charges, as did two other men accused by the prison guard of having relations with Mesa. Several other prisoners accused each other of varying degrees of homosexual involvement, but none of the accused admitted any culpability except Mesa, and he only with Rivera. In June of the following year (1811) medical examinations of the accused were ordered by the civil authorities, but several physicians agreed in detailed opinions that these would be inconclusive. Marroquín was dragged into the case by name when Rivera requested that the bandit be questioned regarding Rivera's behavior in prison. This man, Marroquín asserted, was blameless, but he accused another man, Guadalupe Silva, earlier involved in the accusations and cross-accusations of the prisoners, of involvement with Mesa.

Shortly after this testimony, Marroquín was released from prison with the former inmates, and the investigation was taken up again by the authorities only after Marroquín's death and the reapprehension of Mesa, Silva, and others in 1811. Silva's defense attorney in an 1811 deposition impugned Marroquín's testimony by suggesting that Rivera was his creature, that both "abhorred Silva and abused him because he would not submit to them," and that Marroquín had suborned the testimony of several witnesses against Silva. This charge drew forward a flood of testimony against the deceased Marroquín, painting him as the cruel, unprincipled, would-be kingpin of the prison. One witness affirmed that Marroquín indeed had tried to suborn him to testify against Silva, and another that Marroquín persecuted Silva because the latter "did not agree with [Marroquín's] twisted ideas and perverse faction; [Marroquín] hated other prisoners as well because they did not countenance his thefts and the discord he created, so that there was no other convict in the jail more troublesome [than Marroquín]." Yet another inmate affirmed that Marroquín's bad conduct in the jail was "notorious," and still another that Marroquín hated Silva because of his failure to "humble himself" before the bandit chieftain.

Making sense of the accusations and counteraccusations is a bit difficult, but it appears that Marroquín, in attempting to organize the inmates to suit his own ends, persecuted Silva, Mesa's friend, and that Mesa accused Rivera, Marroquín's cohort, out of revenge. This was substantially the finding of the advising attorney in the case, who also found sufficient circumstantial evidence that Silva and Mesa had been sexually involved with each other, however, to recommend moderate punishment for them (two years at hard labor on public works projects for Silva, and remittance to the military authorities for Mesa).

THE REBEL

The next-to-last item in Marroquín's voluminous dossier, which opens the most well-known chapter in his career, is a laconic note from Father Hidalgo's famous Lieutenant José Antonio Torres to the effect that the notary of the Audiencia should give back to Marroquín any property that had been impounded at his capture five years earlier. Marroquín, who had been freed when Torres took the city and emptied the jails in mid-November, duly signed the receipt on November 25, 1810, and received back his property.

The following day Hidalgo arrived in the city at the head of an army of some seven thousand men. What Marroquín had been doing during the preceding few days is not clear, but presumably he was sufficiently visible so as to come to the notice of the insurgent chief, who probably knew something of him from years before. At some point during the next two weeks, most likely toward the end of November, Hidalgo drew Agustín Marroquín into his inner circle of trusted lieutenants and commissioned him a captain in the insurgent forces. A Guadalajara ecclesiastical official, Dr. Velasco, later described the scene with a pen dipped in acid, referring to Marroquín as Father Hidalgo's "repugnant bodyguard"

> whom Hidalgo made a Captain in an officers' staff meeting, and by the most theatrical act declared him free of any ill fame [*libre de toda nota*], receiving from him an oath of loyalty, and blessing him placed the epaulets upon shoulders which still bore the two hundred lashes placed there by Justice in our streets fourteen months before such a quixotic scene.[6]

The freeing of Marroquín and his rapid absorption into the inner circle of Hidalgo's cohorts almost certainly helped to alienate prominent creole commanders in the insurgent forces, such as Ignacio Allende and Mariano Abasolo, who abhorred the marginal social elements attracted to the movement and deeply mistrusted its popular base, and with whom in any case the priest was already on very bad terms.

Whatever Marroquín's relationship to Miguel Hidalgo or the insurgent movement as a whole, and whatever his other activities at Guadalajara and after, it is certain that he was centrally involved in the infamous mass executions of several hundred European Spaniards that took place in the city during the latter two weeks of December 1810. The evidence for this is his own confession and the accounts of witnesses and subsequent writers on the period. Precisely why Hidalgo ordered the executions has never been made clear. Hidalgo himself claimed that the executions were ordered to placate his Indian followers. Later historians claimed that Hidalgo did it out of simple viciousness, or alternatively that he essentially overreacted to continual rumors and some evidence of plots against his life by Creoles and *gachupines*. On the whole, Hidalgo's own argument of pressure from the popular sectors of his supporters is the most credible explanation.

The executions began on the night of December 12 and continued for the rest of the month. Although the chronology of the executions and of Marroquín's role in them is difficult to reconstruct with any precision, it seems likely that he was involved in them at the start and intermittently thereafter. Marroquín himself, in brief testimony after his capture with Hidalgo and others in the spring of 1811, claimed that he had carried out the execution of one contingent of forty-eight Europeans, on a date unspecified, as he was on his way out of the city to scout the approaching enemy forces. Apparently this was done in conjunction with another insurgent commander named Alatorre, who had received a warrant from Hidalgo's own hand with the names of European prisoners being held in the Colegio de San Juan. Alatorre delegated the task to Marroquín who, with his men, conducted the prisoners to the *cerro* (hill) de San Martín, a few miles distant from the city, beheaded the prisoners, and left the bodies in a pit the insurgents had dug. The same Dr. Velasco who penned the disdainful description of Hidalgo's commissioning of Marroquín added to the account a lurid tableau of the executions in which the prisoners were naked and were "yielded up to the barbarous fury of the Indians, who killed them with lances, throwing their bodies

into the depths of the canyon." Informed testimony implicated Marroquín in still more instances of mass executions,
although he himself denied this; and several other incidents,
some possibly apocryphal and some based on solid documentation, give a picture of Marroquín's relationship to these
events and the apparent coolness with which he gave himself over to the political executions of European Spaniards
in Guadalajara in these months.

On January 17, 1811, the enormous but untrained and
unwieldy insurgent army led by Miguel Hidalgo met a quick
and decisive defeat at the hands of a much smaller but mili-
tarily more effective royalist force led by Félix María Calleja,
royalist commander in chief and future Mexican viceroy, at
the bridge of Calderón, about thirty miles east of Guadalajara. Hidalgo and his lieutenants fled north from Guadalajara, hoping to regroup and eventually gain support from
the United States, but these hopes were not to be realized.
Betrayed by a one-time insurgent officer in the north of New
Spain, Hidalgo and a large party were captured at Acatita
de Bajan, between Saltillo and Monclova, on March 21, 1811.
It is quite clear from accounts of the capture that Hidalgo's
twenty-man mounted escort, which surrendered without resistance, was commanded by Agustín Marroquín, another
indication of the confidence the insurgent leader had placed
in the highwayman. In the meantime Marroquín, who apparently had been with Hidalgo since the flight from
Guadalajara, had not been idle. He admitted under interro-
gation in Chihuahua that while the party was on the road
between Matehuala and Saltillo they had encountered a car-
riage with two European Spaniards and their families inside, and that Marroquín himself had ordered the men
executed on the spot. After the capture at Bajan, Marroquín
was jailed in an improvised prison cell in Chihuahua's former
Jesuit college. On May 10 he was led with two lesser officers
to the city's Franciscan convent and executed by firing squad.
A terse entry appended to Marroquín's criminal dossier in
Guadalajara the following September acknowledged that it
was well known that the highwayman had been brought to
justice in Chihuahua the preceding spring, and that one of
his former associates, Felipe Rodríguez, had been arrested
as an insurgent and was at that time in jail in the city.

The career of Agustín Marroquín is a clear and particularly well-documented example of the way in which social

deviance and marginality can overlap or conflate with rebellion. Moreover, whether crime or delinquency was antecedent to rebellion, or rebellion to crime or delinquency, is not always so clear in the Mexican context. Now, that acts of criminality or delinquency should occur within the context of revolutionary violence, or that criminals and delinquents should be injected into the insurgent moment, would by no means be unusual in the history of rebellion in general, or of collective violent protest in the early modern period in particular. And arriving at a quantitative assessment as to whether one set of such collective phenomena—say, the French Revolution, the classical European grain riot, or the uprisings of the common people in early modern Italian cities—was more characterized by nonprogrammatic criminal behavior than another would just as obviously be impossible. Nonetheless, one is left with the impression in the Mexican case that there was an even greater than usual characteristic fluidity between the two types of social phenomena.

This leads us to ask to what degree Marroquín and other insurgents were organically a part of the collectivities in whose names they took up arms against the constituted authorities. In the case of some, their embeddedness in the matrix of family, clan, town, and region, despite the signs of their delinquency and the evidence that they and their families availed themselves of the rebellion to enrich and advance themselves socially, lends some credibility to the view that their actions as insurgent chieftains resonated with the thinking of the rebels they led. In the case of Marroquín, however, it is exceedingly difficult to imagine, and there is no evidence to indicate, that he had even the faintest ideological formulation in his head when he participated in the mass executions in Guadalajara or the other actions ascribed to him, any more than did the plagues sent by God to scourge the Egyptians in the biblical account of Exodus. Certainly his career shows no hint of social banditry, or of connectedness to any community, except possibly a criminal one, or to any interest other than his own; indeed, this is one of the essential characteristics of the sociopathic personality. That there were a great many other individuals similar to Marroquín in their relationship to the collective behavioral and ideological phenomena of the independence rebellions, even if their activities were not so egregiously magnified, is evident from the documents of the time.

NOTES

1. Unless otherwise indicated, "Spaniard" as used here connotes a person of Spanish ancestry born in the New World.

2. The *fuero*, an ancient corporate charter extended to the military and the Church, entitled its members, among other privileges, to trial by their own rather than by civil courts.

3. *Sociopathy* is generally defined in psychiatry as an antisocial personality disorder characterized by (1) inability to sustain consistent work behavior; (2) failure to accept social norms with respect to lawful behavior; (3) inability to form an enduring attachment with a single significant other; (4) aggressiveness; (5) impulsivity, or failure to plan ahead; (6) disregard for the truth; and (7) recklessness.

4. Pulque is a traditional Mexican intoxicant made from the fermented juice of a certain species of cactus.

5. *De profundis*, "from the depths," is taken from the prison memoirs of the same title (1897) by Oscar Wilde.

6. Quoted in José Ramírez Flores, *El gobierno insurgente en Guadalajara, 1810–1811* (Guadalajara, 1969), pp. 95–96.

SOURCES

The documentation on Agustín Marroquín was drawn overwhelmingly from unpublished archival sources in Biblioteca Pública del Estado, Guadalajara, Mexico—sec. "Criminal," bundles 1, 6, 9, 18, 21, 25; and in Archivo General de la Nación, Mexico City, Mexico—sec. "Operaciones de Guerra," vols. 4A, 145; and "Historia," vol. 584. A vast literature in Spanish, English, and other languages exists on the Mexican independence struggles, although only occasional references to Marroquín occur in it. The most important recent historical treatments in English are Hugh M. Hamill, Jr., *The Hidalgo Revolt: Prelude to Mexican Independence* (reprint, Westport, CT, 1981); John Tutino, *From Insurrection to Revolution in Mexico: Social Bases of Agrarian Violence, 1750–1940* (Princeton, 1986); Brian R. Hamnett, *Roots of Insurgency: Mexican Regions, 1750–1824* (Cambridge, 1986); and Timothy E. Anna, *The Fall of the Royal Government in Mexico City* (Lincoln, 1978). On Mexican banditry in the nineteenth century, see Paul J. Vanderwood, *Disorder and Progress: Bandits, Police, and Mexican Development* (Wilmington, DE, 1992, rev. ed.); and the articles in *Bibliotheca Americana* 1 (November 1982), dedicated to the theme "Social Banditry in Nineteenth-Century Latin America," Paul J. Vanderwood, ed., particularly Christon I.

Archer, "Banditry and Revolution in New Spain, 1790–1821," pp. 58–59; and William B. Taylor, "Sacarse de pobre: El bandolerismo en la Nueva Galicia, 1794–1821," *Revista Jalisco* 2 (1981): 34–45. The major works of Eric Hobsbawm are *Primitive Rebels: Studies in Archaic Forms of Social Movement in the 19th and 20th Centuries* (New York, 1965); and *Bandits* (New York, 1969). On the criminal justice system in late colonial Mexico, see Colin M. MacLachlan, *Criminal Justice in Eighteenth-Century Mexico: A Study of the Tribunal of the Acordada* (Berkeley, 1974). The period of insurgent control of Guadalajara is treated in detail in José Ramírez Flores, *El gobierno insurgente en Guadalajara, 1810–1811* (Guadalajara, 1969).

2

Maria Antônia Muniz: Frontier Matriarch

John Charles Chasteen

As noted in the introduction to Part I, Dom Pedro I proclaimed Brazil's independence from Portugal in 1822 with a minimum of conflict or bloodshed. Yet the imperial ambitions of Dom João VI (1808–1820) and Dom Pedro I (1820–1831) caused considerable trouble for the inhabitants of the region far to the south, the *banda oriental,* or eastern bank, of the Plata River. Both the Spanish and the Portuguese coveted control of this magnificent river system. During the colonial period the Spanish saw the river as a vulnerable path to the famed *plata* (silver) mines of Potosí in Bolivia. The Portuguese saw the Plata River as the most convenient way to reach their western inland regions of Mato Grosso. After Argentina's independence in 1816 and Brazil's in 1822, the two Latin American behemoths continued to press for advantage in the area; both ignored the challenge of the Uruguayan caudillo José Artigas, who fought for independence of the region. In 1828 the British forced Argentina and Brazil to recognize an independent Uruguay as a buffer state between them, but for years both of the larger nations continued to intervene in Uruguayan politics.

The people who lived in the disputed territory suffered and profited in their no-man's-land. Maria Antônia Muniz lived in the region for an incredible ten decades, from her birth in 1762 to her death in 1870. She married, brought up thirteen children, and, after the death of her husband in 1824, indirectly managed the family estates.

John Chasteen's essay raises various historical issues. For Maria Antônia, the frontier was a land of opportunity, much as the U.S. frontier was portrayed by the historian Frederick Jackson Turner. Frontier families, like most families in Latin America, were large and extended. Maria Antônia's experience suggests, however, that among family members competition may have been as common as the more idealized notion of cooperation. The Indian and mestizo gauchos, or cowboys, contrast strongly with members of more settled indigenous communities. Issues of royalism or patriotism, of empire or independence, seem to have been less intense in this region, overshadowed by the competition between Brazil and Argentina and by the harshness of day-to-day life. Political independence per se apparently affected Maria Antônia's family only slightly. We might ponder also the lives and roles of women on the frontier. Chasteen paints Maria Antônia as a tough survivor, but he leaves open the question of whether she ruled over her family like a strong-willed matriarch, or more passively allowed her husband and sons to shelter and protect her.   .

John Charles Chasteen, associate professor of history, earned his doctorate at the University of North Carolina at Chapel Hill, where he now teaches. He has received Social Science Research Council and Fulbright grants to support field research in Brazil and Uruguay. He is the author of *Heroes on Horseback: A Life and Times of the Last Gaucho Caudillos* (Albuquerque,1995) and the coeditor with Joseph S. Tulchin of *Problems in Modern Latin American History: A Reader* (Wilmington, DE, 1994).

In the summer of 1866 news from Paraguay arrived at a ranch house in southern Brazil. The allies (Brazil, Argentina, and Uruguay) had lost four thousand dead and wounded in an attempt to take the Paraguayan stronghold at Curupaití. The wife of the house learned, to her relief, that her two sons with the army were all right, and one of her nephews had become a hero. But another of her nephews had died. At the spinning wheel sat her mother, Maria Antônia Muniz, the grandmother of these four soldiers. She had lived already over one hundred years and had seen too many wars. She had presided over a family divided by the struggles of the period, the formative years of Brazil's southern borderland. Hers was a family that had turned upon itself, on one occasion family members killing one another before her very eyes. To her, the present carnage of Curupaití and the name of its hero were merely echoes of the past. As the wooden wheel whirred and the woolen yarn twisted between her calloused fingers, she sang to herself. Her children and grandchildren had often heard her songs, which she had made about her own life. "'Twas in the village of San Carlos that I was born and raised," she sang, "and it's noble blood of Portugal I carry in my veins."

Shortly before 1760 an aristocratic but impoverished ancestor had come to the vast no-man's-land between the New World empires of Spain and Portugal. The Portuguese Crown had built a citadel, Colônia do Sacramento, deep in territory claimed by the Spanish. This wide expanse of rolling and well-watered grassland was still a wild frontier, occupied only by dwindling tribal bands of nomadic Charrua Indians, by a few thousand drifting gauchos, and by tough longhorn cattle that had run wild and thrived, their herds numbered in the millions. A son of this noble ancestor had married the daughter of the garrison commander at Colônia do Sacramento, and the young couple went to claim land and cattle in no-man's-land at a place called San Carlos. Maria Antônia was born there in 1762.

Soon after Maria Antônia's birth, a Spanish army arrived to push the Portuguese out of San Carlos, which lay in the disputed territory. Her parents fled with the baby and three older children to the citadel at Colônia. The Spanish army besieged and captured the town, and Maria Antônia's mother died during the fighting. Within a few years, Spanish authorities allowed her father to resettle in San Carlos, where Maria Antônia and her three brothers grew up in the care of their unmarried aunts. Always in search of unclaimed land, the Muniz family left San Carlos about 1773 and occupied land farther north at a place called Herval, many miles from the nearest neighbor but much closer to the major Portuguese settlement at Rio Grande. In 1784 a mixed Spanish and Portuguese expedition passed by the Muniz house, surveying a strip of neutral territory between the competing empires. Once again, as in San Carlos, the Muniz claim fell in no-man's-land.

Life in no-man's-land was dangerous. Maria Antônia's father kept his blunderbuss loaded in case a party of Spanish soldiers, freebooting gauchos, or hostile Charruas should appear. But the land was there for the taking, and Muniz could have the meat and sell the hide of any longhorn he could catch. He could also brand all the cattle and horses that he found on his land and try to tame them, but for these operations he needed the help of gauchos.

The gauchos were mostly Guaraní Indians who had become Christians in the Jesuit missions on the edge of the disputed territories. The missions had sent men out to harvest the wild herds of no-man's-land, and these men had learned the skills of mounted herdsmen. When the missions were destroyed in the 1750s, many Guaranís had come to live on the rolling plains, where they could easily survive by killing wild cattle. Maria Antônia's father had lived on the plains for years, but he could never ride, rope, and brand the way a gaucho did. He probably never learned to throw a *boleadora* (the three tethered stones that a gaucho could send whirling through the air to entangle the legs of a running animal). Muniz knew that the gauchos might be enticed by the offer of good wages to come for a week or two and help him. Although it cost them nothing to live from the wild herds, they liked to have some silver coins to buy the few amenities they wanted, or to gamble, which they passionately enjoyed.

It was hard to get a gaucho to stay for long, however, even with good pay, so Muniz almost certainly had a few slaves. They would have sown wheat, which grew well in the soil of Herval. They also raised mules, which men from the north bought to take to the distant mines of central Brazil; in the fall, Muniz took some of the mules to carry his wheat and hides to a riverbank. There, twenty-foot sailing boats passed on their way to Rio Grande where Muniz could sell the wheat and hides to buy sacks of salt and sugar, cloth and ribbons for Maria Antônia's feast-day dress, a fine beaver hat, and a bottle of wine or two. He could also buy Paraguayan tea if he already had learned to appreciate its bitter taste and stimulating effects. Sooner or later, almost all newcomers did come to like this tea, and besides, Brazil did not yet produce much coffee.

By the 1780s, five or six other Portuguese families had settled within a few miles of Muniz. The Amaro da Silveira brothers were the first of these. They were sons of one of many poor Azorean families sent by the Portuguese Crown to populate the disputed lands. Maria Antônia married Manuel Amaro da Silveira when she was fourteen years old. To find a priest the wedding party had to ride to a Spanish outpost two days away, and when they did not return for a week, those who had stayed behind to prepare the wedding feast began to fear a calamity. Almost a century later, Maria Antônia still enjoyed telling the story of how the wedding party had waited at the outpost, delayed for days by the absence of the priest, who finally appeared to perform the ceremony.

Manuel built a house for his bride on one of the highest hills in no-man's-land. From there, one almost could see Portuguese territory to the north and Spanish territory to the south. Manuel set about rounding up and branding the wild longhorns on his claim, and Maria Antônia spun and wove, washed clothes and cooked (almost certainly with the help of one or two slave women), and began to bear and raise children. Her first son, José, was healthy, but the second died in infancy. Then she had two more sons, Hilário and Jerônimo, and a daughter, Maria Antônia. João, Vasco, Dionísio,

Manuel, Balbina, and Francisca followed. The last of these was born in 1788, and Maria Antônia then stopped having children for ten years, but when her son Dionísio died in adolescence, she began again. She had three more girls, and a boy, whom she named Dionísio. In all, thirteen children survived to become adults.

A large family brought advantages in the early days of settlement. The Amaro da Silveira girls helped their mother and eventually married sons of the families settled nearby. The boys learned to ride and rope and throw the *boleadora* better than their father or grandfather ever could. They also learned to use guns. In 1801 there was a war, and the oldest three boys learned to use a sword and a lance as well. José and Hilário were captured by the Spanish in that war, but relatives of their grandfather in Spanish territory managed to win their release. The war had gone very well for Portugal. The Portuguese army had captured all of the no-man's-land where Herval lay and had pushed the Spanish far to the west. From now on, Herval would be part of Brazil. Families that were already well established there got title to the property they claimed, especially if the family had aristocratic pretensions like Maria Antônia's. The Crown rewarded the officers of its victorious army with more grants of land. The Amaro da Silveira family profited in both ways.

The half-century that Maria Antônia spent raising her thirteen children (roughly from 1775 to 1825) were the formative years of the Brazilian borderland. During this time, families of settlers were brought in from the Azores, virtually all the pastureland was distributed and settled, and the settlers were able to push the Spanish out of land that they had claimed for three hundred years. The strength of the Portuguese settlement in the borderland was its homogeneity and greater sense of attachment to an imperial purpose. Although they acquired the gauchos' skill and eventually abandoned the cultivation of wheat altogether, families like Maria Antônia's maintained a strongly European community life that distinguished their society from that of their Spanish-speaking neighbors. Symptomatic was the greater importance of the state religion in the Brazilian borderland. Maria Antônia had a heavy Bible bound in leather and wood, and on Friday evenings it was customary for one of her sons to read aloud from it. Occasionally, she led family and slaves in singing a repetitive *terça,* one third of the rosary. Churches were more frequent on the Brazilian side of the border, and

periodically they sent traveling revivals through the countryside. Three-day caroling trips were popular for January's
feast of the Three Wise Men.

By contrast, the Spanish borderland remained less populated, and its inhabitants had more diverse racial and
geographic origins. Land title there was not granted to the
occupants but was sold in huge tracts to speculators at
the viceregal court, and conflict frequently arose between
the absentee landlords and the actual occupants of the land.
Spanish authorities envied the thriving settlements of the
Portuguese borderland and recommended the adoption of
Portuguese methods. But they had accomplished little when
the Spanish-American wars of independence began in 1810.

Turmoil in the Spanish borderland meant opportunity for
the Portuguese borderlanders. Herval became a permanent
military camp, the starting point of repeated invasions of
Spanish territory. These expeditions brought back hundreds
of thousands of cattle as the spoils of war. Finally, in 1820
the Brazilian borderlanders conquered the entire area of
present-day Uruguay. The families of Herval and other borderland areas of Brazil flooded into the occupied territory
and acquired large areas of land there. Maria Antônia's family profited in this way, too.

The Amaro da Silveiras received at least four royal grants
in the names of various family members. They used their
income to buy more land, cattle, and slaves, and with the
added income they bought still more. By the year 1824, when
Maria Antônia's husband Manuel died, their family owned
about one hundred and fifty square miles of pasture, seventeen thousand semiwild longhorns, four hundred tame longhorns, almost one thousand horses in various stages of
domestication, and fifty-four slaves. (By now, fifty years after Maria Antônia's father had come to Herval, the slaves
had learned all the skills of the gauchos.) The widow's house,
described for the purposes of the probate inventory, was solid
but plain, and the family had few luxuries of any kind despite their large holdings. For the Amaro da Silveiras, cattle
and land were not means to an end but an end in themselves.
Like most of the lords of the borderland who would follow
them in the nineteenth century, Maria Antônia and her children had lived in the backlands all their lives, and their aspirations were those of rural people in a traditional culture.

Maria Antônia was sixty-two years old when her husband
died. She was proud of the wealth she and her family had

built. But troubled times lay ahead for the family. To begin with, this huge collection of pasture and animals was the work of more than one generation. Maria Antônia's oldest sons, José and Hilário, were in their fifties by the time they inherited legal title to the land on which they lived. And there were problems with the distribution of the inheritance. After her husband's death, Maria Antônia's sons and sons-in-law quarreled so terribly that she preferred to entrust the administration of her remaining property (half of the total at Manuel's death) to a neutral party: Domingos Amaro da Silveira, her husband's son by a slave woman. Manuel had always taken a special interest in Domingos, who could read and write (something Maria Antônia could not do), and the old man's will had manumitted him and left him land and cattle. The other Amaro da Silveira men liked and respected Domingos but did not feel they had to compete with him. He managed the huge estate for eight years, sending his sons to study in Rio Grande and eventually becoming a slave owner himself.

When Domingos retired in 1832, Maria Antônia had to find a new administrator for her property. These were conflictive times in the borderland. The Uruguayans had recently broken free from Brazil (itself now independent from Portugal), and they repaid their old enemies by raiding destructively into the Brazilian borderland. No more could Uruguayan cattle be extracted by the thousands with impunity, and the Brazilian government itself exacted a tax on the animals imported legally. In addition, passions ran high throughout Brazil as Conservatives and Liberals disputed key questions of the country's political organization. When Firmina Amaro da Silveira married Juca Teodoro Braga, a famous war captain from the glory days of 1811–1827, old Maria Antônia thought her new son-in-law was just the man to defend the family's interests, and she made him administrator of her property.

Braga stopped the fighting over land, but the family found other things to fight about. One night in 1833, Maria Antônia's eldest daughter (who had always been her favorite) knocked on the door in the middle of the night with her crying children. Her husband had just been killed by a group of men who came in the night to cut his throat. This death was the third in a series of revenge killings among the Amaro da Silveiras and their in-laws. So that her daughter's family would not have to return to the house where this episode occurred, Maria Antônia moved her own household to a new residence a couple of miles away, and the young widow occupied the original hilltop homestead. The old woman had barely gotten accustomed to her new house when another disaster struck. Enraged by her preference for Juca Teodoro Braga, her pampered youngest son, Dionísio, had awaited his chance and finally shot Braga in the back on a hunting trip.

The murder happened only days before the whole borderland was convulsed by the beginnings of the Farrapo War, a ten-year secessionist attempt led by the radical Liberals. In Herval, people held divided loyalties. The Farrapos championed an open border favorable to the borderlanders, but a tradition of military service to the empire pulled the sentiments of the people of Herval in another direction. Maria Antônia's sons and grandsons enlisted on both sides. Her son Vasco became a Farrapo leader so devoted to the cause that he refused to spare the property of the family when the Farrapos ordered requisitions. Her recently widowed daughter, who maintained outspoken loyalty to the empire, soon suffered these requisitions. In 1839 men arrived to tell the old woman that her son Vasco had died at the hand of one of her grandsons, the eldest son of her favorite daughter and the future hero of Curupaití.

The Farrapo War dragged on, ravaging the family's herds and exacerbating old resentments. Maria Antônia's sons José and Hilário had become deadly enemies because of a dispute over their inheritance. Neither could tolerate the presence of the other without threat of violence. One day in 1844, Hilário went to visit his eighty-two-year-old mother at her house. After the midday meal, he and the two men with him lay down in a bedroom for a nap, and while they were asleep José arrived with his son João Pedro. Awakened by voices from the other room, Hilário arose and walked out to greet the visitors. The two brothers were stunned at having come unexpectedly into each other's presence in their mother's parlor. They mumbled a greeting and then sat down dumbly in front of Maria Antônia and the others. Later, the old woman recalled the terrible silence that fell over the room and the words that José cried when he suddenly leaped up: "Because of this heartless fiend I am ruined and miserable!"

The fight that ensued before her very eyes was a confused nightmare. Afterward, even the participants did not know quite what had happened. By that time José was on his horse, calling repeatedly for his son João Pedro. But João Pedro and his uncle Hilário lay dead in a pool of blood on Maria Antônia's parlor floor. Before Hilário's companions could reload their guns, José rode away and fled south into Uruguay where he would remain for many years.

Finally, in 1855, Maria Antônia gave up the matriarchal household that she had maintained for thirty years and went to live with her daughter Francisca. There she spent her last fifteen years, spinning wool and singing about her long life. She continued to grieve over the deaths of her children (she survived eleven of them) but could rejoice in the fertility of her eighty-four grandchildren. One of her multitudinous great-grandchildren, born in the year of Curupaití, listened with special attention to the stories of his family. These were the stories that Maria Antônia had loved to tell about an aristocratic ancestor or about a wedding party that disappeared for one week, as well as the tragic stories the old woman seldom told but that could be collected from uncles and aunts on the long winter evenings of the borderland. Finally, during the first quarter of the twentieth century, this great-grandson wrote down these stories, more or less as they appear here.

SOURCES

The great-grandson who collected the family's oral traditions, and supplemented them with court documents and other archival materials, was Manuel da Costa Medeiros. His manuscript was published, many years after his death, as *História do Herval: Descrição, física e histórica* (Porto Alegre, 1980). The historical context for Maria Antônia's life was drawn from Chasteen's research on the nineteenth-century social and political history of the Brazilian-Uruguayan borderland in the nineteenth century, conducted at the Arquivo Público do Rio Grande do Sul and the Arquivo Histórico do Rio Grande do Sul, both in Porto Alegre, Brazil; and the Archivo General de la Nación, with its Sección Judicial, in Montevideo, Uruguay. For a comparison of the frontier discussed in this essay with others in the region, see David J. Weber and Jane M. Rausch, eds., *Where Cultures Meet: Frontiers in Latin American History* (Wilmington, DE, 1994).

II

The First Republican Generations: Between American Barbarism and European Civilization, 1825–1875

The generation that dominated the independence era bore confusion and hardships, but their prevailing mood was one of hope and expectation. In contrast, Latin Americans who experienced the first fifty years of independence suffered from dashed hopes and frequent pessimism as the glories of the late Bourbon period faded into memory while the promises of republicanism seemed a chimera. The security, certainty, and prosperity of the enlightened monarchy gave way to poverty, stagnation, insecurity, and civil conflict. What had appeared to be a single society during the colonial period proved after independence to be an archipelago of peoples, regions, and conflicting interests.

Elites in the cities struggled to develop an active cultural life and to reconcile their ideals of European civilization with the realities of American discord. They had the advantages of leisure time; of relative tranquility; of access to universities and to other intellectuals and their libraries; and of the opportunity to meet and exchange views with foreign visitors. Authors wrote about and discussed their own work and European poetry and novels and groped their way toward an authentic American voice. Some writers, such as Juana Manuela Gorriti of Argentina, had to flee political unrest at home. Gorriti, safely in Lima, Peru, after a brief and unhappy marriage to a Bolivian president, joined other writers in *tertulias* (discussion groups) where they read and talked about their work. Music, even opera, had wide popular appeal. Mexicans took pride in Angela Peralta's fame as an interpreter of the great European operas and in her efforts to write and perform truly Mexican works.*

Although shaken by conflicts between anticlerical and conservative forces, the Catholic Church still dominated education and retained its colonial aura of grandeur and formality in major cities. In the countryside or on the frontier, priests might be found who emulated the selfless dedication and devotion of early sixteenth-century friars. The small circles of educated elites sometimes felt alienated from their own nations and from the Europe they so admired. Many Latin American urbanites were, like their famous contemporary Domingo F. Sarmiento, author of *Life in the Argentine Republic in the Days of the Tyrants; or, Civilization and Barbarism,* simultaneously attracted to and repelled by their crude compatriots.

Most people in Latin America lived in rural areas and small villages, distant from the few comforts and amusements offered by the cities. In the countryside, nature—and human beings—remained untamed and relatively untamable. Political rebels as well as bandits commandeered horses, cattle, and crops. The new republican governments, based in major cities and allied with urban elites, struggled to replace imperial justice and administration in the volatile countryside. They had little success. Political and family feuds could poison an entire region; the feuds intensified whenever they became linked to national political parties or leaders. Carlota Lucia de Brito's story demonstrates how in Brazil a local feud intersected with Liberal and Conservative politics, leading to violence and tragedy in the untamed northeastern state of Pernambuco. Punishment ultimately came from the distant imperial government in Rio de Janeiro, and a temporary order was achieved (Chapter 3). In Paraguay, a relatively homogeneous and compact nation dominated by a traditional caudillo president, a judge drew on Hispanic legal tradition to defuse the conflict between Rosa Dominga Ocampos and her Spanish lover. In this case, the judge ensured social harmony by seeing that neither party lost face before the community (Chapter 4).

Sometimes the country, towns, or indigenous peoples rose up against the capital cities and the political and economic control they represented. By the 1870s most Latin American countries had experienced at least one major conflict pitting the provinces against the capital city. In Peru the rebellion that Juan Bustamante reluctantly headed had regional as well as indigenous roots since indigenous communities had strong agricultural and familial ties to their regions. Even when the provinces won, as happened in 1852 in Argentina, the cities proved too strong to be dominated. Ultimately, the cities tri-

---

*For a discussion of the society of elites, and of Gorriti and Peralta in particular, see Judith Ewell and William H. Beezley, eds., *The Human Tradition in Latin America: The Nineteenth Century* (Wilmington, DE: Scholarly Resources, 1989), 82–102, 114–86.

umphed over their captors, suggesting either that the outsiders had fought primarily to join the elite or that urban culture, with its ties to Europe, was too powerful to be overcome.

What of the special regions called frontiers? On the fringes of empire—to the far south in Argentina and Chile, in the Amazon or backlands of the Brazilian *sertão*, in the Venezuelan Orinoco or Guayana highlands, in the Colombian llanos, to the far north in Mexico—there frequently remained groups of unconquered Indians. Unlike indigenous settlements nearer to the European and mestizo population cores, the Indians who lived on the fringes dwelt in relative peace for the early part of the century. But as commercial agriculture and mining expanded, and as settlers fanned out from more populated areas, soldiers and priests began pacification of the frontier. On the Argentine pampas, indigenous peoples, like their Indian counterparts in the trans-Mississippi west in the United States, at first lived unmolested by the national government. By the 1880s, however, they had succumbed to the rush of soldiers, speculators, and ranchers into their homeland.

One's chances in life varied with residence in city, town, country, or frontier; with personal or family connections; with access to land or skills; with race; and with gender. Although many independence leaders espoused the liberal goal of freedom from servitude for all peoples, practical political and economic concerns meant that many blacks remained either enslaved or apprenticed until midcentury (or later, in the cases of Cuba and Brazil). Racial discrimination was more subtle than it was in the United States, but it existed. Most Creoles and persons of more European appearance looked down upon blacks, *castas,* and Indians as less civilized than themselves and perhaps incapable of improvement. The elite's political principles followed from their misguided social assumptions.

It is more difficult to generalize about what changes women experienced in the first decades after independence. At times, and in some places, it appears that wealthy or elite women were able to escape some of the restrictions enforced against their sisters. Some women could wield power and influence in national politics, acting through their husbands or fathers. For example, we should recall the power and influence of Encarnación, the famed wife of the Argentine caudillo Juan Manuel de Rosas. Of course, presidents and their wives could more easily escape the restrictions that constrained other, less grand individuals. In other cases, notions of family honor and pride seem to have limited wealthy women more than they did their poorer sisters. Rosa Dominga Ocampos, a nonelite woman of Paraguay, apparently enjoyed a good deal of personal and sexual freedom.

Some studies have suggested that women found their opportunities and status in 1850 reduced from what they had been under the Bourbon monarchs. Other researchers have pointed out that after independence *tertulias,* charitable organizations, and political conflicts may have given women some space in which to increase their experience, autonomy, and influence. It is difficult to determine the extent to which gender affected people's lives quite apart from questions of class, residence, race, and education.

What was the relationship between the social history as seen in these essays and the turbulent political history of the period? Perhaps the bitter civil wars reflected, in part, personal ambitions (Carlota Lucia de Brito), ethnic or regional frustration with central governments, or even a kind of anomie and confusion that followed the erosion of the Iberian colonial order. Liberal and Conservative parties advanced and defended their rival political programs, but historians have suggested that overt ideological cleavages represented only one level of what really was at stake.

In some ways the nineteenth-century conflicts meant a continuation of the hopes of the Independence Wars. In the very broadest terms, people fought over whether to recreate the enlightened Iberian society of the late eighteenth century or the liberal, western European society of the nineteenth century. In more personal terms, people struggled to keep or to expand any small advantage that they possessed, sometimes by calling on old traditions, sometimes by embracing modern ways. By the 1870s, after fifty years of struggle, the issue had been resolved largely in favor of the liberal European modernizers. The excitement and appeal of these early years of national life are in that one can see real alternatives competing for control of the future. How might Latin America be different today if all judges had been as wise as one Paraguayan jurist and all communities as closely knit as that of Rosa Dominga Ocampos in Paraguay?

3

Carlota Lucia de Brito: Women, Power, and Politics in Northeast Brazil

Joan E. Meznar

Brazil experienced less upheaval upon independence than did the Spanish-American nations. Under the 1824 constitution, Emperor Pedro I (1822–1831) allowed upper-class Brazilians to exercise some political influence, especially at the local and regional levels. Pedro I abdicated in 1831 in favor of his five-year-old son, Pedro II. A decade of disorder and uncertainty subsided in 1840 when young Pedro II began his official rule. His forty-nine-year reign represented political and legal continuity and generally was remarkable for its stability, moderation, and prosperity. Brazilian intellectuals worried less about the issues of civilization and barbarism, the conflicts between order and reform, than did their Spanish-American counterparts.

Still, rural areas and small towns in Brazil often experienced violence that belied the nation's reputation for tranquility. The central government, like the colonial Iberian administrations, could not control all of the vast national territory. Regional political leaders, allied with the rural poor and with backcountry bandits, enforced order with informal personal armies. Elites held together their networks of family, friends, and retainers by dispensing favors, protection, and jobs. Thus, when Emperor Pedro II in Rio de Janeiro dismissed a Liberal ministry and called on the Conservatives to govern, the effects rippled far beyond the capital.

Carlota Lucia de Brito, an attractive young woman, was allied with her lover, a local politician, and his Liberal friends in a small town in the northeastern state of Pernambuco. In 1848, when the emperor changed ministries in Rio, the region erupted into a bloody feud between Liberals and Conservatives. Carlota ordered the assassination of a Conservative enemy and was condemned to life imprisonment by an imperial court for her role in the crime.

Carlota's story demonstrates not only that patron-client networks protected women but also that they sometimes allowed women, at least in backwoods areas, to act independently. The subliminal issues of family and individual honor often intersected with overtly political issues. Politics as practiced in midcentury Brazil was complex.

41

So, too, was justice. Did Carlota's sentence punish her for the crime of murder, for being a political enemy of the party in power, or, perhaps, for being a woman who had become too strong and independent?

Joan Meznar has taught at Mount Holyoke College and the University of South Carolina and is now an associate professor at Westmont College in Santa Barbara, California. She received her Ph.D. from the University of Texas in 1986 and has held numerous fellowships from the Tinker Foundation, Fulbright-Hays, and the National Endowment for the Humanities. She continues to focus her research on the world of small farmers in northeastern Brazil from 1850 to 1900.

Politics in nineteenth-century Brazil centered primarily around family. Patterns of power and deference within it prepared each member for a role in the larger society. Families, by both portraying and reinforcing patron-client relationships, incorporated and thus perpetuated the acceptance of a social hierarchy with "protectors" at the top and "protected" at the bottom. The father's responsibility lay in protecting and controlling the women and children. To the fathers and older sons fell responsibility for preserving the family's integrity, in particular, for safeguarding the "honor" of female relations living within the household. The virtue of the women thus reflected the control men had over female family members. Men shaped the political world in which women lived. Women's most important political role appeared to be to acquiesce to the marriages that strengthened the extended family alliances upon which local politics rested. But women, at times, also acted as catalysts for political change. Some of the women who most directly influenced politics were not bound by traditional family roles; they exemplified an alternative to the ideals of a rigidly hierarchical society while functioning under the constraints of that very order. Carlota Lucia de Brito, the mistress of a powerful Paraiban politician, had a dramatic impact on political life in one Brazilian province during the midnineteenth century.

Carlota was a survivor. A refugee from catastrophic drought, she rebuilt her life in a new community, battled prejudice, and fought for her lover's political position. She survived a death sentence (commuted to a life term in the penal colony on the island of Fernando de Noronha) and finally died a free, very old woman in Recife around the turn of the twentieth century. The resilience that characterizes her story points to a strong, unusual woman, but her struggles were shared by many other Brazilian women. Carlota's story illuminates issues of class, gender, politics, and justice in nineteenth-century northeastern Brazil.

For those who lived in the backlands, in the northeastern *sertão,* periodic droughts severely disrupted normal life. About every thirty years the intensity of the drought would push men, women, and children from their familiar world, forcing them to begin anew in an area with more plentiful rainfall. All levels of society could be affected by the drought that scorched crops and destroyed fodder. The wealthy, bemoaning the loss of their cattle, often found refuge with relatives in the coastal region. The very poor, sometimes the last to leave because they had nowhere to go, died of hunger or exposure while searching for relief; the luckier of this group swelled the indigent contingent in the towns. The middling group, usually owning at least some portable property, also moved to the urban centers to rebuild their lives. For all, drought meant drastic change. Families, by and large, attempted to move together during droughts; the bonds of blood would help ease the transition and earn acceptance into a new community. Often, nonetheless, drought disrupted families as well. Fathers and brothers, insisting that women and children move immediately to healthier surroundings, might stay with the family goods until the last hope of salvaging crops and herds was gone. In the flight from the scorched backlands, adults and children succumbed to disease and death, destroying family balance. Lashing out against the hopelessness of their situation, men turned to banditry, abandoning their wives and children. And women who felt tied to undesirable marriages used the disruption to free themselves from unwanted husbands.

Drought years altered social conditions in both the countryside and the towns. Population exploded in the areas unaffected by the drought, pressuring the minimal social services available. The ties of familiarity and even of patronage and camaraderie that had bound backlanders to the city dwellers disintegrated. While the swelling mass of the poor frightened the staid urban society, many profited from the misery of others. Women and young girls from the backlands arrived in the towns laden with all their earthly possessions, trusting that the value of their gold jewelry would keep them clothed, fed, and sheltered until they found a new means of survival. The value of gold, in response to the sudden supply, always dropped precipitously. Townspeople bought up the cheap gold, saving it for the inevitable price rise when they would realize handsome profits. Once all their ornaments had been sold, women from the interior who had lost the protection of male kin might find in prostitution their only alternative for replenishing cash reserves and thus assuring survival.

In the drought of 1845, Carlota Lucia de Brito was among those who left the backlands of the province of Pernambuco and settled in the town of Areia. Situated in the humid *brejo* region of the province of Paraíba, Areia was not subject to dryness. An important market center in the midnineteenth century, it served as entrepôt for the coastal plantation region and the cattle-ranching *sertão*. Its merchant families also maintained close commercial ties with Recife, a major port and capital of the province of Pernambuco. The prosperity and wide-ranging connections of Areia's elite families placed the town among the most influential in provincial politics. Carlota arrived in Areia with a daughter, but no husband. She claimed to be a widow and later would be implicated in the murder of her husband. But in 1845 she was concerned primarily with building a new life. While hers had certainly not been a life of luxury, neither had it been one of penury. She had owned some land, she survived the move to Areia, and she quickly settled into a situation that seemed rather comfortable: she came under the protection of Areia's leading Liberal politician, Joaquim José dos Santos Leal. Apparently a woman of considerable beauty, Carlota did not possess the social status (nor did her family have the political ties) necessary to make her an acceptable wife for a member of the Santos Leal family. Nevertheless, she was soon installed in Joaquim José's town home and behaved as though the two had indeed legally married. She had found an important male protector, but in forfeiting the acceptable role of an "honest" woman, she became a target for accusations against her own and her lover's morality. While many sons of important Brazilian families enjoyed liaisons with women who were not their wives, these affairs were to remain discreet. Townspeople who readily accepted even frequent forays to the local houses of prostitution would pass harsh judgment on those men who, they believed, flaunted immorality by openly living with women they were unwilling to marry.

From 1844 to 1848 the Liberal party controlled the government ministries in Rio de Janeiro, the capital city of the Brazilian empire. Liberal ascendancy in the capital was reflected in the provinces. In 1846, Joaquim José dos Santos Leal, lieutenant colonel and commander of Areia's National Guard, was elected to and served in Paraíba's legislative assembly. His chief Conservative opponent was Trajano Alipio de Holanda Chacon, another illustrious citizen of Areia who had served as deputy in both the national and provincial assemblies, as president of the province of Paraíba (1839–40), and as municipal judge of Areia from 1840 to 1848. It was during the Liberal ascendancy that Carlota and Joaquim José set up housekeeping together. Townspeople, suspicious and envious of Carlota, could do nothing but murmur. Trajano Chacon (Joaquim José's neighbor in town), however, let it be known that he considered Carlota nothing more than a prostitute; neither he nor Carlota disguised the distaste each inspired in the other.

In 1848 the Liberal party fell from favor, and Conservatives once again occupied the chief imperial ministries. Three years after Carlota's flight from drought, the provinces of Pernambuco and Paraíba entered a period of serious political upheaval. In Recife, a newly formed party of the Praia (composed primarily of disgruntled Liberals) challenged the Conservative government for power. Armed rebellion ensued. Driven from Recife, Praieira leaders fled north, seeking adherents as they went, hoping to return with greater strength to Pernambuco. The movement did not gather much momentum in Paraíba, with the notable exception of the town of Areia. Politics there, as elsewhere, was closely tied to family interests. The Conservatives of Areia, led by Trajano Chacon, despised the Santos Leal Liberals. Their animosity in town and provincial government preceded the Praieira revolt and would survive the collapse of the Praieira movement. But the heightened tensions caused by the rebellion (the Santos Leal faction supported the Praieriros who were opposed by Trajano Chacon's Conservative allies) would bring sinister consequences to both families.

When loyal government troops quashed the revolt, members of the Santos Leal family suffered not only a defeat and prison terms but also the humiliation of losing to the Conservative faction. Liberals, potential traitors to the imperial government, were forced out of local public office. Even the family space of the defeated Liberals was violated. The home of dona Maria José dos Santos Leal (Joaquim José's mother) was requisitioned to serve as headquarters for the imperial troops that defeated the Praieira movement. The looting that accompanied the stay of government troops in the Santos Leal house was so thorough that even the diadems from images in doña Maria's home altar were stolen. When, that same year, Joaquim José dos Santos Leal (from the safety of his family ranch in the interior of Paraíba) ran against Trajano Alipio de Holanda Chacon for a seat in the national Chamber of Deputies, few in Areia doubted that Trajano Chacon would win the election.

After Joaquim José's flight from Areia following the defeat of the Praia, Carlota took charge of his business in town. She also took the initiative in expanding her role as benefactress to loyal Liberals. Among her duties was that of serving as liaison between her lover's more humble clients and the Church. Much of local life was tied to the Catholic Church. All the important passages from birth through marriage to death were channeled through the local church. Parish priests oversaw the spiritual well-being of their flock while also providing the framework in which temporal duties could be performed. Besides baptizing children, marrying couples, and burying the dead, the priests explained government decrees and collaborated with political authorities to ensure an orderly society. Just as the family imparted to its members the values of deference, so also did the Church, while confirming the importance of families, instill values that contributed to an orderly, hierarchical community. Carlota, herself only a marginal member of the society that the Church promoted, became responsible for helping her lover's supporters assume the role of upstanding citizens. She arranged, among other things, church baptisms and marriages for those who could not afford the parish fees.

In 1849 the town priest, Father Francisco de Holanda Chacon, was also Trajano Chacon's brother. One afternoon, while Carlota conferred with the priest about an upcoming baptism, Trajano arrived to pay his brother a visit. Furious at finding a "prostitute" in Areia's vicarage, and in an apparent effort to drive home his political and moral superiority over his Liberal opponent, Trajano openly confronted Carlota: he attempted literally to kick her out of his brother's house. For a woman who possessed a measure of social prestige, the accusation of leading an irregular life, coupled with the humiliation of being expelled from the vicarage, proved unbearable. In her anger at this affront, Carlota saw the opportunity to avenge both her own and her outlaw lover's honor. She decided to contact old relations in the *sertão* and commissioned Trajano's murder.

While Joaquim José (still avoiding a prison term for his role in the Praieira revolt by remaining far from Areia) probably knew little or nothing of Carlota's plan, his family in town supported her attempt to avenge his honor. Carlota charged Antonio Brabo, a cousin of Joaquim José's from the interior, with executing Trajano Chacon. Brabo, in turn, solicited the aid of one of the *agregados* (tenant farmers) of the Santos Leal family, a man named Antonio José das Virgens, locally known as Beiju, who lived by favor on Santos Leal land. Beiju refused Brabo, but, after Carlota herself intervened, he accepted his duty to his patron and, encouraged by her promises of reward and protection, agreed to cooperate. Carlota's extended family thus joined with the Santos Leal clan in the determination to execute Trajano Chacon.

After several unsuccessful ambush attempts, Brabo and Beiju finally succeeded in killing Trajano Chacon on September 5, 1849, the very day that Trajano defeated Joaquim José in the contest for a seat in the Chamber of Deputies. To many in Areia the murder seemed to be revenge for the electoral defeat; Joaquim José, of course, became the prime suspect for ordering the crime. With Conservatives firmly in power in Areia after the Praieira debacle, the quest for justice reflected party as well as family animosity. Conservatives determined to bring the Liberals to justice while the Chacon family sought to avenge the death of one of their own.

Carlota immediately sent messengers to her lover, who remained hidden in the backlands of the province, urging him to flee even farther from the justice to be dispensed by Areia Conservatives. Although Carlota had planned the crime, Joaquim José tacitly accepted responsibility, thus fulfilling his duty to protect his woman; he knew that if he stayed in Paraíba he would be held liable for Trajano Chacon's death. Carlota eventually joined him in his flight from the province. The Conservative thirst for vengeance, however, would not be satiated without bringing the criminals to justice in Areia. The deputy police chief of Areia, José Pereira Copque, relentlessly pursued leads concerning the Santos Leal group throughout the northeast. In March 1850 he finally tracked down Joaquim José, the latter's brother Manoel José, and Carlota in the interior of the province of Rio Grande do Norte, only to find them heavily armed and prepared to resist capture. Copque believed it imperative to seek reinforcements before engaging the fugitives in a gun battle, and in so doing allowed them to escape. The Santos Leal family had a wide network of friends throughout the northeast who gave the fugitives cover and provisions to help them in their flight. For their part, the Chacons had influential ties to provincial authorities in the region and managed to circulate descriptions of the fleeing group to police chiefs in the surrounding provinces.

Early in 1851 those accused of the murder of Trajano Chacon were sentenced in absentia. By that time it had become clear that Carlota had planned the crime. She and Beiju were sentenced to death; Joaquim José to twenty years in prison, and Manoel José to twenty-three years and four months imprisonment (Antonio Brabo had been killed by a slave). The search for the accused continued; they were finally captured on May 16, 1851, in the province of Piauí and sent back to Areia.

Meanwhile, in May 1851 the emperor granted amnesty to those who had participated in the Praieira revolt, ordering that "an eternal silence enfold all the facts about which the amnestied group might be questioned regarding their complicity in the rebellion that recently took place in the province of Pernambuco." The Conservatives could no longer hope to punish the Praia group, but they could still make Joaquim José and his supporters pay for the murder of Trajano Chacon.

The outlaws were finally brought to Areia in early December 1851, only a few days before the yearly holiday honoring Our Lady of the Conception, the town's patron saint. What a contrast the criminal Carlota presented to the Holy Mother of God! The inhabitants of Areia took seriously their duties toward the town patroness; her feast day was always prepared with elaborate care. Devotion to saints in northeastern Brazil long had reinforced the importance of protection in a paternalistic society. As with human relations, there existed a large variety of degrees of power among the saints. In rural Brazilian society, personal relations of patronage and protection provided the surest guarantees of security and immediate improvement of living conditions. The same occurred in dealing with saints. A system of duties and obligations guaranteed supernatural action. Not all saints possessed the same power; some proved stronger by exerting more influence on their own patrons, and thus assured greater miracles for their devotees. Devotion to a certain saint indicated acceptance of that image as powerful to bargain effectively with the supreme patron, God.

Our Lady of the Conception, the patroness of Areia, was one of the representations of the Virgin Mary most closely associated with motherhood. Her devotees believed that as the mother of God, she would influence her son on their behalf and that as the town's chosen patroness, she dispensed special protection and favor to its inhabitants. The Virgin ranked second only to Christ in most Brazilians' perceptions of supernatural power. Some even believed that Mary's role as mother made her more powerful than her divine son, for in the family hierarchy children must defer to their parents. Yet, overall, the Virgin's role appealed to the populace not so much for her authority as for her maternal compassion: the same attitude Mary had displayed toward her son at the foot of his cross would also be manifested toward her "children" in Areia. Carlota's image as "murderess" and "prostitute" sharply contrasted with the image of Mary's compassion and virginal motherhood, which Areia was preparing to celebrate.

The townspeople well knew that the powerful Santos Leal family would attempt to keep its two sons from paying the legal consequences of the crime they had committed. Family responsibilities included protecting its members from the law. But political rivalry between Conservatives and Liberals had reached such a point by 1851 that it was impossible to protect Joaquim José and Manoel José from justice. At one time important local political leaders, they were brought into town chained to their mounts, in a humiliating display of power eroded. The president of Paraíba instructed Areia's deputy police chief not to release the Santos Leal brothers under any circumstances; they were to be considered prisoners of the state. Carlota, not a part of the Santos Leal family, did not enjoy the same attempts at protection as did her lover. She, however, also counted on family support. Her relatives in Pajeú das Flores, province of Pernambuco, attempted to have her removed to their town's jurisdiction in order to stand trial for the murder of her husband. But Father Francisco Chacon petitioned the president of Paraíba to guarantee that Carlota would pay for the death of his brother and not be sent to Pernambuco to be tried for the death of a less important man and possibly be released or sentenced to a less rigorous penalty. Father Chacon's petition, sent all the way to the minister of justice of the Brazilian empire, succeeded in keeping Carlota from benefiting from her family's attempt to protect her. Once again, she alone would be responsible for her survival.

With the accused finally captured and in Areia, a jury was assembled to try them. Most of the earlier sentences were upheld, with the exception of Carlota's, now changed from death to life imprisonment. Only Beiju, a poor retainer who at one time had enjoyed the protection of the Santos Leal family, was sentenced to death for the murder of Trajano Chacon. Despite petitions for imperial clemency, he was hanged in 1863. Carlota, Joaquim José, and Manoel José were sent to the island prison of Fernando de Noronha.

Escape from the island was practically impossible. The only recourse left the Santos Leal family was to request authorities to bring their boys back to the mainland. Once the brothers were on the mainland, the family could supply them with some amenities and even conspire to free them by force. In 1865, dona Maria, in a display of lofty maternal responsibility, petitioned the president of the province to transfer her sons to the prison of Paraíba, since they were blind and sick and suffering and she wanted to give them the aid she owed them as their mother. Her petition was not granted. Joaquim José died on Fernando de Noronha, and Manoel José eventually returned to Areia, blind and crazed from his prison experience.

Carlota, on the other hand, survived. She, who had accompanied Joaquim José in his flight through at least four northeastern provinces and stood trial with him in Areia, quickly abandoned him once they reached Fernando de Noronha. It was clear to her that her erstwhile lover needed protection far more than he was able to offer it and that she had to manage to protect herself. Once again, she sought the company of a powerful man, this time the director of the penal colony. For more than thirty years she lived as comfortably as possible on Fernando de Noronha. In 1889 the Brazilian emperor was deposed. The new republican government commuted life sentences to thirty years in prison. Carlota was free at last. In 1890 she left the island and settled in Recife, where she spent her last days in charge of a boardinghouse for young men from influential families in the interior who came to Pernambuco's capital to study.

The Santos Leal family continued to play an important role in Areia politics. Carlota's crime did not relegate them to political obscurity or even political impotence, but it did exacerbate tensions at a particularly volatile time. Had Trajano Chacon not been murdered, Joaquim José dos Santos Leal probably would have continued to be a major political force in the town. Yet Carlota's story must be understood as more than simply the account of a woman who ruins one man's life. Carlota knew she would never be accepted as a full member of the community she entered when she moved to Areia in the drought of 1845. She had refused to confine herself to a role others sought to impose. She was not willing even to subject herself fully to the man with whom she lived. The self-assertion and independence of this woman, who moved beyond the boundaries of family hierarchy perceived as so vital to social order, contributed, in the final analysis, to the community's outrage against the Santos Leal family. It was bad enough that Carlota lived openly in concubinage with Joaquim José, but a man who could not keep his woman in check should suffer for that crime as well as for any others that grew from that inability. Ultimately, even though Carlota ordered the murder, Joaquim José was responsible for it. Only in the context of patriarchy can the political and family revenge against the Santos Leal brothers be fully understood.

Carlota well knew the options available to women without influential husbands. Rather than conform to the place reserved for her in a stratified world, she determined to move upward. It was, after all, impossible to maintain the ideal hierarchical society when nature and politics conspired to disrupt order. Those who understood the fragility of hierarchy, who individually survived its disruption by disaster, would chip away at the standards of accepted authority. But they remained subject to a system still gasping for survival. Carlota, for all her strength and independent ways, was fully dependent on men until the end of her very long life.

SOURCES

The most complete account of Carlota's crime is in Horacio de Almeida, *Brejo de Areia,* 2d ed. (João Pessoa, Paraíba, 1980), pp. 61–75. My account here is based also on manuscript documents from the Arquivo Nacional and the Arquivo

Histórico da Paraíba. This research was made possible through a National Endowment for the Humanities Travel to Collections Grant.

4

Rosa Dominga Ocampos:
A Matter of Honor in Paraguay

Thomas L. Whigham

Historians have paid scant attention to Paraguay. An isolated colonial backwater, this peaceful agricultural region, populated by friendly Guaraní Indians, developed into a mestizo society that generally lacked the extremes of wealth and poverty found in more important parts of the empire. The Jesuits chose Paraguay as a hospitable field in which to develop an extensive and idealistic mission area. Paraguayan leaders, much like the Central American elites who scorned union with Mexico, chose autonomy over absorption into the Argentine confederation at the time of independence.

The early republican history of Paraguay often has been dismissed as a simple tale of backward caudillos (José Gaspar Rodríguez de Francia, 1816–1840; Carlos Antonio López, 1840–1862, and his son, Francisco Solano López, 1862–1870). The inland nation seemed oblivious to the liberal European values that represented progress and that were beginning to penetrate some of the other Latin American countries. Historians cite the disastrous War of the Triple Alliance (1865–1870), which robbed Paraguay of 60 percent of its male population, as further evidence of the irresponsibility of traditional caudillos. Yet if Paraguay's splendid backwardness is examined more closely, one finds that its caudillos tried to reconcile economic development with the maintenance of traditional communal values. Some of these Hispanic and mestizo values even may have offered a more effective, and less costly, development model than that provided by Europeanized urban society.

The progress of the 1847 legal suit in which Rosa Dominga Ocampos sued her Spanish lover for breach of promise reveals both positive and negative aspects of López's Paraguay. A woman's honor was analogous legally to a possession that could be stolen, and even a woman of modest social background could go to court and insist on compensation. Women had limited legal and civil rights, but Rosa could appear before the court alone without the intercession of a male relative. Paraguayan society, although tightly knit, was no egalitarian utopia, however. Whereas Paraguayans accorded their former Spanish masters high status and respect, even though they sometimes resented them, they discriminated against people of darker skin and

53

considered them to be inferior. Perhaps most significantly, Thomas Whigham's essay demonstrates the tension between the community's desire to compensate an individual for his or her grievances and its longing to guarantee community harmony by encouraging a truce or reconciliation between litigants.

Thomas L. Whigham received his Ph.D. from Stanford University and is an associate professor of history at the University of Georgia. He belongs to a group of historians examining the uniqueness and creativity of Paraguay in the late colonial and early national era. Whigham has published *The Politics of River Trade: Tradition and Development in the Upper Plata, 1780–1870* (Albuquerque, 1991).

A visitor to Paraguay in the midnineteenth century would discover a land that was quiet and isolated in the extreme. The great muddy rivers that surrounded the inland republic gave it a picturesque appearance as they bathed its verdant landscape, rich with flowering trees and all manner of exotic plants and animals. Yet these same waters had long served as a barrier, as a warning sign that Paraguay wanted no truck with the outside world. Nearly thirty years had passed since the taciturn dictator and doctor of theology José Gaspar Rodríguez de Francia first elaborated a policy of nonintercourse with neighboring states, a policy well justified by the violent political realities of the day. Both Francia and his corpulent successor, Carlos Antonio López, faced the threat of foreign expansionism and both adamantly refused to accept anything less than recognition of national independence. Paraguayan society might prosper or decline, they believed, but only on terms that were specifically Paraguayan in context.

The authoritarian nature and staunch isolationism of Paraguay's government encountered no resistance in the countryside. There the tiny landed elite pursued its traditional interest in stockraising, while the small farmer, or *kokuejara,* occupied himself with the cultivation of maize, tobacco, and manioc root. Social life was in every way limited to the family, the church, and the *pulpería* (general store). And if infusions of information and new habits from beyond the frontier were few, they were not much missed in a rustic world dominated by Hispanic values. The dictators in Asunción might periodically take advantage of foreign contacts in commerce, but rarely did any outside influences trickle down to the average Paraguayan, whose passive acquiescence in this unchanging pattern of life was generally taken for granted.

So it had always been for Rosa Dominga Ocampos, a young woman of modest background from the interior farming village of Capiatá. Until the late 1840s she contented herself with the usual pursuits of girlhood in the Paraguayan countryside. These included domestic chores, babysitting, tending animals, rolling cigars, and preparing the maté gourd in which was drunk yerba maté, the fragrant green tea so popular throughout the southern third of the continent. As she matured, her thoughts probably focused more and more on marriage, perhaps with a wealthy older man who could provide for both her and her mother. This is where the trouble started. In 1847, now at age twenty-four, Ocampos became the victim of mean-hearted local gossips who claimed that she was about to bear a child out of wedlock. The squabble that ensued might have gone unnoticed were it not for her reaction. Rather than meekly accept the damage that malicious rumor might cause her reputation, Ocampos decided to fight back through legal means.

Estupro (seduction or breach of promise if the woman consented voluntarily to the sex act) was a serious offense under Spanish legal precepts. An individual's reputation was central to the scheme of balances within the community, and a charge of *estupro* could upset all of these balances. Only a woman with a good reputation could bring such a charge before the authorities since known prostitutes and "women of loose morals" had no legal recourse against mistreatment. Nonetheless, in the Paraguay of the 1840s it was still odd for any woman who felt wronged by her lover or betrothed to appeal to the law.

The judicial system available to Rosa Dominga Ocampos inherited much from the colonial past, including an array of vaguely defined rural judgeships. In some districts, municipal *delegados* (military commanders) fulfilled judicial as well as administrative functions. Regardless of the nomenclature, all judges were responsible to and appointed by the central government in Asunción.

Ocampos, in testing the legal waters, first met in a short session with a *juez territorial*, the Paraguayan equivalent of a circuit judge, and he evidently advised her to drop the matter. She flatly refused. In early 1848 she decided to bypass intermediate levels and recorded her complaint with the interim vice president of the republic, Juan José Alvarenga. The latter had been an important jurist even during the colonial period, and perhaps Ocampos expected him to give her case a careful and sympathetic analysis.

In the *demanda* (complaint), Ocampos maintained that life in Capiatá had become difficult for her. Having lost her father at an early age, she now faced the shameless gossip of local busybodies. Specifically, she had become romantically linked with a Spanish resident, Martín de Abazolo, who had taken full advantage of the "weakness of her sex." Having plied her with assurances of his love and a promise of marriage, Abazolo had slept with her on several occasions, or so she claimed.

Ocampos swore that she had taken Abazolo at his word—for he was a gentleman—and that the two even had gone so far as to petition Carlos Antonio López for permission to wed. Government consent was needed because Dr. Francia earlier had outlawed marriage between Paraguayans and the hated Spaniards. Although in dealing with foreigners López often acted with as much caprice as Francia, he nevertheless recently had seen fit to alter the marriage law on a case-by-case basis. Perhaps López thought to curry the favor of individuals who, although no longer a threat to the state, could potentially strengthen the regime through their support. In any case, on this occasion, as with other elderly Spaniards marrying their local paramours, López evidently offered no objections, and Ocampos began to plan her trousseau.

Almost overnight, however, the relationship began to turn sour. Abazolo appeared at the Ocampos residence less and less and, when confronted with these absences, made a startling accusation: he claimed that his now former fiancée had become pregnant by a mulatto who worked in her household. This was indeed a serious charge. As in other areas of Spanish America, Paraguay maintained a culture that was deeply conscious of race. Any mention of a possible dalliance with a mulatto could spell social ruin, even for someone from a relatively poor background. This explains the eagerness with which Ocampos sought to clear her name, as well as her willingness to pay the high fees for stamped paper (on which all state petitions had to be written) and for the services of legal advisers and professional scribes. Given the gravity of the issue involved, Ocampos had no intention of allowing her own illiteracy to stand in the way of vindication. She knew that a relationship with a European, even an illicit one, might bring considerable advantages, but with a mulatto, never!

In her plea to Alvarenga, Ocampos presented herself as the aggrieved party. She was not, in fact, pregnant, as a visit to a midwife in nearby Pirayú had confirmed, nor had she experienced a miscarriage. Abazolo's betrayal and false public utterings, she maintained, made it impossible for her to remain silent. As her reputation was irretrievably tarnished, she demanded some kind of compensation from the Spaniard. Ocampos emphasized that she acted not out of malice "but only to obtain vindication, to satisfy her gravely offended honor."

Even if her portrayal of these events was basically accurate, Ocampos clearly stood to gain from any xenophobic feelings she might encounter in Alvarenga. Since late colonial times, when they controlled the all-important Asunción *cabildo* (city council), Europeans had been regarded in Paraguay with some distrust. Although always a small minority in the country, they possessed a commercial acumen that brought them success even in bad times, and Paraguayans envied as much as hated them.

The local Spaniards proved the obvious victims of the 1811 *cuartelazo* (barracks revolt), which brought independence to Paraguay. Given the uncompromising spirit of the times, it was no surprise when the new revolutionary junta sought to wrest control of the bureaucracy from the Spaniards. But the Paraguayans went even further, casually stripping their former colonial masters of any influence in commerce and in the Church. Abandoning the idealistic platitudes of equality and brotherhood for a less lofty expediency, the government erected stiff precautionary measures against all Spaniards, from the lowliest day worker to the highest member of the mercantile elite. In this manner, the Paraguayans gave vent to their hatred.

Dr. Francia, himself the son of a foreigner, was no exception. As supreme dictator, he strove to dismantle those institutions most visibly connected with the Europeans, not excluding the priesthood, which he reshaped to suit his own needs. Inclined to suspicion by his temper and situation, Francia took no chances, and beginning in the late 1810s, he exiled those Europeans whom he considered dangerous and harassed those who remained in Asunción with massive fines and forced contributions. Adding humiliation to contempt, he also forbade them from riding horseback, a traditional perquisite of gentlemen. In response to such pressures, many Spaniards fled into the countryside, where they hoped to lead quiet lives until the advent of a more sympathetic regime. There Europeans like Abazolo invested their capital in land and cattle, kept their heads low, and secured informal alliances with Paraguayan women.

In his own account before Alvarenga, Abazolo protested his complete innocence and sought to portray Rosa Dominga Ocampos as little more than a common gold digger. He had been the victim throughout and not Ocampos, toward whom he had always shown the proper decorum. After all, had he not been the one to formulate the marriage contract in the first place and to seek the appropriate licenses from the president of the republic? Abazolo was at least in his midfifties at the time and in all of his years in Paraguay had never made trouble for the government. Now a village hussy had made a fool of him by charging him with *estupro*. He was in no mood to be generous.

According to Abazolo, the real trouble had started when word reached him that Ocampos had boasted publicly of being pregnant, a great surprise to him indeed since, despite her claim to the contrary, they had never shared a bed. The Spaniard stated that the woman refused to confirm or deny her pregnancy, which was, to his way of thinking, a tacit confession of wrongdoing. Moreover, she declined to return any of the gifts he had given her, although he had tried on several occasions to reclaim them.

Still further evidence of Ocampos's illicit behavior soon came to light. Her mulatto lover, Domingo Benítez, actually visited Abazolo and confirmed the nature of his relationship with Ocampos. Other citizens of Capiatá then stepped forward to swear that they also had knowledge of her pregnancy. As for the midwife's report, Abazolo dismissed it out of hand. The woman might conceivably have miscarried at some point in the recent past, but that she had been pregnant by Benítez was beyond doubt.

If anyone's honor had been offended, Abazolo concluded, surely it was his own. He stood accused of seduction and breach of promise, both completely specious charges, and the woman who denounced him had been manifestly unfaithful and was therefore unworthy of the government's consideration. Her "lack of morals had corrupted the neighborhood," and Abazolo begged the interim vice president to silence her once and for all.

At the distance of over 140 years it is difficult to choose between the merits of the different charges and counter-charges. Standards of evidence in 1840s Paraguay allowed for the admission of hearsay, and sifting through the many layers of rumor would present a formidable task in any event. On the surface, Abazolo's case is the weaker. His litany of witnesses is not supported by sworn affidavits in the extant documentation. At the same time, an alleged pregnancy should have offered easy opportunities for confirmation, but no record exists to show that this was done. For her part, Ocampos was hardly a disinterested party, but a preponderance of evidence does seem to favor her position.

In the end, Alvarenga's approach to the whole matter proved less than Solomonic. Falling back on his legal prerogatives, he passed all of the paperwork on to lower officials and requested a judgment from a district-level justice of the peace, José de la Paz Berges. Although only in his midtwenties, Berges already had made a name for himself as an efficient functionary of the López government and had risen quickly in the state bureaucracy. His later career was likewise notable and included service as Paraguayan delegate to a mixed-claims commission in Washington, DC, and a stint as foreign minister of the republic before and during the disastrous Triple Alliance War (1865–1870).

In his resolution of the Ocampos-Abazolo difficulties, Berges rendered a judgment in keeping with common sense and with Paraguayan social reality. The small society of Capiatá would be rife with intrigue and jealousy in any case and what the present situation called for was maximum toleration and flexibility. Therefore, Berges ordered the two parties to attempt a reconciliation, to forget their past differences and recriminations, and to work out a solution that could salvage honor on both sides. He granted them five days in which to present a plan.

On May 15, 1848, Berges approved the final terms of reconciliation between Rosa Dominga Ocampos and Martín de Abazolo. The latter agreed to pay the young woman thirty-four pesos in silver as a token of sincere regret over the whole affair, and in accepting this rather generous sum—enough to purchase a small herd of cattle—Ocampos effectively brought the relationship back full circle. In closing the case, Berges declared both parties essentially blameless. True, they had fallen victim to malicious gossip, but none of this loose talk had any basis in fact. No *estupro* had occurred. If they now desired, they were free to continue their lives together with their reputations intact. And this is exactly what Berges advised them to do; the government had spoken.

The judicial records do not indicate whether the couple continued on the path to a happy marriage. One suspects that Abazolo was angry for having lost so much cash, but he could have regained the money simply by marrying the woman. No matter—from the viewpoint of the state, it was enough that order had been restored to the community and that Berges had mandated a "Christian reconciliation." Whether that really ended the matter or not is something we doubtless shall never know.

The case of Rosa Dominga Ocampos and Martín de Abazolo illustrates much about Paraguayan society in the midnineteenth century. For one thing, it shows how a small-town environment easily transformed idle gossip into a heated legal feud. To be sure, Paraguay was not alone in this regard; a similar chain of events might well be imagined in rural areas of the United States or Europe in precisely the same historical period.

What, then, is specifically Paraguayan about this whole affair? The answer lies in the unusual degree to which Hispanic legal tradition retained its force within the independent republic. Certain social theorists have mistakenly argued that the process of nation building ripped apart much of the older sense of community, leaving little more than a void in its place. This phenomenon, it is supposed, explains the nearly desperate search for identity that Latin Americans experience in the present day. In Paraguay, however, traditional values clearly lived on after independence, with the state periodically intervening, as in this instance, to reinforce established standards of behavior. Elsewhere, French, and to a much lesser degree North American, models already had begun to erode the old patterns. Paraguay was different. As an absolutist in the Bourbon mold rather than a Bolívar-style revolutionary, Dr. Francia modified only those elements of the colonial system that might restrain his authoritarian leadership. In almost all other respects, the tenor of the colonial past remained fixed in Paraguay, even years after Francia's death. Changes did occur under Carlos Antonio López, but only very slowly.

For Rosa Dominga Ocampos, there was something beneficial in all this, since the conservative traditions permitted a direct appeal to the highest authorities for advice as well as judgment. Alvarenga and Berges acted as manifestations of the paterfamilias principle, each guiding the litigants with a fatherly hand in the direction of a satisfactory reconciliation. That Ocampos should turn to the state for help might surprise those who view Hispanic culture as a sort of prison for women. Ocampos knew differently. Primitive and isolated though it might be, Paraguay still afforded her ample opportunities to press for restitution of her honor.

SOURCES

Documentation on Rosa Dominga Ocampos, including all affidavits and pleas, can be found in Asunción's National Archive, Sección Nueva Encuadernación, vol. 2680. This archive, especially its Sección Judicial Criminal, also provided many details as to legal procedure in 1840s Paraguay.

III

The Fin de Siècle Generations: The Tension between Decadence and Progress, 1870–1900

A new spirit pervaded the last quarter of the nineteenth century in Latin America. In most areas the Europeanized urban liberals had defeated the traditionalists and were strengthening the new order, which would finally replace the old Iberian one. Progress in all forms loomed large. New buildings, city parks and avenues, railroads, streetlights, refrigerated ships, and industries were all visible signs of the modernization that had been dreamed of for much of the century. Railroads and armies drew the formerly lawless frontiers more closely into national orbits.

Science and technology, and the people who could best manipulate them, ushered in the new millennium. Some individuals adapted better than others to the challenges and to the feeling that their world was crumbling and a new one fighting to emerge. The couple Emilio and Gabriela Coni of Argentina offered simultaneously the benefits of medical science and the increasing control that the liberal elites assumed when they began to pass public health legislation for the rest of the population (Chapter 6). Most of these winners lived in major cities, in islands of modernity and centers of national power and wealth.

Other Latin Americans lagged behind, either ignored or patronized in the new age. A new poverty sometimes accompanied the new progress. Former frontiers had become safe for settlement, but what would become of the gauchos and Indians already living in these regions? Some changes rendered helpless the people and institutions that in the past had served as buffers between the national elites and the rural poor and indigenous groups. Police and armies had become more efficient national institutions, which threatened the local patronage of regional caudillos. The Church hierarchy had grudgingly accepted a more limited national role as part of its newly structured alliance with Liberal politicians.

Some individuals or groups who challenged the new age met defeat. The Mexican sage Nicolás Zúñiga played the clown, and few of his compatriots recognized that the dictator Porfirio Díaz was the real joke (Chapter 5). An Indian leader such as Mandeponay used the Church to protect his people in Bolivia, but his successors would have to seek other solutions and allies to fit their own times (Chapter 7). Cuba and Brazil outlawed slavery in the 1880s but relegated former slaves to the margins of national life. However much creole leaders might despise the colored masses as inferior to European peasants, they had to acknowledge that Indians, mestizos, *pardos,* mulattoes, and blacks formed the citizenry of their modern nations. Beneath the glittering facade of liberal progress lay the decadence of unresolved social and economic inequality.

The last quarter of the century also saw a resurgence of major conflicts, which were again cast in political terms. The dismantling of old empires and institutions had left behind a feeling of insecurity about what would replace them. The costly independence struggle of Cuba demonstrated the sad impotence of Spain. The shining empire of Dom Pedro II fell in 1889 with hardly a whimper. Colombia had its War of 1,000 Days (1899–1902), and Uruguay its final conflict between Liberals and Conservatives in 1903. The War of the Pacific (1879–1884) destroyed Bolivian and Peruvian optimism and assured Chile's ascendancy, albeit a Chile chastened by the bloody struggle between president and parliament in 1891. In Venezuela the Andean hordes of Cipriano Castro took over the nation in 1899. Political parties to represent new, dynamic economic interests emerged in Argentina and Chile. These struggles and, in some cases, "new men" highlighted the sense of the decay of the old age and the birth of the new.

Do these individuals constitute a single generation? Surely not, for they had neither a common background nor common attitudes toward issues of their day. They shared only in the anxieties and contradictions that marked the end of the nineteenth century in Latin America. Sometimes in their individual lives, and certainly collectively, they exemplify the tensions between progress and decadence.

5

Mexican Sartre on the Zócalo: Nicolás Zúñiga y Miranda

William H. Beezley

The rule of dictator Porfirio Díaz in Mexico has become synonymous with the modern, positivistic dictatorships of the late nineteenth century. Díaz first seized power in 1876 with the battle cry of "effective suffrage and no reelection." He surrendered power between 1880 and 1884, but he retained the top office after that until 1911. Nonetheless, elections were held at four-year intervals (six-year intervals after 1904). The stability that Díaz's long regime provided allowed Mexico at last to enjoy a burst of economic development. Agriculture for commercial export expanded, thousands of miles of railroads linked Mexico to U.S. markets, and a modest industrial complex appeared.

The political and intellectual elite and the Catholic Church hastened to sing Díaz's praises as the necessary gendarme of Mexico. Most prominent in the chorus were his technocratic advisers, known collectively as *científicos* (scientific men), who followed the positivist philosophy of the Frenchman Auguste Comte. Few people dared publicly to criticize either the government or positivism. Many in the growing middle class depended on the expanding government bureaucracy for employment. Entrepreneurs needed the goodwill of government officials to secure their concessions and investments.

Still, some Mexicans questioned the benefits of the new progress. Farm and industrial labor saw their standard of living fall while food costs rose drastically. Employers called in the army or the *rurales* (national police force) at any sign of workers' restiveness. The *científicos* praised education, but they did little to invest in rural public schools. On the whole, they preferred foreign immigrants to native mestizos and Indians.

Nicolás Zúñiga y Miranda was born around 1856. He became a kind of "wise fool" in Mexico City, where he was known for his scientific inventions and earthquake predictions. He confirmed his role as a fool when, in 1896 and in 1900, he ran for president against Díaz, but in running he also drew attention to the farcical elections in a way that made Díaz uneasy. If all must feign compliance with a dictatorship in order to avoid reprisal, then what outlets are there for frustration? As the story of Zúñiga y Miranda illustrates, poking fun at government values, even indirectly, both can provide a release for frustration and begin to undercut the solid front of the regime.

William H. Beezley, Neville G. Penrose Chair of Latin American History at Texas Christian University and coeditor of this volume, has become well known both as an interpreter of Latin American popular culture and as an expert on Porfirian Mexico, 1876–1910. His publications include articles on teaching, sports history, and Mexican historiography. Among his recent books are *Judas at the Jockey Club and Other Episodes of Porfirian Mexico* (Lincoln, 1987); with Colin MacLachlan, *El Gran Pueblo: A History of Greater Mexico* (Englewood Cliffs, 1994); and *Rituals of Rule, Rituals of Resistance* (Wilmington, DE, 1994), with Cheryl Martin and William French.

Modernization, with its attendant crumbling of traditional society, causes some human wreckage. Marginal persons, fools, vagrants, town drunks, all in some way qualify as the human damage of so-called progress. These derelicts lurch through the community, engendering laughter that on inspection reveals a great deal about society's paradoxes and anxieties and what Jean-Paul Sartre called "bad faith" in the midst of change. These individuals, these characters, appeared in multitudes in the past. In the midst of the disheveled society that followed the gold rush in California, for example, there appeared Norton I, self-proclaimed emperor of the United States and protector of Mexico. Norton I, like other socially acceptable fools, personified Cervantes's judgment of Don Quixote that he was "mad in patches, full of lucid intervals." During the flurry of modernization in Mexico promoted by Porfirio Díaz there appeared a "fool" who expressed social apprehensions and represented popular humor.

Nicolás Zúñiga y Miranda belongs to a long and vigorous tradition of mirth and fun, which in Mexico stretches back into the early nineteenth century and includes an emphasis on billingsgate. Ribald commentators were no respecters of rank. They were as ready to poke fun at the misadventures of former President Antonio López de Santa Anna and his wooden leg as they were at the confusion of a country bumpkin in the city. Don Nicolás represents one facet of political raillery during the dictatorship of Porfirio Díaz that survives today. It includes as well numskull jokes about the people of Lagos, Jalisco. These stories lampooned all of the town's residents, but in particular satirized the city fathers. No doubt also Mexicans told political jokes and anecdotes about the

dictator and his regime. Much of this humor has not survived, but accounts do exist of the mock challenger to the
dictator, Zúñiga y Miranda.

Nicolás Zúñiga y Miranda was born in the city of Zaca-
tecas sometime before 1856. The precocious child of a provincial elite family, he had tutors from his third birthday
on. One teacher, a priest, steered him toward the priesthood;
Nicolás wanted to study engineering. His father sent him at
sixteen to Mexico City to study law. Immediately upon his
arrival in the capital city, his misadventures began. He mistakenly took a room in a hotel that normally rented by the
hour to lovers. When the young student, who had been reared
as a gentleman, heard an argument develop between an in-
sistent lover and his companion, who seemed to have changed
her mind, he determined to rescue the woman's honor.
Dressed in his bedclothes and a serape, Nicolás burst into
the room and discovered that he had interrupted a playful
couple who were engaged in a mock lovers' quarrel. Moreover, he had to face a local policeman summoned by the angry couple.

His troubles continued at the law school, where his tall,
broomstick-thin appearance, drooping moustache, and mode
of dress led to many jokes. He ignored the catcalls and dedicated himself to his studies, which included mathematics
and geology. In his spare moments he practiced his hobby of
astronomy, which he had begun under the direction of one of
his tutors. His fellow students viewed him as a humorous
eccentric.

This apparently harmless eccentric unsuccessfully predicted comets, floods, and other cataclysms. He had no
greater success with his seismographic invention, which, he
claimed, could indicate in advance the time of earthquakes.
When he announced his campaign for the presidency in 1896,
he immediately became the choice of the lawyers with whom
he had attended law school and of the university students
who demonstrated in rallies throughout the city. Thus he
became the classic jester, deflecting genuine criticism of the
regime through laughter.

Don Nicolás's comic characteristics can be analyzed. Humor, according to one theory, can be defined as the playful
impulse deriving pleasure from an instance of life's ambiguity. This explanation stresses the element of play that
leaps from words, phrases, actions, and situations in which
the expected is replaced by something else, revealing an

unsuspected equivoke. A certainty suddenly can be perceived in different ways; ambiguity allows incongruity as one possible perception of the situation. An individual's inability to catch the equivocal character of a word, phrase, action, or situation means that he or she does not get the joke.

Humor performs several social functions. There are jokes that help in the acculturation process, that help in adjustments to new social situations, that serve as cautions against unacceptable or dangerous social behavior, and that act as safety valves for protest and frustrations of all kinds. Joking becomes subversive to political, economic, and social structures insofar as it suggests that principles are not immutable but equivocal. Yet joking cannot itself serve as an agent of social change or revolution because the successful toppling of an institution removes the ambiguity and therefore the humor. The humor substitutes for action that may be risky or impossible. On the other hand, jokes substituted for positive action may hurt society by allowing correctable situations to continue unchanged because no one will protest or act to set matters right.

Social sublimation through the safety valve of joking, sociologist Anton C. Zijderveld has suggested, may be encouraged, even manipulated, by the powerful as a technique to manage conflict and protest. As tempting as it may be to blame the governing elite for bad jokes, atrocious puns, and numskull riddles, it hardly seems likely that any government would manufacture and broadcast jokes deliberately. However, as a technique for managing conflict, for the elite to encourage or at least to ignore antigovernment jokes seems well advised.

This brings us back to Zúñiga y Miranda. The description of don Nicolás provides us with a graphic example of his ambiguity and, therefore, of his humorous character. His effect, through humor, was to confront the Porfirians with a display of Sartre's "bad faith," that is, with the pretense that something is necessary that is actually voluntary. Zúñiga y Miranda reminded Mexicans of all ranks that presidential elections did not have to go uncontested, that Porfirio Díaz did not have to be unchallenged, that technology did not have to come from abroad, and that inventions did not all perform as advertised. Above all, he revealed the people's bad faith because they had adopted the attitude that Díaz was indispensable and that technology was the equivalent of progress. Their notions had produced a collective contented sigh while society awaited modernization. This, don Nicolás performed in a social comedy creating doubts about the Díaz regime. His inadvertent humor offered more than a simple safety valve; it was a form in which to demonstrate graphically the incongruities in everyday Mexican life.

Always dressed in a sombrero with a tall, glittering crown, an elegant frock coat, clean spats, and black, highly polished shoes, Zúñiga y Miranda epitomized the old Mexican elite. Traditional Mexican males invested as much as they could afford in their sombreros. Social standing was expressed from the high, ornate, heavy felt hats of the upper ranks to the small, straw, nearly flat sombreros of the poorest peon. Don Nicolás represented traditional Mexico at a moment of change.

The Díaz government, in its quest for modernity, launched a series of fashion regulations. State governments and the governor of the Federal District decreed pants laws, requiring all adult males to wear European-style trousers while in town. Naturally, a brisk pants-rental business appeared at the city limits of major towns. The government of the Federal District continued with its plan to westernize the appearance of Mexicans. This resulted in a series of required uniforms for different occupations. Porters, hack drivers, and streetcar conductors all had distinct uniforms, including caps to replace the sombrero. Corner newspaper boys dressed in black-and-white vertically striped pants and shirts until Porfirian officials learned that North American tourists avoided these boys because they assumed them to be some kind of prison labor.

The Díaz elite abandoned Mexican clothes for those of European cut, donning tailored coats and trousers, ties, collars, and homburgs. Zúñiga y Miranda thus was an ambiguous figure, representing the Mexican elite to the lower ranks and symbolizing traditional society to the Porfirian plutocrats. This image was accentuated by don Nicolás's drooping moustache, the traditional facial hair. Porfirian government officials and the social *científicos* (Mexican followers of the positivist philosophy of Auguste Comte) replaced their moustaches with trimmed beards, sideburns, goatees, and other European styles.

Because Zúñiga y Miranda roamed the capital's streets and gave his interviews, speeches, and prognostications on street corners, he appealed to the folk tradition of melodrama. For decades there had been street festivals on religious and civil holidays. Carnival, Holy Week, Independence Day, and the Cinco de Mayo each had official rituals, but these were overwhelmed by popular celebrations in the streets. These popular festivals included itinerant puppet theaters, Judas burnings, clowns, and social reversals by the crowds, who acted simultaneously as spectators and participants. Don Nicolás represented a heritage that reached back through the colonial society to medieval Europe and perhaps even earlier. He performed as the classic clown, exaggerating his actions to reveal that which caused either unspoken or unconscious conflict in the society. Thus he overstated the purpose of his mechanical inventions and made hyperbolic claims for the utility of science.

Don Nicolás burst into public consciousness in May 1887. His observations of the heavens led him to predict that at the end of the month there would be an earthquake that would send shocks throughout central Mexico from its epicenter in Oaxaca. He went to the editor of *El Siglo XIX* and explained his conclusions. The paper published don Nicolás's startling prediction along with a sarcastic sketch of this self-made man of science.

On May 24, the day he had predicted for the earthquake, churches filled with Mexicans praying for help. Even the students who had jeered him at the mining and law schools decided to take no chances. Every hour seemed an eternity until at eleven o'clock at night in Mexico City the gas and oil street lamps began to sway, and the capital endured a mild tremor. The following day, don Nicolás was acclaimed for his scientific ability. His father purchased one thousand copies of the issue of *El Siglo XIX* that carried the sketch of his son and the story of his astronomical skills.

His second earthquake prediction did not turn out so well for his reputation. He made a series of astronomical studies that persuaded him of an approaching earthquake that threatened all of the buildings in the republic; during the quake four volcanoes would erupt, new mountains would appear, and the entire Mexican population would perish, to be replaced by a new race. His scientific efforts took him away from his classes for days of intensive investigation, and he determined that August 10, 1887, would be the day of this holocaust. Again he went to *El Siglo XIX*, and the editor eagerly published his story.

Priests sang the Mass; the faithful and the unfaithful made confessions; many made pilgrimages to the Virgin of

Guadalupe. On the evening of August 9, the eve of the apoca-
lypse, reports circulated that smoke columns could be seen
rising from the volcano Popocatepetl. Near panic gripped
Mexico City through the next day and night until the dawn
of August 11. Then people relaxed—and many blamed don
Nicolás for misleading them. Other individuals believed that
his warning had saved them because he had given the faithful enough time to offer sufficient prayers to prevent the
catastrophe. His fellow students believed him to be a fool.
He was swung up in the air like a Holy Week Judas effigy in
the open patio of the National School of Jurisprudence (today, the open-air theater of the Ministry of Public Education). For half an hour he was tormented with taunts and
sticks. When he was lowered, his sombrero looked like an
accordion and his frock coat was in tatters. He himself dismissed the entire episode by blaming his sources, not his
science. Society at large laughed at him.

Don Nicolás created mirth by taking seriously what he
was not supposed to and by becoming a character of public
derision. Posing as a man of science, he represented a Hispanic tradition of comic figures that served as a parody and
a signal of social ambiguity. For example, Spaniards who had
gone to the colonies to make their fortunes and then returned
home with their riches were called *indianos* and became the
butt of humor in their home country because they seemed
more colonial than Spanish. The *indiano* became synonymous
with new wealth and appeared as a stock satirical figure in
contemporary Spanish literature. Nineteenth-century nov-
elists continued this tradition in the literature of the frontier by using laughter to defuse stressful situations, and, on
other occasions, by using it to create tension. Humor was
also used as a device to undermine authority by challenging
it with laughter.

What great fun for the lower ranks to watch don Nicolás
try to master modern science and technology! Like the foreigners with their locomotives, factory engines, pumps,
presses, and steel plows, don Nicolás produced machines that
did very little for most everyday Mexicans, since a majority
of them lacked either the money to ride the trains or the
skills necessary to work in the factories. His seismograph
promised to predict earthquakes; railroad promoters promised to bring prosperity, the plow salesman an end to drudgery. None of it came to pass, but it sounded good and looked
modern. Like the Zuni clowns who covered themselves with

excrement and mud when they danced, don Nicolás carried his inventions through the streets, displaying things that much of society regarded as abhorrent, or at least as improper and astonishing.

What pleasure for the Porfirian elite to observe Zúñiga y Miranda attempt to master science and technology! He, like those people whom the elite viewed as the downtrodden, retrograde, and primitive lower classes, mixed superstitious predictions and sham science. His wild efforts at invention fit perfectly the elite's perception of indigenous naïveté and stolid ignorance.

For both segments of Mexican society in the 1890s he provoked laughter by exaggerating the stereotype that each group held of the other. At the same time, underneath the humor of his caricature was the growing confidence many Mexicans had in technology as a remedy for their concerns. His inventions might not work, but they did indicate the areas of life that everyday Mexicans believed needed to be explained and, if possible, controlled. Zúñiga y Miranda's performances provided a key to popular attitudes toward modern technology and aspirations for its application.

Equally relevant to his contemporaries were his one-man melodramas of Mexican politics, that is, his campaigns in presidential elections. Don Nicolás ran for the presidency in 1896 and 1900. He conducted his campaigns on street corners, especially those in transitional neighborhoods where the rich were pushing the poor out toward the city limits.

President Díaz found nothing amusing or quaint in Zúñiga y Miranda's initial efforts. The dictator recognized that this comical character, a betwixt-and-between figure, represented a social danger. Don Nicolás acted as though the regime's democratic pretenses were real. In so doing, he disrupted the orderly social system that had been erected so carefully by Díaz and his advisers. The laughter of the people at the challenge to Díaz was anxious as well as amused because the everyday order was being disturbed. By the 1890s the authoritarian administration of Díaz had become a consensual arrangement, and Zúñiga y Miranda threatened to undo the balance.

Liberal journalists attacked don Nicolás's candidacy, declaring that he made Liberal ideals appear ridiculous and that he outraged society with his mockery of sacred political rights. One undercurrent in such newspaper opposition was the journalists' belief in the priority of lucid, rational political argument in written form over the street-corner theatrics of a populist politician, even of one whom the editors regarded as a buffoon populist. The arrogance of the literate Liberals limited their appeal, and they resented don Nicolás's ability to capture public attention by seeming to mock their programs.

In his lucid intervals, don Nicolás, like such fools as California's Emperor Norton, revealed a sensitivity to social problems and popular concerns. The emperor issued decrees in San Francisco commuting John Brown's death sentence on the grounds of insanity, directing that a bridge be built from Oakland to San Francisco, and supporting aerial experiments. The challenger to Porfirio Díaz offered voters a sincere plan for Mexican progress. His political platform called for land reform to increase food production, elimination of pulque production to end drunkenness, and endorsement of European clothing and shoes. His agrarian proposal aimed at making Mexico more productive than Argentina by dividing the land into small plots to be sold on credit with ten years to pay, by offering loans for the purchase of farming equipment and seed, and by demanding no repayment of loans until after the first harvest. He planned to eliminate the problems associated with pulque by giving prison terms without parole to its producers. His fashion regulations echoed those of Díaz; he wanted to prevent men from entering the national capital in white peasant pants that he believed were indecent and displayed the backwardness of the people. He declared that if any man could not afford the obligatory trousers and shoes, the articles would be provided by the government, and the individual could pay for them by working on the crews paving the capital's streets.

Mexican police halted don Nicolás's 1896 political campaign. They arrested him on a charge of drunk and disorderly conduct. A night in jail and a four-peso fine stunted don Nicolás's enthusiasm, and he retired from the political arena until 1900. Díaz had had the candidate arrested because he represented a challenge, apparently a mild one but symbolically fundamental, to the orderly system. His campaign blurred the hierarchy and thus created feelings of unease by revealing society's bad faith. In this respect, don Nicolás was a marginal man and a dangerous one for his political challenges to the Porfirian myth of consensus.

His activities imp wd Madero

During the interval between the 1896 and 1900 elections, Díaz decided that Zúñiga y Miranda actually deflected criticism by his antics. Consequently, the dictator welcomed don Nicolás's participation in the new election. Once the "fool" joined the campaign, he served the views of both the traditional masses and the *científico* elite. For the dispossessed population, Zúñiga y Miranda provided his theater of the absurd, mocking all the highfalutin' talk of Mexican democracy. For the elite, he provided a living tableau of the ridiculous results from attempts by semieducated Mexicans to win a role in government. Don Nicolás thus provided an object of humor for all the witnesses. This humorous spectacle gave those individuals who did not benefit from Porfirian progress the strength to stand straight beneath the repressive yoke, not the rage to throw it aside. Laughter renewed the courage to live with reality rather than instilled the bravery to dream new worlds.

Don Nicolás retired as a political candidate after 1900. His last political effort came in 1909, when he offered his assistance to General Bernardo Reyes, who briefly considered an election campaign against the dictator. Reyes rejected his help and soon discarded his own presidential ambitions. But another challenger appeared in the 1910 campaign, who took don Nicolás's place. Díaz mistook this new aspirant, Francisco Madero, for a fool; he misinterpreted the Antireelectionist challenge as another streetcorner melodrama. Too late the dictator learned that the short, squeaky-voiced vegetarian from Coahuila took Porfirio at his word. Madero dressed and acted the part of the elite and, above all, sanctioned or not, was nobody's fool.

Don Nicolás, the sanctioned fool, this Sartre on the Zócalo, ultimately had misled the dictator. After abandoning politics, he directed his attention to more general problems, which he wanted to solve with the help of the great men of history. He became a Spiritualist and believed that he received direct counsel from Aristotle. He claimed, for example, that the Greek philosopher had instructed him to negotiate a peace settlement during World War I. A lifelong bachelor, don Nicolás became a favorite with neighborhood children, who loved his stories and his phantoms. His conversion to spiritualism only added to the popular derision about his prognostications, which continued now and again until his death in 1927.

SOURCES

Works on don Nicolás are limited but see the brief biography, Guillermo Mellado, *Don Nicolás de Mexico (el eterno candidato): Vida, aventuras y episodios del caballero andante, Don Nicolás de Zúñiga y Miranda* (Mexico City, 1931) and both *Diccionario porrua* 2:2354 and Carleton Beals, *Porfirio Díaz: Dictator of Mexico* (Philadelphia, 1932), p. 318. A full-fledged study of a similar character is William Drury, *Norton I: Emperor of the United States: A Biography of One of America's Most Colorful Eccentrics* (New York, 1986). For an example of a similar individual from Caracas, see "Duque de Roca Negras," *Venezuela Up-to-date* 19, no. 1 (Spring 1978): 22.

Theories of humor and its social functions are discussed in William H. Beezley, "Recent Mexican Political Humor," *Journal of Latin American Lore* 1, no. 2 (1985): 195–223; Rose Coser, "Some Social Functions of Laughter: Humor in a Hospital Setting," *Human Relations* 12, no. 2 (1959): 171–82; Charles Winick, "Space Jokes as Indicators of Attitudes toward Space,"*Journal of Social Issues 17, no.* 2 (1961): 43–49; and Anton C. Zijderveld, "Jokes and Their Relation to Social Reality," *Social Research* 35, no.2 (Summer 1968): 306.

Sanctioned clowns receive consideration in two articles: Arlene K. Daniels and Richard R. Daniels, "The Social Function of the Career Fool," *Psychiatry* 27, no.3 (1964): 219–29, in which is discussed the fool in rigid or oppressive social situations; and Lucile Hoerr Charles, "The Clown's Function," *Journal of American Folklore* 58, no. 227 (January 1945): 33. Charles used the Cross-Cultural Survey of the Institute of Human Relations, Yale University, as well as drawing on her own understanding of Jungian psychology and her years of practical experience in the amateur and professional theater.

The interaction of humor and politics is explored in Alan Dundes, "Laughter behind the Iron Curtain: A Sample of Rumanian Political Jokes," *The Ukrainian Quarterly* 27 (1971): 50–59, esp. 50–51; Stanley H. Brandes, "Peaceful Protest: Spanish Political Humor in a Time of Crisis," *Western Folklore* 36, no.4 (October 1977): 334–35; and Jan Harold Brunvand, " 'Don't Shoot, Comrades': A Survey of the Submerged Folklore of Eastern Europe," *North Carolina Folklore Journal* 11 (1973): 181–88.

Peter Berger discussed Sartre's construct in *Invitation to Sociology*, reprinted as "Society as Drama," in *Drama in Life: The Uses of Communication in Society*, edited by James E. Combs and Michael W. Mansfield (New York, 1976), pp. 41–43. Also see Hugh Duncan, *Symbols in Society*, reprinted as "Axiomatic Propositions" in the same collection, p. 37.

The outstanding work on the Porfirian period for those who read Spanish is Daniel Cosio Villegas's nine-volume study. See especially *El Porfiriato: Vida política interior*, vol. 2, in the *Historia moderna de Mexico* (Mexico, 1972). William H. Beezley discusses society in these years in *Judas at the Jockey Club* (Lincoln, 1987).

6

Emilio and Gabriela Coni: Reformers, Public Health, and Working Women

Donna J. Guy

By the end of the nineteenth century, Argentina bristled with confidence and optimism. After the conflicts that had resulted in Juan Manuel de Rosas's overthrow in 1852 and the subsequent dispute over whether Buenos Aires should become the national capital (resolved by 1880), the nation settled down to enjoy peace and prosperity. With its fine public educational system, its broad avenues and public buildings, and its prosperous middle class, Buenos Aires became the Paris of Latin America. Thousands of European immigrants streamed into Argentina, residing primarily in the capital and drawing attention to critical urban problems.

Gabriela Laperrière, a French schoolteacher and journalist, was one of these immigrants. After her marriage to Emilio Coni, a Buenos Aires doctor and city council member, she continued to write, became a factory inspector, and, like her husband, joined the Socialist party. Both worked for implementation of measures that would improve the lot of the working class in the capital city.

A belief grew in Argentina that the traditional political parties were exhausted and incapable of leading the nation into the twentieth century. The immigrants, the growing working class, and the concomitant penetration of European ideologies encouraged the rise of new parties. The Radical Civic Union and the Socialist party proposed an end to the laissez-faire philosophy of the old Liberals. They advocated a more activist government, one that would assume some responsibility for the wellbeing of its citizens. Buenos Aires and other cities became the major beneficiaries of the new social reforms, heightening the disparity between the quality of life in rural and urban areas of the country.

The careers of Emilio and Gabriela Coni illustrate some unresolved dilemmas that accompanied the new politics of social welfare. Civil liberties had not been a strong part of the Hispanic tradition, so few Argentines criticized Emilio Coni's efforts to control people's behavior for their own and for the public good. With the best of intentions, Coni saw illness as a metaphor and implicitly blamed the poor

77

for their tuberculosis or syphilis. In the hands of liberal reformers science and technology could become additional tools with which to manipulate and control the less educated and the powerless. What were the implications of having the *científicos* (scientific men) replace the traditional caudillos and political bosses as the intermediaries between governments and their citizens?

Donna Guy is professor of history at the University of Arizona. After publishing the economic and political study, *Argentine Sugar Politics: Tucumán and the Generation of Eighty* (Tempe, 1980), she turned her attention to gender and family topics in the prize-winning volume, *Sex and Danger in Buenos Aires: Prostitution, Family, and Nation in Argentina* (Lincoln, 1991). She currently is at work on a study of children, family, and the state in Latin America.

D r. Emilio R. Coni and his wife Gabriela exemplified the commitment and dedication of health workers and social reformers in the Argentine capital city, Buenos Aires, during the late nineteenth and early twentieth centuries. Confronted by rapid population growth, outbreaks of epidemic and pandemic diseases, and inadequate housing, the Conis helped shape public policy and private efforts aimed at reducing the alarming rates of infant mortality and communicable diseases. To accomplish their goals they identified women who worked and the work that women performed in the home, the factory, and the bordello as subjects for reformist activities.

Emilio was a *higienista* (public health physician) and, intermittently between 1880 and 1909, a member of the Buenos Aires health board. Gabriela Laperrière de Coni had her own multifaceted career as a journalist, novelist, factory inspector, and feminist Socialist activist. Although we know little about their private lives, their influence on public health strategies and protective labor legislation for women and children are important contributions to the history of Buenos Aires.

Both Conis wanted to improve women's health, but they disagreed about the best way to accomplish this. Emilio exemplified the nineteenth-century male liberal reformer. A doctor and city council member, he wanted first to control and then to change the behavior of women in order to make sure that they raised healthier children. In contrast, Gabriela had little experience wielding power and authority. She, too, wanted to keep the children of Buenos Aires healthy, but Gabriela believed that this goal could be met without coercion. A feminist Socialist, she believed that women would be better mothers if they were given more control over their lives. Therefore, she worked to relieve women of household tasks, of unhealthy working conditions, and of ignorance.

Physicians and social reformers in Argentina had to contend with a number of factors. From the 1860s until World War I, the country experienced unprecedented growth and modernization. During this time the young nation encouraged European immigrants to come and provide the labor and technical expertise needed by Argentine agriculture and industry. Argentina's search for a foreign-born work force coincided with the exodus of millions of Europeans who traveled to the New World in search of economic advancement and a new life. Between 1857 and 1890 the country's population tripled.

Argentine cities, particularly the capital and port of Buenos Aires, were completely unprepared for rapid urban growth. In 1854, Buenos Aires had a population of 90,000. In fifteen years it had almost doubled to 177,000, only to increase to 670,000 by 1895 and to 1,575,000 in 1914. Most of the population growth was due to the arrival of Europeans or the migration of native-born workers from the Argentine interior. As the city grew, unsanitary living conditions and exposure to epidemic diseases threatened to decimate the newly arrived working class.

In 1858, Buenos Aires experienced its first yellow fever outbreak, and in 1871 more than thirteen thousand residents died from the disease. Epidemics of cholera, measles, and smallpox also periodically ravaged the city until the 1890s, while tuberculosis and syphilis were persistent causes of both infant and adult mortality. The city's first response to these problems was the creation of a municipal public health board in the 1850s and the subsequent passage of ordinances to control the purity of water and food and the disposal of garbage. Throughout the latter part of the nineteenth century teams of physicians and neighborhood officials periodically entered tenement houses and businesses in search of unsanitary conditions or people infected by disease.

By 1873 the University of Buenos Aires began to teach principles of hygiene, or public health, at its medical school. Graduates of these courses formed the next generation of public health physicians, and many of them were called upon to serve in municipal hospitals and to formulate city ordinances. With the advice of the *higienistas,* Buenos Aires officials began to target specific groups of potentially infectious individuals, such as prostitutes, beggars, wet nurses, and domestic servants, and monitor them from a medical as well as, in some cases, a police perspective. At the same time, health officials began campaigns of public education to inform city inhabitants, both rich and poor, of the need to practice good health habits within the home. Strained by limited budgets and having few medicines with which to treat the many diseases that threatened Buenos Aires, physicians and public officials came to rely on a combination of modern water and sewer systems, vaccinations, increased hospital and clinic facilities, and preventive medicine based upon principles of hygiene in order to protect the city's health.

EMILIO R. CONI (1854–1928)

Emilio Coni was among the first class of doctors at the University of Buenos Aires to graduate with a specialization in public health. Considered a brilliant student, he soon embarked on an equally impressive career of public service. Even before he graduated he had collected and analyzed health statistics. Subsequently, he continued his statistical work, proposed and implemented public health programs in Buenos Aires, and published more than thirty books and pamphlets. Many of his ideas came from his reading in the field and from his observation of European public health organizations during trips abroad.

The young *higienista,* an idealistic liberal reformer, was convinced that Buenos Aires could be a healthier city provided that it had laws to enforce good medical practices. All he had to do was convince the ruling urban elite of the need to implement an extensive public health program to control, as well as to cure, sick inhabitants.

The formation of a municipal organization controlled by *higienistas* was one of Emilio's main goals. The proposed Asistencia Pública (Public Assistance) would centralize the administration and improve the efficiency of hospitals, laboratories, cemeteries, garbage collection, slaughterhouses, and social services. Without the vigilance of disinterested physicians, health conditions in the city would be at the mercy of doctors and politicians who might be unscrupulous or poorly informed. From the late 1870s until the early 1890s, Emilio worked unceasingly, often without compensation, to implement Asistencia Pública.

His years of public service spanned the critical decades from the 1870s until the 1920s. Emilio had started his career fighting epidemics, and many of his authoritarian tendencies were reinforced by the need to take swift, often arbitrary action in order to contain the spread of diseases such as cholera or smallpox. Teams of health workers literally had to invade tenement houses, identify the sick, isolate them, and disinfect or destroy their possessions. Because of his early experiences fighting the disease, Emilio favored mandatory smallpox vaccinations. He was willing to advocate often unpopular policies because he believed that the public's interest in health matters should take precedence over individual rights.

Emilio's determination to control individuals for the sake of the group's health can be seen clearly in his campaign against syphilis. In January 1875 the Buenos Aires municipal council had legalized female prostitution in licensed bordellos, provided that the women be examined twice each week and, if necessary, treated by a private physician. Emilio believed that medical examination of the prostitutes should be more rigorous and conducted by city physicians and that infected women should be more securely isolated in municipal hospitals. He began to campaign for these reforms in 1877 when he published an article that blamed infected prostitutes for all of the deaths from syphilis of infants in the city orphanage.

Doctors at the time had no simple cure for syphilis and few effective treatments for gonorrhea. They did know, however, that syphilis could be inherited by the children of infected mothers. Many European and Argentine physicians in the late nineteenth century also believed that women infected men but that men rarely infected women. Since prostitutes had many sexual partners, they were considered to be medically dangerous as well as immoral. Consequently, European authorities sought to control syphilis by monitoring female prostitution. The Buenos Aires ordinance of 1875 was a pale reflection of European laws, and, therefore, the young *higienista* believed that the alarming incidence of venereal disease in Buenos Aires would not be lowered without a more comprehensive system of medical control.

For similar reasons he began to advocate municipal medical inspection of wet nurses who could transmit syphilis through their milk. The hiring of a woman who had given birth recently to provide milk for another's infant was a common practice among middle- and upper-income families in different parts of the world. Medical discoveries during the nineteenth century had revealed that the mortality of infants nursed by these women depended upon the level of care provided the babies and the wet nurses' health and milk quality. Furthermore, poor women supposedly often ignored their own children's needs in order to have breast milk for sale. Emilio urged mothers to either breast-feed their own infants or seek medical examinations of any wet nurses they hired. He recommended that the authorities create a system to inspect potential wet nurses and to regulate their business.

In 1880, Emilio was asked to join the Buenos Aires municipal council as a member of the Public Health Board. During his short time on the board he supported many neighborhood petitions to have women evicted from their lodgings because they were suspected prostitutes. He was unsuccessful, however, in his efforts to modify undesirable aspects of the bordello ordinance. Frustrated by the lack of action on his proposed health ordinances, such as new laws covering bordellos and prostitution, Emilio resigned from the board in 1881 and worked for other provincial and municipal authorities as a specialist in medical and census statistics.

Emilio envisioned a public health system that, in addition to protecting urban inhabitants, particularly children, from contagious individuals, complemented the work of charities and ultimately replaced charitable institutions. He wanted health care for indigents and the protection of poor and unwanted children. He was one of the first defenders of vagrants and successfully launched a municipally sponsored program to provide transient men with lodging and breakfast. He started hygiene programs in the schools and had milk distributed to schoolchildren. He translated pamphlets on sex education for children and adults as part of a campaign to inform the public of the dangers of venereal disease.

At the same time as he strove to bring about social and medical reform, Emilio was quite willing to sponsor municipal or national laws to take civil liberties away from alcoholics and to confine female prostitutes in medically supervised bordellos until they either married or died. He also advocated a ban on alcohol and tobacco consumption as a way to lower the incidence of tuberculosis. His advocacy of coercive and charitable laws, fines, and public education demonstrate that he often had conflicting ideas on how to improve sanitary conditions in the city. While he hoped that people would learn about hygiene and voluntarily change their habits, he also was willing to force them to live healthier lives.

In 1887, Emilio established the first comprehensive service in Buenos Aires to register and monitor wet nurses. Subsequently, he worked on a number of national, provincial, and municipal committees related to public health issues. Then in 1890 the *intendente* (mayor) of Buenos Aires invited Emilio to study the causes of infant mortality. Two years later Emilio's committee published its report, and the Patronato y Asistencia de la Infancia (Children's Welfare Board) was established. The committee recommended ways to provide better services to poor and defenseless children and thereby reduce infant mortality. Their suggestions included encouraging parents to put children up for adoption rather than abandon them; instituting more rigorous and scientific vigilance over wet nurses; preventing children from working more than six hours per day; and teaching mothers about nutritious liquids and foods to feed young children.

By this time Emilio was at the peak of his energy and highly respected by city officials in Buenos Aires. Again the mayor called upon him, this time to reorganize completely municipal health facilities. With his typical zeal, Emilio set out to change the world, or at least the city. He divided public health facilities into two categories, Asistencia Pública and Administración Sanitaria (Sanitary Services). Within these institutions he organized an ambulance system, introduced evening medical clinics, centralized many hospital facilities, and defined standards for burials, autopsies, and disinfection of localities contaminated by infectious diseases.

He was willing to do almost anything to implement his program and often ended up in acrid oral and written battles with the mayor, the city council, and the principal charity of Buenos Aires, the Sociedad de Beneficencia, an organization run by prominent society ladies that controlled most hospital services for women. A dispute with the new mayor in 1893 led Emilio to resign once again from municipal service. He left for Europe where he spent several years representing Argentina in a number of public health matters. When he returned, he stayed away from Buenos Aires until the turn of the century when he was invited back to the city to serve on the Public Health Board.

At the same time as he returned to the health board, Emilio began his great campaign against tuberculosis. He was president of the international commission on the prevention of tuberculosis in Latin America, and, in May 1901, he founded the Argentine Anti-Tuberculosis League, serving as director of the league's clinics until 1909. Earlier public health campaigns had led to a decline in mortality from yellow fever, cholera, smallpox, and other epidemic diseases. In their place, tuberculosis had become a major cause of illness and death among children and adults. Emilio set out to conquer tuberculosis, but once again he encountered resistance from public officials who were reluctant to commit scarce municipal funds to a campaign that would need vast amounts of money. Moreover, Emilio was bitterly disappointed by the scarce numbers of private citizens who were willing to pay dues to and support the league. By 1917, at the end of Emilio's career, he had concluded that only the national government had the resources necessary to finance the expansion of hospitals, centralize hospital administration, and, eventually, lower the incidence of diseases such as tuberculosis in Argentina. He drafted a law to carry out his program, but it was not acted upon. He died in 1928, embittered and frustrated by government officials who did not heed his expert advice.

In contrast to his boundless energy in pursuing the ideal of healthy children, his interest in mothers, particularly if they were working women, was more limited. Emilio saw all women as potential mothers. Since he assumed that women bore primary responsibility for *puericultura* (child care), he believed that they needed to learn how to take care of their children and how to keep the home hygienic. For good mothers and mothers with good intentions, he had unbounded time, energy, and ideas. All he needed was the financing, either public or private, for his programs.

On the other hand, while Emilio's writings demonstrated an awareness of the latest developments in public health technology, he rarely contemplated the impact of industrialization and modernization on women workers. Not until after the death of his wife did he go into factories nor did he concern himself with industrial health conditions unless they threatened children. After all, in his estimation working women were merely ignoring their primary roles as mothers.

Emilio's concern for women and children was part of his great campaign to make Buenos Aires a healthier place in which to live. At times he worried about the need for coercive measures to prevent the spread of illness, but he justified their use to protect all of the city's inhabitants. A biographer once wrote that Coni was "not the physician of the individual but rather of the collectivity; he was the physician not just of the ill, but also of the towns and cities." Without such dedicated doctors, cities like Buenos Aires would have been unable to control many of the health problems brought on by rapid population growth.

GABRIELA L. DE CONI (1866–1907)

Gabriela's early biography sheds little light on her preparation for a political career. In fact, we know little about her at all. Born in France and trained as a schoolteacher, Gabriela worked for several French newspapers before migrating to Argentina as a young woman. As Emilio's wife (there are some indications that she may have been married prior to meeting him), she continued her interest in writing, and only after 1900 did she turn most of her energy toward politics. Her brief political career was truncated by her death in 1907 at the age of forty. Despite the disparate lengths of their activist years, Emilio and Gabriela both deserve to be remembered for their efforts to improve the health of the working class, particularly of mothers and children, and to find appropriate ways to maintain safe and hygienic conditions in the home and workplace.

Emilio's and Gabriela's approaches to these problems were as different as the span of their careers. Emilio formulated public health policy to protect the city as a whole and ill children and indigents as groups. He concentrated on teaching urban mothers how to keep children healthy and on providing medical services for the poorest city residents. Gabriela focused on a somewhat different group. Deeply influenced by her husband's efforts to reduce infant mortality and prevent tuberculosis, she also was committed, as a Socialist and feminist, to the defense of working-class women and children. Hence, Gabriela targeted the unhealthy factory and the working-class home as the objects of her scrutiny, and she championed the political, economic, and hygienic rights of women and children who worked and lived in those environments. Unlike the unemployed and the desperately poor, working-class people in Buenos Aires often earned too much to qualify for the municipal programs established by her husband, yet they were too poor to escape the need to work in insalubrious factories and businesses.

When, then, did Gabriela develop her political ideas? Her novel, published in Paris in 1900, indicated that she was committed to social reform even before she began to be active politically. Her principal female character, Anita Kerven, was a young teacher who became a doctor and worked at the Children's Hospital. Anita was guided in her career by a kindly physician, Dr. Mendel. From him she learned many secrets of science and medicine and the difference between good physicians and those who were incompetent or inhumane. Anita also married a physician, Eduardo Larsan, who was both well trained and caring. These fictional characters had much in common with Emilio and Gabriela, although Gabriela herself never became a doctor. Nevertheless, it is clear that she learned much from her husband about the plight of sick children, and she used her knowledge to buttress her own political speeches about unhealthy working conditions.

Gabriela began her political career in 1900 as the press secretary for the Argentine National Council of Women, but she resigned that same year because of the council's conservative policies. After that, she became Buenos Aires's first factory inspector. As a member of the city's board of health, Emilio probably suggested that the mayor appoint Gabriela to the position. One of the goals of the league to combat tuberculosis that Emilio headed was to encourage factory owners to ensure the health of their employees. In August 1901, three months after the Argentine Anti-Tuberculosis League began to operate, Mayor Adolfo Bullrich named Gabriela L. de Coni to be an inspector of city factories employing women and children. Her job was to visit the factories, analyze their hygiene and health conditions, and prepare a report that would be sent to the national congress.

Gabriela took her assignment seriously and prepared an in-depth four-part study. Her first report, delivered in November 1901, was designed to tell the mayor of her personal fears and anxieties about the unhealthy working conditions that she encountered. She was disturbed that children less than ten years old were working and that the air was filled with all kinds of impurities that could damage workers' lungs. Her recommendations culminated in her April 1902 proposal that protective legislation for women and children be enacted.

The law suggested by Gabriela consisted of eighteen articles and copious explanations in footnotes. Children were to be banned from factories and workshops until they were fourteen and could prove that they had been vaccinated for smallpox. They could work for only six hours per day. Women and children over eighteen could work eight hours but not before 6 A.M. or after 6 P.M. They would also be forbidden from working in factories considered dangerous or immoral. Finally, all women and children would be guaranteed Sundays off, and lactating mothers would have a room within the factory where they could breast-feed their children.

Although Gabriela did not live to see all aspects of her legislation enacted, parts of it were incorporated into another piece of protective legislation presented to the congress by Joaquín V. González in 1904. Although González's bill was rejected by the Socialist party as well as by the congress, the cause of protective legislation was, nevertheless, a key issue for Argentina's Socialist party. Indeed, it was Socialist Deputy Alfredo L. Palacios who drafted the legislation that was finally passed by the congress in 1907.

As Gabriela explored the factories of Buenos Aires, she realized that her position as inspector could help the campaign against tuberculosis. Accordingly, less than a month after her appointment, she wrote Dr. Samuel Gache, president of the league established by her husband, and offered to give talks about hygiene in the home, nutrition, and other topics related to the antituberculosis cause. As she put it, "Surely there are many female apostles, more competent and appropriate than myself, who could talk to upper-class women, but I want to serve the working women because they are more threatened and less prepared to combat disease, and thus their needs are more critical." Gache was delighted to have Gabriela's help and accepted her offer. By October 23, 1901, after less than one month, Gabriela already had given ten conferences.

Her 1902 speech to the Unione Operari Italiani (Italian Workers' Union) was published by the Argentine Anti-Tuberculosis League, and it enables us to recapture the intelligence and social commitment of an unusual woman. Gabriela, after citing a number of recent publications on the subject, identified the causes of tuberculosis to be "alcoholism, unhealthy habitations, poor nourishment, excessive physical, mental, or moral labor, and poor hygiene." She informed her audience that these perils endangered men and women alike, although men tended to suffer more frequently from alcoholism while women and children experienced more poor health from working too strenuously. This was especially true for women, who were expected to perform domestic chores in addition to salaried labor, and Gabriela described the daily schedule of a typical working woman:

> The typical working-class woman has to be in the factory at 6 A.M.; if she is a mother and married, she arises at 4 or 4:30 to prepare breakfast, dress her children, and sweep and straighten out her lodging. Of course I am presuming all of this can be accomplished in an hour and a half, and the woman lives close to her place of work. At 11 A.M. she returns home, makes a fire, and prepares lunch for her family, all within an hour and a half. Some factories—very few—grant them two hours, others one. . . . At 6 P.M., having finished her work at the factory, she must begin the preparation of dinner, washing the dishes, and the children, if they need it. She must also mend, sew, iron, etc. . . . How many hours do these beasts of burden, these women who are perhaps pregnant, have to rest? Add them up yourselves: by 9 P.M., they have worked without rest for seventeen hours and not for themselves, but rather *for others,* for this family they have given birth to.

Throughout 1902 the league's magazine continued to publish speeches and reports by Gabriela. In September the league responded favorably to her suggestion that soup kitchens be set up near factories so that inexpensive but nourishing meals would be available for workers. Such establishments would eliminate the need for women to cook for their families at lunchtime. Given the insufficient financial base of the league, no soup kitchens were established immediately. Nevertheless, by 1917 subsidized restaurants were operating throughout the industrial parts of the city under the auspices of the Salvation Army, the Sisters of the Sacred Heart, the Sisters of Mary the Provident, the St. Vincent de Paul Society, the Charity Dames, the Conservation of the Faith Society, the YWCA, the League for the Protection of Young Women, the Irish Sisters of Mercy, and the Dowry Society for Working Women. Most of these establishments served working-class people full-course meals at very low prices.

Other activities undertaken by Gabriela after 1902 had a more immediate impact. Working more directly through the Argentine Socialist party, which had been organized in the 1890s, Gabriela was the first woman to support Socialist politicians at public political meetings. The only female member of the party's Executive Council in its early years, she was also one of the founders of the Centro Socialista Femenino (Socialist Women's Center) in 1902. The center endeavored to organize dressmakers, espadrille makers, telephone operators, and cigarette workers. Gabriela's support for the Centro Socialista Femenino was evident when she tried to use her influence as an inspector to mediate labor disputes between factory owners and striking women. In November 1904 she represented the women on strike against La Argentina Espadrille Factory after management had refused to accept an eight-hour work day. Gabriela bravely addressed more than eight hundred angry women workers, exhorting them to stay away from their jobs until their demands were met. Eventually, Gabriela's formal efforts to mediate the strike were rejected by the factory owners because she was not an employee.

Until national legislation mandated an eight-hour day for men and women, striking workers could rarely force employers to limit the number of work hours, although they could obtain higher wages. Gradually, Gabriela came to the conclusion that women should not offer their services to factories unless it was a matter of economic necessity. Instead, they should accept financial privation in order to make sure that their children were cared for and fed. Of course, for many workers in Buenos Aires unemployment was unacceptable. Given the prevailing high rents and low salaries in the city, it was usually imperative that women and young children contribute to the family income if they could.

News of Gabriela's activities after 1904 is impossible to find. Her tumultuous and active career as a defender of the rights of women and children ended as suddenly as it had commenced. According to the memoirs of Enrique Dickmann, a prominent Socialist physician, Gabriela was forced out of the party after she left Emilio for another man. More likely, she already was stricken with the illness that caused her death on January 7, 1907. Her brief, but intensive, efforts to defend working women and children and document their abuse had to be taken up by others.

Alfredo Palacios and Emilio Coni continued Gabriela's campaign to enact municipal and national legislation to protect the working class and provide government-sponsored inexpensive medical care. In 1913 the Argentine feminist Socialist Carolina Muzzilli wrote a prize-winning study of the conditions faced by working women. Gabriela's work for the Argentine Anti-Tuberculosis League was continued, partly by municipal public health education programs, partly by the hygiene classes offered by the Socialist popular university program, the Sociedad de Luz (Society of Light), and partly by charitable organizations.

Emilio's work was also carried on by others. When he died in 1928 his plan to provide a centralized and well-financed program of hospital care and preventive medicine in Buenos Aires and other Argentine cities had not been fully implemented and funded. Twenty years later, during the presidential administration of Juan Perón (1946–1955), Dr. Ramón Carrillo, a *higienista* as dedicated as Emilio, started an ambitious program that incorporated many of Coni's 1917 suggestions. Under Carrillo's guidance, a new national program rapidly expanded the number of hospital beds, doctors, and nurses ready to serve public health needs. Because of the availability of penicillin and other modern medicines, communicable diseases that had endangered women and children finally were scientifically controlled.

CONCLUSION

The careers of Emilio and Gabriela Coni set the course for future public health programs and strategies to help mothers and working women. Efforts to ameliorate the health problems and working conditions of women and children appeared to have common goals but in fact were quite different. Generally speaking, these goals could be divided into two categories: plans to help women and children by regulating their behavior and health; and programs to give women more control over their jobs as mothers and as workers through education and improved working conditions at home and in the factory. One strategy sought to control women, the other to empower them.

Municipal programs to improve the nourishment and health of poor children were vital to the well-being of the inhabitants of rapidly growing cities. Planned by members of the governing class, the programs rarely contemplated the problems of the working-class mother who had to combine child care with salaried labor. Similarly, programs to monitor medically suspect women such as prostitutes and wet nurses rarely considered the fact that these women could contract diseases as easily as they could infect others. While these programs may have had laudable goals, often they were resisted by those whom they were supposed to benefit because they were too coercive.

Socialist feminist plans to help working-class women offered a different approach to the problems of public health. Reformers geared to helping working women and children ignored the need to provide public health information to the middle and upper classes. They also presumed that insalubrious conditions in the home or factory would affect women and children more than men, and they believed in the ability of the working class to demand health reforms in the workplace. When strikes and labor demands were not successful, people like Gabriela de Coni suggested that women and children withdraw from the labor force, an often unrealistic strategy.

Countries like Argentina and cities like Buenos Aires needed a combination of programs, some multiclass as they were in Emilio Coni's dream, others class-specific and sensitive to gender issues as in the feminist-Socialist vision of Gabriela. The aspirations of both Conis relied upon the commitment of personnel and funds by private and public agencies. Over the years, many of their plans reached fruition. In 1918, Emilio published a book documenting the various agencies providing social, medical, economic, and charitable services to the working class in Buenos Aires. In his book he took credit for initiating many public facilities. He also acknowledged Gabriela's role in suggesting many programs aimed at working women. Together they left a legacy of concern about public health, child care, and working conditions that would continue to spur public and private efforts to tackle the social and medical consequences of modernization.

SOURCES

Among the books and articles written by or about Emilio Coni, see Dr. Emilio R. Coni, *Higiene pública: El servicio sanitario de la ciudad de Buenos Aires* (Buenos Aires, 1880); idem, *Memorias de un médico higienista* (Buenos Aires, 1918); idem, *Higiene social: Asistencia y previsión social. Buenos Aires caritativa y previsor* (Buenos Aires, 1918); Ernest A. Crider, "Modernization and Human Welfare: The Asistencia Pública and Buenos Aires, 1883–1910" (Ph.D. diss., Ohio State University, 1976); Osvaldo Loudet, *Figuras próximas y lejanas al margen de la historia* (Buenos Aires, 1970); idem, *Médicos argentinos* (Buenos Aires, 1966); Drs. Horacio Madero and José Penna, *La administración sanitaria y asistencia pública en la ciudad de Buenos Aires*, 2 vols. (Buenos Aires, 1910); Estela Pagani and María Victoria Alcaraz, *Las nodrizas de Buenos Aires: Un estudio histórico, 1880–1930* (Buenos Aires, forthcoming); and Hugo Vezzetti, *La locura en la Argentina* (Buenos Aires, 1983).

For materials about Gabriela L. de Coni, feminism, or the Argentine Socialist party, see Maryfran Carlson, *Feminismo! The Women's Movement in Argentina from Its Beginnings to Eva Perón* (Chicago, 1988); Nicolás Cuello, *Acción feminina* (Buenos Aires, 1939); Gabriela L. de Coni, *Proyecto de ley de protección del trabajo de la mujer y del niño en las fábricas presentado á la Intendencia Municipal* (Buenos Aires, 1902); María Carmen del Feijoó, "Las luchas feministas," *Todo es Historia* 128 (January 1978): 6–23; Enrique Dickmann, *Recuerdos de un militante socialista* (Buenos Aires, 1949); Asunción Lavrin, "The Ideology of Feminism in the Southern Cone, 1900–1940," Wilson Center Working Paper, no. 169 (Washington, DC, 1986); Maryssa Navarro, "Hidden, Silent, and Anonymous: Women Workers in the Argentine Trade Union Movement," *The World of Women in Trade Unions,* edited by Norbert Soldon (Westport, CT, 1985); María Silvia Ospital, "Un antecedente del proyecto de ley nacional del trabajo: La labor de la Sra. Gabriela de L. de Coni (1901–1904)," *Investigaciones* 1 (1976): 68–95; and Richard Walter, *The Socialist Party of Argentina, 1890–1930* (Austin, 1977).

7

Mandeponay: Chiriguano Indian Chief in the Franciscan Missions

Erick D. Langer

Bolivia enjoyed a rather splendid isolation during the quarter of a century following independence in 1825. The Catholic Church, the state, and elites generally ignored the country's indigenous population as long as the Indians paid tribute, which was the principal source of government revenue in the first years of the republic. By midcentury, an economic renaissance had begun. Foreign and local capital revived silver mining and made possible some agricultural expansion. Greater profitability of commercial farming naturally inflated the value of land and threatened the isolated harmony of many Indian communities. By what tactics could the Indians guarantee their economic and cultural survival?

Passive accommodation would mean the rapid loss of land and of cultural autonomy, and the transformation of independent farmers into a pool of reserve day workers for plantations owned by others. Rebellion would mean even quicker destruction. Ethnic and regional differences among those whom others termed *Indians* also limited the possibility of real unity among Bolivia's indigenous people. The state, even if it had wanted to protect the indigenous population, increasingly embraced a laissez-faire ideology that tacitly favored the wealthy and powerful. Individuals such as Manuel Isidro Belzú in Bolivia and Juan Bustamante in Peru, who tried to enact reforms, met with derision from their recalcitrant colleagues and even death.

Mandeponay, chief of the Chiriguano Indians from 1868 until 1904, combined the skills of a caudillo and of a traditional chieftain. The Chiriguano chief found a solution that worked—for a while. He invited one powerful institution, the Church, to place a check on the encroachments of the government and the elite. Still, the Franciscan fathers pacified as they protected, and their exhortations to the Indians to be good Christians and good citizens ultimately undermined the cultural autonomy of Mandeponay's people. So, too, did Mandeponay's policy of encouraging Indian migration to Argentina to seek jobs. In the short run, it gave the Indians independence, but in the long run, it threatened communal unity.

We cannot but admire the wily stratagems of a proud chief who secured the best deal he could for his people and himself in a

93

changing world. Yet as historians we might ask what Mandeponay's story tells us about the "development of underdevelopment." How and why did the modernization of Bolivia contribute to increasing misery in the countryside?

Erick Langer, associate professor of history at Carnegie-Mellon University and adjunct associate professor at the University of Pittsburgh, received his doctorate at Stanford University. He has done research on the rural society, ethnicity, and economy of southern Bolivia. His published works include *Economic Change and Rural Resistance in Southern Bolivia, 1880–1930* (Stanford, 1989); and, with Robert H. Jackson, *The New Mission History* (Lincoln, 1995). He currently is completing a volume on contemporary indigenous movements in Latin America.

Mandeponay became chief of the Macharetí Chiriguano Indians when his chieftain father, Taruncunti, was murdered in 1868. A group of Chiriguanos from Cuevo cut open Taruncunti's mouth from ear to ear because he had betrayed the Indians' cause and spoken to the Franciscan missionaries. Taruncunti's brother and a niece also were killed and a number of his relatives kidnapped and taken to Cuevo. Mandeponay, the oldest son of Taruncunti and the next in line for the Macharetí chieftainship, was not present and so escaped the massacre. Filled with rage, he immediately asked that a mission be established in Macharetí as revenge for his father's death. Within one year the missionaries had built a fort at the Indian village. Despite a concerted attack by dissident Chiriguanos while the fort was still unfinished, the mission at Macharetí had become a reality. As we will see, there was more than just revenge as a motive for Mandeponay's request.

Together the murder of Taruncunti and Mandeponay's request for the establishment of a mission were one episode in the conquest of the Chiriguanía, a vast region of rugged jungle-covered Andean foothills in southeastern Bolivia, ranging from one hundred miles south of Santa Cruz to almost the northern outskirts of the city of Tarija on the edge of the desolate Chaco region. The Chiriguanos had held out against Spanish forces since colonial times. Viceroy Toledo mounted a large expedition against this ethnic group in the 1560s, but he suffered defeat at the hands of the Chiriguanos, who effectively used guerrilla tactics to combat the better-armed Spanish soldiers. Only in the late colonial period did Indian resistance weaken. After the failure of the

Jesuits to convert the Chiriguanos in the first half of the eighteenth century, the Franciscans finally achieved some success. In the late eighteenth century the friars, based in Tarija, established a string of prosperous missions in the Chiriguanía. However, patriot guerrillas and their Chiriguano allies during the wars for independence destroyed the missions and sent the Spanish friars packing.

The Chiriguanos were known as fierce warriors since the sixteenth century, when they migrated from what is now Brazil into southeastern Bolivia. They were able to survive the onslaught of the Spaniards and early republican society because of their military organization, their political decentralization whereby a number of regional chiefs lorded it over chiefs of allied villages, and the training in the art of ambush and weapons that every Chiriguano boy underwent at a relatively early age. The Chiriguanos were superb practitioners of guerrilla warfare and frequently raided white settlements throughout the early republican period. The village-based military society, the warriors' unconditional obedience to their chiefs, and the perpetual state of warfare between Chiriguano village alliances as well as against the whites kept the Indians well trained in all manner of death and destruction.

The Chiriguanos were largely left alone until the 1840s, when the Bolivian economy began to quicken again. The government set up a series of military forts along the Chaco frontier on the southern borders of the Chiriguanía. Also, settlers from Tarija entered Indian territory and joined the small garrisons in periodic raids deep into the frontier, destroying Chiriguano villages and kidnapping women and children. However, the cattle that the settlers brought proved even more destructive. Buoyed by increased demand for cattle in the highland silver mines, the colonists drove their herds into the Indians' cornfields. As a result, entire villages lost their means of subsistence and either had to migrate farther north, into the core of the Chiriguanía, or submit to the settlers and work for them under extremely poor conditions as hacienda peons. Many villages resisted violently the encroachment of the white settlers, but in the long term this proved futile.

The only other alternative was for the Chiriguanos to accept a Franciscan mission on their territory as a way of preserving their homeland. By the 1840s the Bolivian government had retreated from its earlier anticlerical stance and, in fact, encouraged the Franciscans from the Tarija convent to resume their missionary activities as a way of neutralizing the still formidable Chiriguano military threat along the frontier. By 1854, under increasing pressure as settlers and cattle ranches encroached on their land, Chiriguano chiefs in Itau (1845), Aguairenda (1851), and Tarairi (1854) had accepted the establishment of missions as the lesser evil.

Machareti, farther to the north, became the next goal for the settlers. This location was particularly strategic, for it was the main meeting place between the Tobas, adept Indian horsemen who controlled much of the Chaco, and the Chiriguanos. Taruncunti led the resistance to the establishment of the mission in Tarairi and, in alliance with the Guacaya Chiriguanos, attacked the mission in 1855. The assault failed. In revenge for this attack the mission Indians of Tarairi joined with the soldiers in the military colonies farther south and launched a punitive expedition on Machareti. This expedition was completely successful, and as a result of the sacking of Machareti and the capture of numerous women, the place was abandoned by Taruncunti's people. Only a small faction of Machareteños, under the leadership of Guariyu, returned to Machareti six years later after making peace with the missionaries. Taruncunti, outraged by this betrayal, attacked with his people and allied Tobas, wiping out the new settlement. His erstwhile subordinate Guariyu barely escaped naked to the safety of the hillside. Flush with success, Taruncunti marched on Tarairi but again failed to take the mission.

Mandeponay was a young boy during these assaults and counterassaults and probably did not participate in these wars. His father certainly inculcated in him a fierce sense of independence and of Chiriguano ethnic identity. However, Taruncunti could see that his position was tenuous at best on the frontlines in the war against the white settlers. In his later years, in exile in an allied Chiriguano village, he became convinced that he would have to live with the whites and that friendship with the missionaries held the key to the reestablishment of Machareti as the most important Chiriguano settlement. In 1866 he decided to visit Tarairi mission and make peace with the Franciscans. Settlers were already moving their cattle herds into the Machareti area, and Taruncunti saw that returning his people to the area was the only way of maintaining his claim there. Almost certainly, Mandeponay, as the oldest son and heir apparent of his father, helped Taruncunti negotiate with the friars on the conditions for the Chiriguanos' return to Macharetí.

Despite his wishes, Taruncunti could not move his people back to the old settlement. The Chiriguano bands farther north, in Guacaya and Cuevo, who knew that if Taruncunti buckled under white pressure they would be next, refused to let him return to his ancestral grounds. Deeply suspicious of Taruncunti's motives and his steadily improving relations with the missionaries, they launched a sneak attack on Ñaunti, where Taruncunti was hiding, and killed the old chief. It is in this way that Mandeponay became chief of the Macharetí Chiriguanos and invited the friars to establish a mission at his birthplace.

For the Tarija Franciscans, gaining Macharetí was the greatest triumph of their careers as missionaries in republican Bolivia. Mandeponay controlled more than three thousand individuals, including the dissident band under Guariyu, almost certainly the largest concentration of Chiriguanos in the whole region. Moreover, establishing a mission at Macharetí helped alleviate the constant threat of Toba and Chiriguano alliances against the whites, since it was the chief of Macharetí who traditionally controlled Chiriguano-Toba relations. This move isolated the Tobas and made possible the colonization of the vast Chaco regions on the border with Paraguay. The Tobas, who were well known to the white colonists from Argentina to Bolivia as cattle and horse thieves, relied on the Chiriguanos in Macharetí to provide them with corn, a crop that the nomadic hunting and gathering Toba groups found impossible to cultivate in the difficult climate and soil of the Chaco desert. Traditionally, Tobas came after the rainy season to help the Machareteños harvest their corn and, in return for their labor, received part of the crop. The Franciscans hoped that the Tobas might even be persuaded to accept the missionaries among themselves if they got to know the fathers when they came to work and trade with the Macharetí mission Indians.

Mandeponay knew that he had a strong bargaining position, and he was able to get concessions that none of the other Chiriguano chiefs ever got once they agreed to have missions. For one, Macharetí had only a single central plaza. Unlike earlier colonial missions, the Franciscans could not force the Indians to convert if they did not want to, for there were no soldiers to back up forced conversions and the subsequent modifications in behavior required of the converts. However, the missionaries in the Chiriguanía usually segregated *neófitos* (converts) from the heathens as a way of better indoctrinating their charges and preventing the heathens' "savage" ways of life from infecting the Christianized natives. To do this, they had the converts build their houses around a separate plaza, which would assert in spatial terms the separation of heathens and *neófitos*. The *neófitos* gradually received different authorities as well and lived according to the dictates of the missionaries, not the traditional chiefs. This Mandeponay did not permit when setting up the Macharetí mission. Instead, converts and heathens all lived around the one central plaza, although each group lived along different streets. The settlement's layout, however, allowed Mandeponay to maintain his authority over the whole mission population.

Mandeponay made sure that he kept his authority even over his father's old nemesis, Guariyu. Despite serious misgivings, the missionaries and Guariyu had to accede to Mandeponay's demands; Guariyu kept his group separate from the larger group, but he was placed under the chief's overall jurisdiction. Mandeponay himself never converted to Christianity and kept up traditional customs, much to the chagrin of the Franciscans. For example, he had six wives, clearly a violation of Christian injunctions. There was little the friars could do. It was Mandeponay who ran the mission and kept everyone in line. When problems arose, the missionaries had to rely on this traditional chief to correct them, and thus they needed his full cooperation. In Chiriguano society, the chief played an extremely important role in regulating the community and had tremendous power over his followers. Mandeponay kept up the custom of giving large feasts, to which he invited the whole mission population. Showing his largess in this fashion, the chief was able to bind the mission Indians in a web of reciprocity. The feasts thus not only served to demonstrate his wealth and power, a desirable attribute in any Chiriguano leader, but also created ties of mutual obligation upon which Mandeponay could call when necessary.

Mandeponay's example was very important, and, as a result, the friars had little success in converting their charges to Christianity. In 1882, at the apogee of the mission's population and fully thirteen years after the foundation of the mission, only nine families out of a total of over six hundred had converted. In the past five years, only three families had been baptized. Obviously, Mandeponay maintained a significant hold over his people, as evidenced by the tiny number of conversions. The chief clearly wanted to have his cake and eat it too: enjoy the protection of the missionaries and maintain the cultural integrity of his people and their land without giving up anything essential in return.

At this, Mandeponay was remarkably successful. In 1890 the missionaries decided to try and modify his behavior. In 1888 a new Franciscan had arrived from Italy. Terencio Marucci was appalled by the licentious behavior of Mandeponay and the liberties he enjoyed with his many wives. Not only did Mandeponay maintain a harem but his son, Napoleón Yaguaracu (also called Tacu), also kept three wives. Many of the chief's "soldiers" practiced polygamy as well. At first, the Franciscans called upon local authorities to punish Mandeponay for his unlawful behavior, but the officials refused to antagonize the powerful Chiriguano ally. The authorities had very good reasons not to punish the chief of Machareti. In the late 1880s the national government began to explore the uncharted reaches of the Chaco beyond the foothills of the Chiriguanía and support colonization of that region. To accomplish this settlement they needed Mandeponay's support, for in his capacity as the head of the Machareti Chiriguanos he possessed extensive links to the Tobas and other Chaco tribes. The Daniel Campos expedition in 1886, for example, employed a number of Machareti Indians to act as porters and attempted to use Mandeponay's influence to keep hostile Indian bands at bay. Other, later expeditions into the Chaco also usually made an obligatory stop at Machareti to get Mandeponay's assistance and gather intelligence from the Indian chief.

After their appeal to the authorities brought no results, the missionaries resorted to ostracism, isolating Mandeponay from the rest of the mission as much as possible. At first, they reported some success, asserting that now Mandeponay found himself "scorned by many of his soldiers and is fearful of some punishment." This optimism, however, did not last long. With Mandeponay cut out of the authority structure, the unconverted Chiriguanos, the vast majority, refused to obey the missionaries. Afraid that they would lose much of their liberty in this crackdown, many Chiriguanos either left the mission for the Guacaya region, where the whites only recently had penetrated, or simply went out into the countryside adjacent to the mission, away from the influence of the friars. In one year the mission lost over 700 individuals, or about 20 percent of the total population of 3,577. The missionaries were forced to back down. They asked Mandeponay to resume his duties in 1891, which immediately helped get things under control at the mission. Mandeponay exiled a troublemaker, helped return a number of families who had fled into the hills, and prohibited polygamy among the *catecúmenos,* those who had made a commitment to converting to Christianity and were learning the requisite rules.

The reincorporation of Mandeponay into mission life occurred just in time. In 1892 the last revolt of the Chiriguanos broke out under the leadership of a messianic leader, Apiaguaiqui, from Ivo. Apiaguaiqui called himself a *tumpa* (messiah) who would rid the Chiriguanía of its white interlopers and return all lands lost to their rightful owners. By this time, colonists had insinuated themselves in virtually every corner of Chiriguano territory and were forcing the Indians to work as poorly paid peons on their ancestral lands. Guacaya had fallen to the settlers in a war in 1874; the Franciscans from Potosí took the opportunity to establish a new mission in the area. Even Cuevo, at the heart of nineteenth-century Chiriguano resistance, in 1887 had accepted the establishment of a mission after the Cueveños' attempt at building a huge fence to keep out colonists' cattle had failed. Only Ivo and a scattered number of smaller settlements remained outside the control of the settlers.

The 1892 war was doomed to failure from the start because no mission Indian chiefs joined their brethren from Ivo. A number of Chiriguano chiefs visited Apiaguaiqui to determine whether to follow the rebel leader or not. This group included Mandeponay, who by this time was among the two or three most powerful Chiriguano chiefs in the whole region. He refused to join in the growing movement but, on the other hand, also never denied Apiaguaiqui's claims. Although the missionaries and local authorities liked to believe that Mandeponay was their ally, in fact he was only against bloodshed and remained essentially neutral during the conflict. The assembly of Apiaguaiqui's followers declared war on the whites in January 1892, and Mandeponay, when he got the message, is reputed to have said: "War is bad. There is no advantage in it. It means no homes, no

chicha [corn beer, used as a staple in the Chiriguano diet]."
It was rumored, however, that his son Tacu left to join the
movement.

The Indians under Apiaguaiqui had planned to revolt
during Carnival, when the whites would be celebrating and
most men would be drunk, but the rape and murder of a
Chiriguano woman by a colonist during a New Year's fiesta
brought about a premature uprising. The Chiriguano army
gained control over an extensive territory between the River
Parapetí and Camatindi, a few miles north of Macharetí. At
this point, the Indian warrior bands suddenly retreated to
the vicinity of Ivo to celebrate their victory over the white
colonists. Almost certainly, the failure of the movement to
spread among the missions just outside this area precipitated this retreat. Thus, the refusal of Mandeponay in
Macharetí and of the Cueveños in the new mission limited
Apiaguaiqui's success and doomed the movement. Reaction
by a hastily mobilized militia and some troops from the regular army was swift. The Ivo Indians and their allies fought
bravely from a hillside near Ivo with their bows and arrows,
spears, knives, and occasional firearms. They hastily dug
trenches and erected walls of fallen trees, but even this tactic was of little use against the much better armed whites. A
bloody pitched battle at Curuyuqui, where the fighting soon
degenerated into hand-to-hand combat, decided the fate of
the rebels. As a result of this battle and the subsequent repression, six thousand Indians were killed or taken prisoner.
Those Indians who survived were given to white families in
the region, and some children were sold to work as servants
in households in Sucre, Monteagudo, and other towns.

Mandeponay, it seems, had been right. Violent resistance
was futile. Rather, it was necessary to adapt to changing
circumstances. The mission was the most viable alternative
to becoming exploited hacienda peons or fleeing into the
Chaco to join the Tobas. On the mission, the Chiriguanos
enjoyed their own authority structure and, to a large extent,
despite pressure from the missionaries to change their ways,
were able to maintain many traditions. For example, while
the friars forbade consumption of the beloved *chicha*, such
an injunction had little effect in a mission such as Macharetí,
where the heathen population remained so large. In the af-
termath of the 1892 uprising, Mandeponay gained even more
power. In 1894 his archrival Guariyu, who had to a certain

extent been a counterweight to Mandeponay's influence, was sent with his followers to a new mission, San Antonio de Padua, to help control the Tobas who were congregated there.

Mandeponay's plan of preserving Chiriguano ethnic identity and projecting political power from the missions could not work in the long term. Although adults had a choice of converting or not (something which they rarely did, leading a missionary to exclaim in frustration that "to baptize an Indian adult who is in perfect health is the same as asking for pears from an elm tree"), all children above age seven were required to attend mission school. This practice, of course, led to the progressive conversion of the mission population, a process that Mandeponay could do little to halt. Not only were the children taught the catechism, but they were also required to wear European-style clothes and speak Spanish instead of their native Guaraní. They also learned how to play brass instruments for the mission band and some type of craft such as carpentry or shoemaking, and the brightest boys learned some elementary reading, writing, and arithmetic. The girls received instruction in sewing, cooking, and other "womanly skills." The friars also often hired out the children to neighboring haciendas, where they were further imbued with Western ideas and habits. Thus, although the conversion process was lengthy, at least in theory by the second generation the mission population would be completely converted.

The process was more lengthy than the missionaries or national authorities had counted on. It is quite possible that Mandeponay helped delay the inevitable, for there were persistent reports that many families hid their children in the surrounding dense scrub forest to prevent them from being indoctrinated. Mandeponay certainly knew about this circumvention but elected to do nothing to help the friars retrieve the children. Moreover, Tacu refused to hand over his own children, setting a dangerous example for the rest of the mission Indians. Another circumstance that made the conversion problem more intractable was the constant turnover of Indians in the mission. Some families found temporary refuge on the mission during the various uprisings or when the corn harvest was poor in other regions, a recurrent phenomenon in the arid climate of the southeastern Andean foothills. Once families moved on again, the missionaries had to return the children to their parents, making many conversion efforts futile.

Nevertheless, the *neófito* population continued to grow. By the 1890s they constituted approximately one-third of the total population living at Macharetí, which during this period fluctuated between twenty-five hundred and three thousand individuals. Although mission residence patterns gave Mandeponay a larger say over even those who had converted, in the long term his authority was threatened by the ever-larger Christian population on the mission. The converts tended to heed the friars more and thus obviated the necessity for an intermediary such as Mandeponay. The number of mestizos who lived either on mission grounds or in the near vicinity also increased significantly during the 1890s, from about two hundred fifty at the beginning of the decade to double that number at the end. It was clear to Mandeponay that Chiriguano ethnic identity was threatened even in the relatively benign conditions of the missions.

Another threat to traditional ways of life was the increasing integration of the mission Indians into the market economy. The mission's natural pastures and scrub forest provided abundant fodder for the cattle that the Indians were beginning to raise. By the 1890s mission residents raised over seven hundred head of cattle themselves, in addition to the large herd of almost two thousand head belonging to the mission. In the 1890s a new trail connecting Argentina with Santa Cruz to the north was developed that passed through Macharetí. The Indians began to grow fruits, cotton, and other goods for their own consumption and for sale to the merchants who passed with ever-greater frequency through the mission. However, the land around Macharetí was not as fertile as that at other missions because of the sandy soil and its proximity to the arid Chaco, making agriculture a difficult enterprise. Nevertheless, as more Indians entered the monetary economy, the emphasis on reciprocity through large feasts that showed the generosity of the chiefs, and the art of traditional crafts such as hand-weaving cotton cloth and making beautifully ornamented pottery, slowly began to wane. Instead, many mission Indians refused to participate in the mutual shows of largess; others purchased ready made clothes and iron pots rather than engage in time-consuming artisanal activities.

Mandeponay tried to adapt himself and his people to these changes and used his great influence to provide his followers with the best alternatives. The most important role the Chiriguanos played in the regional economy was not as producers or consumers, but as laborers. All white settlers who received land grants from the government in the Chiriguanía attempted to include as many Indian villages as possible so as to provide an adequate source of hacienda peons for the new estates. Unfortunately, labor conditions were miserable on the haciendas, where the Chiriguanos were treated as virtual slaves, lost their indigenous culture, and were perpetually mired in debt. Mandeponay was very much aware of this situation, and certainly his awareness of labor conditions in the region's estates had led him to ask for a mission rather than subordinate himself and his people to the white colonists. At times, of course, Mandeponay had permitted some of his people to work on surrounding estates. At least the Franciscans, who had considerable clout with the region's landowners as well as local and national authorities, were able to protect the mission Indians from the worst abuses. However, even there, pay was low and conditions far from ideal. How was Mandeponay going to give his people the best possible deal as the valuable labor resource that they were?

The solution presented itself in the 1880s, when a few labor contractors from the sugar mills in Jujuy, Argentina, came to the mission. Jujuy had a relatively large rural population, but most lived in the highlands and, because of their subsistence mentality, rarely came down to the valleys to help harvest the sugarcane. As a result, labor contractors began to look for other sources of workers, particularly among the indigenous peoples of the Chaco. These contractors, knowing full well who had control over the majority of the mission population, offered Mandeponay a fee for each Indian whom he could deliver to Jujuy for the sugar harvest. The deal seemed too good to be true. On the one hand, his people could make more than double the wages that they received in Bolivia. On the other hand, the work was only temporary and did not require permanent migration away from the mission. Mandeponay used the fees that he collected to strengthen his ties with his soldiers and so increase his authority over the mission's inhabitants.

Thus, in the 1880s, with Mandeponay's help, Macharetí Chiriguanos began to trickle over the border into Jujuy, particularly to the Ledezma Valley, to work in the sugarcane harvest. The missionaries were against this temporary migration for a number of reasons. They complained that when the mission Indians returned, the men had been corrupted by their experience in Argentina. The missionaries saw their tutelage over their charges and their efforts at conversion threatened by this absence. Many Indians brought back with them to the mission what the friars considered to be terrible habits. Most returning migrants had learned to fight with knives over even trivial matters, as was the custom among the gauchos of the Jujuy lowlands, creating serious problems of insubordination at the mission. Also, since many of the men had left their wives behind during the harvest, the friars became very concerned about the breakup of family lives. The women and children often had insufficient resources to fend for themselves for the whole period that their men were gone. After they returned, many Chiriguano men, the Franciscans complained, became abusive to their mates, leading to frequent instances of wife beating. The friars also worried about problems of infidelity that the prolonged absence of the men caused. However, Mandeponay's power remained such that despite these misgivings the Franciscans were unable to halt the migration.

In fact, in 1896, Mandeponay, by now an old man, went with his people to Jujuy to supervise the work there. On the sugar plantation he resided in a hut made of sugarcane stalks and leaves, just like the other temporary Indian workers. The owners of the mill gave him a monthly stipend and twelve pesos for every able-bodied man that he had work for at least one month. Even a few Chiriguano women joined the caravan; they did not work in the fields but remained home to cook and watch over the meager possessions that they and their spouses had brought along. At the end of the three-month stay, Mandeponay received, as was customary for Indian chiefs to keep them well disposed toward the mill owners, a few mules or mares as going-away presents.

The friars complained in 1896 that not enough able-bodied men remained to carry out even the basic tasks of maintaining the mission. The missionaries could do nothing to stop Mandeponay, but by this time it had become difficult to sustain the large population on the mission anyway. The years from 1897 to 1903 were exceptionally hard. At first, a plague of locusts descended upon the region, wiping out virtually all the mission's crops. For the rest of the century, a prolonged drought dried out the corn plants before they bore ears, creating even worse problems for those who lived on the mission. Also, as the region's inhabitants lacked food, they resorted to cattle rustling, especially from the mission's herds, leading to an even greater breakdown in the mission economy. Hunger drove many of the Chiriguanos, including a number of the boys in the school, to go to Argentina rather than starve at home. Some friars condoned this migration, for they saw little alternative for their charges, despite the cries of outrage from local hacendados who relied on mission labor for their farms.

In the meantime, Mandeponay as well as his sons became wealthier with their trade in mission workers. As a good Chiriguano chief, Mandeponay distributed this wealth to his followers in the form of more expensive feasts, which he supplied with copious amounts of rum. The missionaries, who were already concerned with discipline problems brought about by the migrants' new habits learned in Argentina, were appalled at this drunkenness but again could do nothing about it. They continued to need Mandeponay, especially as the drought got worse, to prevent the mission from losing all its population. In fact, Mandeponay's ability to hold these feasts attracted for the first time large numbers of Tobas and Tapietés (another Chaco tribe), who were affected by the prolonged drought themselves and sought food and refuge on the mission. Thus, Mandeponay maintained his position as the indispensable intermediary between the missionaries and the indigenous population of the region.

This situation could not continue, however. The drought persisted into the twentieth century. Even Mandeponay's ability to purchase large quantities of alcohol could not prevent the Indians from noticing that they had no food for their children and themselves. As a way of keeping the Indians on the mission, Mandeponay became more and more autocratic and, according to the friars, abusive. The feasts, in the context of the increasing commercialization of the mission and the subsequent breakdown of traditional ties among the Indians, were simply no longer adequate for keeping his followers in line. Instead, Mandeponay relied to a greater extent than before on force to maintain his authority. This tactic backfired, especially as the drought worsened. First to depart were the Tobas and Tapietés, who left for regions that had been spared the disastrous crop failures.

The remaining heathens at the mission, Mandeponay's power base, left in increasing numbers as well. Once he had alienated his followers, there was little reason for them to remain. Many instead elected to go to Argentina with their families and to stay there permanently. As the twentieth century arrived, the exodus turned from a trickle to a flood. The missionaries in 1901 had to turn over seventy of their pupils to families leaving the mission, a fact that they blamed on the drought and on Mandeponay's despotism. In 1903, ninety heathen families and forty *neófito* families left for greener pastures. The Franciscans threatened to depose him, and Mandeponay agreed to reform his ways. It was too late. By 1904, three hundred left, more than halving the mission population from its high point in early 1901 of over three thousand. Of the fourteen hundred people remaining, most were *neófitos,* since they had a greater stake in staying on the mission. As a result, for the first time in 1904 the mission contained more Christian Indians than heathens (in fact, twice as many), making Mandeponay's position as intermediary superfluous. The friars could finally act against the old chief, and they deposed him as the supreme Indian authority of the mission. Although Mandeponay continued to send Indians to Argentina, his power was broken, and he died soon thereafter.

What does Mandeponay's life tell us about the human condition in nineteenth-century Latin America? Mandeponay was representative of the leaders of indigenous groups who, during the course of the nineteenth century, were forced to accommodate themselves to the expansion of the frontier into their territories. In a sense, Mandeponay's experience was relatively fortunate; neither he nor his band suffered total extinction as happened to many other, smaller native groups in, for example, the Amazon basin. Mandeponay wielded significant power during most of his long adulthood because he was able to act as an intermediary between his people, as well as to a certain extent other frontier tribes, and national society. Even in these frontier conditions, where the strong subjugated the weak, Mandeponay was able to carve out a breathing space for his people and help them adapt to changing conditions.

Mandeponay's experience shows that even relatively powerless indigenous groups, when led by creative leaders with political savvy and a firm understanding of their indispensability as intermediaries in the ever-changing circumstances along the frontier, were able to maintain a semblance of ethnic cohesion and pride. Tragically, this could be only temporary. The acceptance of a Franciscan mission spelled, through the indoctrination of the indigenous children, the eventual end of traditional cohesion and culture. Also, by bringing the Indians into the regional economy, the missions guaranteed that the Chiriguanos would move away from their customary ways of life. Even so, Mandeponay seized the initiative and gave his people the opportunity to work for much larger monetary rewards than were available in the immediate vicinity of the mission. This Macharetí chief tried to maintain his traditional control over his people by sponsoring more festivals and distributing large quantities of drink. However, this effort failed. The immediate cause for this failure was the prolonged agricultural crisis that afflicted the area at the turn of the century, making it difficult for Mandeponay to keep his people in the region. In the long term, his political project was doomed anyhow; the drought probably accelerated his eventual downfall. By encouraging the mission Indians to migrate to Argentina, he helped expose his people to the full force of the market and to ideas that entered the mission only in a filtered form. This circumstance alone would have converted the Chiriguanos into the agricultural proletariat that by the first decades of the twentieth century the vast majority of these Indians had become.

SOURCES

Sources on Mandeponay, considering his importance in southeastern Bolivia for a generation, are relatively scarce and scattered. The founding of Macharetí and Mandeponay's role in it is related in Antonio Comajuncosa and Alejandro M. Corrado, *El colegio franciscano de Tarija y sus misiones* (Quaracchi, 1884). Numerous reports highlight the conditions in Macharetí and the other Chiriguano missions. Among them Manuel Jofre O., hijo, *Colonias y misiones: Informe de la visita practicada por el Delegado del Supremo Gobierno, Dr. Manuel Jofre O., hijo, en 1893* (Tarija, 1895); A. Thouar, *Explorations dans l'Amérique du Sud* (Paris, 1891); and Doroteo Giannecchini, *Diario de la expedición exploradora boliviana al Alto Paraguay de 1886–1887* are most revealing. In this study, I have relied extensively on the annual reports of the Tarija mission prefects for Macharetí, which are in the archive of the Franciscan convent in Tarija, and on the annual reports of the minister of colonization, available in the Archivo Nacional in Sucre, Bolivia.

For the 1892 revolt the basic secondary source is Hernando Sanabria Fernández's excellent *Apiaguaiqui-Tumpa* (La Paz, 1972). For conditions in the Chiriguanía in the late nineteenth and early twentieth centuries, see Erick D. Langer, "Franciscan Missions and Chiriguano Workers: Colonization, Acculturation, and Indian Labor in Southeastern Bolivia," *The Americas* 62, no. 1 (January 1987): 305–22; Langer and Robert H. Jackson, "Colonial and Republican Missions Compared: The Cases of Alta California and Southeastern Bolivia," *Comparative Studies in Society and History* 30, no. 2 (April 1988); and Langer, *Rural Society and the Mining Economy in Southern Bolivia: Agrarian Resistance in Chuquisaca, 1880–1930* (Stanford, 1988), chapter 6. By far the best analysis of the colonial Chiriguanos is Thierry Saignes, "Une 'frontière fossile': La Cordillère Chiriguano au XIXe siècle" (Ph.D. diss., Ecole des Hautes Etudes, Paris, 1974).

General studies on the Chiriguanos include Bernardino de Nino, *Etnografía chiriguana* (La Paz, 1912); Alfred Métraux, "Chiriguano and Chané," in *Handbook of South American Indians*, vol. 3, edited by Julian H. Steward, 465–85 (Washington, DC, 1948); Bratislava Susnik, *Chiriguanos* (Asunción, 1968); and Lorenzo Calzavarini, *Nación chiriguana: Grandeza y ocaso* (La Paz, 1980).

IV

New-Century Generations: Revolution and Change in the Cities and the Countryside, 1900–1920

The twentieth century witnessed the widespread intensification of trends from previous decades. Revolution, urbanization, and commercial agriculture characterized these emergent forces in Latin American society. Each shaped the national histories of the region through the first two decades of the new century.

The pull of urban opportunities drew migrants from the countryside and immigrants from abroad. The cities underwent dramatic changes with the addition of public services and utilities that were quickly overwhelmed by the burgeoning population. Most dramatic was the growth of the urban masses, who represented a large pool of workers and a potential source of followers for those who sought to organize labor unions or to create mass political machines. The Radical and the Socialist Parties in Argentina, for example, developed huge organizations based on the immigrants in Buenos Aires. Together, their successful political mobilization forced the elites to attempt to preempt popular issues by reforming the political system, extending the franchise to all adult males, introducing secret ballots, and devising modest political changes. The character of urban life and the needs of city dwellers throughout the region find expression in the life story of Lima resident Miguel Rostaing (Chapter 10). His biography also illustrates the salient issues of race and class as well as the ways in which individuals found self-expression in such humble leisure activities as playing soccer.

For those who remained at Latin America's rural margins, life had both new opportunities and new challenges because of the commercialization of agriculture and the expansion of markets—both in domestic demand for food and the international appetite for raw materials. Juan Esquivel, a resourceful Peruvian campesino, encouraged by the opportunities represented by these enlarged markets, audaciously agreed to become a tenant farmer. For years, his luck and hard work made him successful, but ultimately he succumbed to the expanding haciendas, increasingly created as factories in the fields (Chapter 8).

The lopsided development of plantation agriculture in the later years of the nineteenth and the early years of the twentieth century resulted in a huge percentage of campesinos working on someone else's property. Land ownership was a dream for perhaps as many as 80 percent of rural Latin Americans. Moreover, many who worked the land were often terribly exploited and subjected to meager wages, inhuman housing, and starvation foodstuffs. Those who took advantage of these workers often justified their actions in racial or ethnic terms laced with social Darwinian rationalizations.

From the concentration of land in the hands of the few and the exploitation of workers in both the countryside and the city arose two causes for revolution in the early twentieth century. The first of the great regional uprisings came in Mexico. Beginning in 1910, Mexicans went through an era of violence that continued for a decade and resulted in a reconstruction of the nation, starting in 1920, that attempted to benefit its majority. The indigenous population was paid particular attention in the 1920s and 1930s (Chapter 9) and Indianism was made a part of Mexican nationalism. These issues would surface in other revolutions (Bolivia, Cuba, and Nicaragua) and revolutionary movements (Peru, Venezuela, and Colombia). For Mexicans, the revolution created a legacy that inspired a pantheon of heroes (including Emiliano Zapata and Pancho Villa) and endures today. For the rest of the hemisphere, revolution would soon become either the great fear or the great goal of the people.

8

Juan Esquivel: Cotton Plantation Tenant

Vincent C. Peloso

For too long the lives of tenant farmers such as Juan Esquivel existed beyond the historical spectrum where they remained unseen and unheard. In this essay, Vincent Peloso describes the experiences of one ambitious tenant and, by implication, explains the hopes of many of the Andean villagers who left their homes for the factories and fields of lowland Peru. The author opens a window onto the lives of rural Peruvians and indicates the range of contractual arrangements that they made with the landowners.

Esquivel's life story gives meaning to the demands of rural workers throughout the Andes and much of Latin America for agrarian reform—titles to the lands they worked—that inspired uprisings and revolutions for much of the two centuries since independence. His working experience can be compared with those related in the classic novels of Ecuadorian and Bolivian plantation life lived by indigenous peoples, Jorge Icaza's *Huasipungo* and Alcides Argüedas's *Raza de Bronce*. His experience can also be measured against that of revolutionaries from Emiliano Zapata to the current Zapatistas who demand land in Mexico.

This essay tells us about the Peruvians who were not ruling the country, dictating its economy, or signing contracts with foreign investors with the hope of creating a modern economy and claiming a personal profit. Esquivel's Peru is distant indeed from the Peru in the first quarter of the twentieth century shaped by Augusto B. Leguía as president (1908–1912) and dictator (1919–1930). Leguía talked reform for the marginal peoples, especially indigenous highlanders, but practiced almost none. Populist campaigns for Peruvians such as Esquivel remained in the future, although Leguía's development program attracted people to lowland plantations and cities (see the vignette of Miguel Rostaing, Chapter 10).

Vincent Peloso, editor of the cultural history journal, *The Americas*, and a history professor at Howard University in Washington, DC, helped organize Peru's Archivo del Fuero Agrario in Lima. Today, this center, the agrarian archive, is a major resource for scholars and served as the source of information on the life of Juan Esquivel. Peloso has written on peasant problems in numerous articles, examined Peruvian food and culinary patterns, and, most recently, edited with Barbara A. Tenenbaum, *Liberals, Politics, and Power* (Athens, GA, 1996), an examination of Liberalism in nineteenth-century Latin America.

A labor contractor from Peru's Pisco Valley went looking in 1898 for farmhands for the expanding cotton plantations of the Aspíllaga family. He made one stop in the Chincha Valley where, as usual, he went to the village tavern to find recruits. He wanted, he said, men who had the skills and daring to improve their future.

Juan Esquivel listened closely. A black villager, son of a former slave, he had a vision of a comfortable future that would put him, his wife, and children in a better social position than the one they endured. He had little formal schooling, but he knew from experience how to till the soil and from instinct when to plant and when to harvest to get maximum results. He had confidence in his skills, and he believed he had found an opportunity to escape his village for a greater chance to use his abilities.

After the labor contractor bought him and his friends a round of drinks, Esquivel did not resist much when offered a contract. Vaguely worded, the agreement required no cash from Esquivel; he would pay his rent with cotton. A good crop, the contractor suggested, would leave a shrewd tenant with cotton to sell on the open market. Nor did it hurt the recruiter's argument when he shook a few silver soles, Peru's currency, onto the table in the *chingana* (tavern) as an advance on Esquivel's earnings as a cotton farmer on the Hacienda Palto.

Esquivel made the decision to abandon the village where he had grown up and the people he had known to try for a more exciting life. Pisco was not so far away, so he could always return to his village if things did not work out. With his wife and sons and their few possessions, most importantly the farming tools and a pair of oxen, he traveled south. Not far down the desert coast road the Pisco River formed an oasis somewhat smaller than the one they had left in the Chincha region. There the port town of Pisco, with its few wharves, lay alongside the river. Where the rushing streambed fanned out into a gurgling alluvial dribble as it met the Pacific tide, the Esquivels turned left. Facing east toward the distant escarpment of the massive Andean range that hid the river's origins, they walked another six kilometers until they reached the imposing gateway of the Hacienda San Francisco de Palto.

As a new tenant, Esquivel joined a group of thirty-four men and women and their families who also had abandoned their villages for the hacienda. Many young Peruvians, lured by the promise of wages and drawn by curiosity, left their Andean villages in the waning years of the last century. Some of them went to the new towns sprouting on the edges of the reinvigorated copper and lead mines, others to the big cities, especially Lima, and still others sought out the expanding, lively, aggressive coastal plantations.

The Esquivels could sense the energy on the hacienda from the noise made by the workers, shouting and talking as they labored by hand. People daily turned over the soil, planted, weeded, built or rebuilt dikes and water channels, mended fences and buildings, herded animals, and harvested and stored crops. The only machinery to be found on cotton plantations were the deseeding and pressing machines that were used to prepare bales for shipment.

Excitement filled the region because of the renewal of commercial agriculture on the coastal plantations at the turn of the century. Critical to maintaining rural society in the nineteenth century had been an ideology of authority based on force. Until midcentury, slaves and indentured Asian laborers harvested grapes, sugarcane, and cotton on the plantations. When demand for cotton rose sharply both in Peru and on the world market, landowners sought ways to develop commercial cotton, but they conceded that a system of authority based on persuasion had to replace force. They gambled that they could persuade free farmers to assume the risks of producing large amounts of cotton without requiring a major increase in labor or new technology.

Caution governed the efforts to stimulate commercial cotton agriculture. Owners made few technological changes, relying almost exclusively on animal and human power until nearly World War I. They found it much easier to limit the cost of labor than to resist technological change, thus encouraging them to begin to expand production. For a decade after the Chilean War (1879–83), cotton planters experimented with various combinations of tenantry. The experiments yielded valuable lessons, and after 1895 many of the large landowners settled for a contract labor system with two categories.

Farm workers became tenants, meaning that they were hired to live on as well as farm the plantations. Among the tenants, distinctions emerged that proved to be of some economic importance. In the southern coastal valleys, some tenants were called *arrendatarios* (renters, or tenants), a designation that initially meant they enjoyed certain privileges, especially the one of paying a fixed rent in kind. However, most of the resident laborers were *compañeros,* a term peculiar to the southern coast and later dropped for the more widely used term *yanacona* (sharecropper). The sharecroppers usually paid 50 percent of their crop for rent, rather than a fixed amount.

Differences between the two types of resident labor were meant to be sharp. The landowners hoped that by providing a bit of freedom from credit and planting restrictions for some tenants, while placing some restrictions on others, they could reduce their costs, especially in times of low prices for cotton. The ratio of sharecroppers to tenants on a plantation sometimes changed when the market or land use policies intervened. The tenants seemed to enjoy a more favorable social status and have more independence in choosing the mix of cotton and other crops they would plant than did the sharecroppers. At least this was true as long as a fixed-rent labor population was important to the growers. Later, when the *arrendatarios* had outlived their usefulness, the owners did not evict them wholesale from the land, they merely altered the rules that governed tenantry.

The owners of the coastal cotton plantations apparently were confident that they had found the right formula. After 1895 they began to increase the amount of land in production on their plantations. Between 1900 and 1910, cotton exports from all coastal plantations doubled; and, in the next decade, they doubled again. The increased land in use was rented to tenants and sharecroppers, who then were provided with field hands if they needed them. Migrant workers were scarce throughout this era; for this reason, plantation owners sought peasant families to fill the roles of tenant and sharecropper. To help the sharecroppers and tenants, the cotton planters would have liked to hire migrant laborers who could be paid by the week or month when the need arose, such as at harvest time or when a road or dike had to be built. But the number of day laborers was small at the turn of the century, and they commanded high pay. Nevertheless, the owners continued to hope that enough of them would become available at critical times to meet production needs. In any case, whether there was enough labor or not, the landowners seem to have minimized the risk to themselves by passing it on to the resident tenants and sharecroppers.

Hacienda Palto, the plantation that had lured the Esquivels and others, was a medium-size, 460-hectare property. It was the cotton plantation of the Aspíllagas, one of the most powerful families in Peru. They had turned this rather neglected, bedraggled estate into a commercially sound plantation, its warehouses bulging with cotton ready for shipment to consignment houses in Europe. The four Aspíllaga brothers owned Palto and other properties along with other business interests. Their business connections were built along vertical rather than horizontal lines. All of their ventures were related to real estate (the use of the land), whether they were in agriculture, warehousing, banking, shipping, or commerce. A large, productive sugarcane plantation, Hacienda Cayaltí, in the north coast's Zaña Valley, which the Aspíllaga family first had managed for and then bought from a wealthy shipowner, was their earliest successful undertaking in commercial agriculture. They owned several homes and office buildings in Lima and Pisco that they rented. Their offices were located in the capital, where they held positions on the boards of several banks. By the turn of the century, this wealthy family, whose sons had married well, showed little interest in living on a plantation near a small port town. The Aspíllagas preferred the cosmopolitan life, including membership in a prestigious social club in Lima and dabbling in municipal and national politics.

Their reluctance to live in the countryside of Pisco did not mean that the Aspíllagas had little interest in Palto. On the contrary, the extent of their commitment to the plantation and to cotton was evident. They had received numerous offers over the years for the property, and, although tempted in 1891, they held on to the land. It produced a steady, even growing, income for its owners but needed careful and attentive management to produce these profits, so the family hired an administrator to handle the plantation's affairs. The manager had to enforce the contracts drawn between the owners and each individual tenant at Palto.

The rental contract was a vaguely written agreement for the most part, but it was also the instrument that would explain to the tenant how plantation society functioned. No longer would a tenant be linked by the family to a community, with obligations to neighbors and expectations that they would reciprocate if need be. Those obligations ended at the gates of Palto or of any other plantation and were transformed into an unequal relationship with the owner that was based upon certain responsibilities. The expectations, meanwhile, became vague promises.

Although the most attractive contracts stipulated that a tenant could remain on a specific portion of the plantation for three years, contract terms were flexible. In practice, tenant and sharecropper agreements were revised if the manager demanded it or when the owners needed the tenants to keep the land producing. One element in the contract was its list of rewards and punishments. Tenants were to be rewarded for making some kinds of farming decisions under the manager's supervision, for providing their own animals and tools, and with ample room for seeking credit in the marketplace. Tenants could keep their gardens free of pasturing animals. On rare occasions, they might correspond directly with the landowner. This chance to communicate with the owner no doubt was offered for the same reason as other privileges, to make tenants feel like they were more than hired field hands, that they were autonomous farmers in an informal partnership with the owners.

When Esquivel accepted his contract at Palto, he did not recognize that he would need to develop a close working relationship with the plantation's manager. This was something new to him. Although the manager was the owner's spokesman on all matters large and small on the hacienda, he was not the owner. Details about which debts must be paid first—outstanding loans or rent or an owner's option on crops above rent—would have to be discussed with the manager. But there seemed to be no reason why this relationship should prevent Esquivel from becoming a successful cotton tenant.

The manager enforced the contracts and wielded daily authority on the scene, so owners wanted someone who would remind the tenants of the owners, who could identify with the Aspíllagas. Preferably a family man, the administrator was expected to handle the details of plantation management as if the estate were his personal property. The Aspíllagas did not trust a stranger much. For that reason, one of the brothers periodically made a hasty trip to the Pisco Valley, where he checked the condition of the fields, buildings, and equipment and reviewed the account ledgers. A similar visit took place each time a new manager was appointed. The new man received detailed instructions outlining every plantation operation and how the Aspíllagas expected it to be handled. He was instructed to communicate at least once a week by letter with the owners; they especially wanted his judgment on how well the tenants carried out their contractual duties and how the other workers performed their jobs.

The Aspíllagas hired only a few managers for their estate. Usually, these men were recommended through family connections, and they developed their managerial and commercial skills in large farming through on-the-job experience. Their understanding of labor, perhaps the most important element of their profession, was based on attitudes and behaviors common to the elite. These notions included strong negative stereotypes of villagers and other farm workers as people who were slow to learn and who only poorly understood modern work methods. Provincial elites, including plantation managers and accountants, usually looked down on persons of African or Amerindian descent as people "without culture." The owners, thoroughly disdainful of all country dwellers, occasionally reminded their managers to be tactful but firm in their dealings with tenants and other farm workers.

Esquivel's decision to become a tenant was shaped by two factors. One, tenantry, which was already in limited use at Palto for a decade when Esquivel arrived fresh from the north, seemed to be the most independent yet secure form of farming available in the cotton valleys to the person who knew enough about growing cotton to gamble on the size of the next year's crop and who was bold enough to bet his team of oxen on it. Moreover, Esquivel was the right person for the time. Favored for his reliability and productivity and blessed with a strong wife and three young sons who could work in the fields, he did well when others were losing their contracts. When the Aspíllagas raised his rent, Esquivel answered this challenge by renting still more sections of the plantation.

The start was hopeful. Esquivel went to Palto with considerable assets for a village dweller. He owned tools, a team of oxen, and the equipment that he needed to work the animals. But Esquivel took a look around and decided that he did not immediately want a tenant contract. Instead, he settled for a *compañero* arrangement. This made him a partner of the plantation owners, for whom he worked specified fields as a resident laborer. Part of the time he spent working at jobs under the manager's supervision.

The manager assured Esquivel that if he worked at his assigned tasks for a time he could save money, perhaps even enough money to avoid large loans. Esquivel accepted. He worked as an *arriero* (mule skinner), periodically escorting the plantation's mule train loaded with cotton to the warehouses of Pisco where it awaited consignment. Between cotton shipments he tended the animals and wagons and did the regular field work assigned to all workers at Palto—caring for the all-important irrigation system and tending the fields. After the harvest, the raw bales of cotton were hauled off to be sold to English textile factories in Liverpool. Esquivel, as a mule skinner, was paid wages plus meals and given a horse and the tools of his work (spurs, bridle and saddle, blanket, and horse feed, among other gear) by the plantation manager, leaving use of the rest of his meager wage to his discretion.

Esquivel had committed himself to working hard for the owners of Hacienda Palto; all his actions showed this, and the manager responded favorably to him. Despite the manager's skepticism about such agreements, he was impressed with Esquivel's talent and his eagerness to work for the plantation. He recommended to the owners that they allow Esquivel to pay a fixed annual rent in kind. The Chincha farmer thus became one of fourteen tenants at the hacienda who together rented over ninety-seven hectares of cotton land. Over the next few years, he quietly and carefully tripled the land he leased, acquiring command of thirty-three hectares of the plantation and paying five thousand pounds of cotton per season in rent. He was by far the largest and most productive tenant at Palto.

After a few successive seasons of larger and larger cotton crops, Esquivel realized that his family's hard work meant that he had accumulated certain privileges, perhaps even rights. Not the civil rights of a citizen in the political world—of those Esquivel had no real awareness as yet—but the privileges of a tenant who regularly fulfilled the obligations of his contract, paid his rent, and canceled his debt each year on time, and who sent workers when the plantation needed them for jobs not directly related to the production of cotton in his own fields. Patiently, with a regularity that made him and his family predictable, he sent his sons,

Demetrio, Manuel, and Ernesto, to the manager each week to perform the labor services that the plantation demanded of its tenants and sharecroppers.

One son, and sometimes Esquivel's brother, Apolonio, who had joined the family at the hacienda, would spend a portion of each week, depending on the season and the plantation's immediate needs, mending fences and sluice gates, cutting and hauling wood, tending the herds of goats, oxen, and horses, and, especially, clearing the irrigation channels of debris. Juan continued to work occasionally as a mule driver. His wife tended the garden that helped to cut food expenses, harvested the cotton fields when the time came, and performed a variety of other tasks necessary for the family's livelihood.

The most abominable of all the labor required on the plantation was deepening and widening the channels that led to the swamp at the hacienda's edge and into which all its waste drained and collected. Smelly, grimy, and unhealthy as it was, this work paid only a little better than any other. Yet it was a vital task, for without periodic attention to the waste system the plantation's entire irrigation network was endangered and the threat of flooding increased. It was rivaled in importance and repugnance only by the highly dangerous job of building dikes along the river to control flooding from sudden river swells. Many of the country men could not swim, and occasional drownings intensified the awe felt by the workers for the river that held their crops and their lives in its grip.

Esquivel thought he was up to the challenges hurled at him by the manager of Palto. He paid his rent on time, in full, and with few complaints despite the increases that threatened to reduce his family's income. But the rising price of cotton in the Pisco town market, reflecting the world demand, kept Esquivel even with his rental payments. After 1905 world demand for Peruvian cotton continued to support the endeavors of the Palto tenant and his family. In spite of worsening relations between him and the plantation manager, the Aspíllaga family did not give Esquivel any special attention. Indeed, in 1908 the owners once again acceded to his request to rent more land, raising his total holdings to over fifty-five hectares. At the same time, they demanded that he hire more wage laborers to help keep up production and, despite the added cost, Esquivel complied, but only when the owners threatened to evict him if he did not.

One year later the manager reported that Esquivel was harvesting 13,775 pounds of cotton annually and paying 8,111 pounds of it in rent. Meanwhile, he had planted vegetables and corn in parts of his fields and taken on sharecroppers as well as day laborers to meet his production schedule. The owners had in Esquivel at this point a tenant in whom they had made a considerable investment and upon whom they depended for a large portion of the success of their cotton operation in the Pisco Valley.

Not that Esquivel was alone in producing larger amounts of cotton at Palto, but he was representative of the tenants and sharecroppers who lived there. In total, the plantation's fields yielded 108,770 pounds of cotton in 1909 and 105,895 pounds in 1910. The increases in cotton production that occurred at Palto between 1900, when the plantation's total cotton crop amounted to only 81,491 pounds, and 1909, with the introduction of cotton into larger numbers of fields, paralleled the rise to prominence of Juan Esquivel. Between 1901 and 1905 the entire plantation harvested an average of 86,375 pounds of raw, unseeded cotton per year. During the following five years, from 1906 through 1910, Palto yielded an average of 102,447 pounds of cotton per year. The two figures indicate that the yields extracted from Palto's labor force increased sharply, by over three-fourths, after 1906.

Palto's manager insisted that these increases could not be attributed to the industriousness of the tenants. He found much to complain about in the work habits of these families, and old wounds that had been buried in the press of getting out the cotton in the past were now reopened as the owners demanded even greater increases in production. Some of the hostility was precipitated by bad floods. In 1907 several of Esquivel's most productive fields lying close to the riverbank were flooded, making it difficult for him to meet his rent bill.

Esquivel and the Palto administrator argued vehemently over the total amount of rent the tenant owed after the 1907 flood. The manager insisted that the flood was not the plantation's fault and that Esquivel was responsible for the full amount of rent stipulated by his contract, flood or no flood. To the tenant, this position was a bad sign of changing attitudes. Under harmonious conditions, managers were prepared to accept nature's fickle ways and to forgive a portion of the rent that was lost in a disaster not of the tenant's making. But in this case, the manager was insisting upon tacking the loss onto the tenant's debt. Why had he become so inflexible?

The issues most likely to spark arguments between the manager and the tenants were not directly related to the production of cotton. Often disagreements arose concerning maintenance of the plantation. The floods were one instance when the plantation owners had advised the manager that they would not pay for the damages. Therefore, the manager attempted to pass the cost on to the tenants, but some of them resisted. Those like Esquivel, who saw themselves as victims of the poor maintenance of dikes that usually stemmed the river's tides, refused to absorb the cost. Esquivel argued that he should not have to pay rent for those fields in which the floods of 1907 had ruined the cotton plants. In 1908 the tenants of Hacienda Palto banded together in order to argue more effectively with the plantation's manager over proper distribution of the cost of cleaning the drainage ditches.

Credit was also a matter of dispute. From the beginning, Esquivel received few loans from the owners of Palto. The Aspíllagas were unwilling to share the risk of cotton farming with their tenants. That is why they had sought tenants in the first place—to have others who would have to absorb the immediate risks of cotton farming. Esquivel was able to manage tenantry only because he found suitable lenders, small merchants in Pisco who demanded a portion of his crop as collateral. Thus, each year, after he paid his rent and debts to the plantation, Esquivel would settle his loan.

In each year of this practice, with what remained of a crop after the rent going to pay the principal and interest on the loan, and with nothing left, a tenant would need another loan to finance the next season. The loan-debt cycle seemed like an endless trap, with the high interest on short-term loans making them difficult to pay off. This cycle left tenants with little room for dealing with calamities. Still, Esquivel could point to a growing number of oxen in his stable, and to his wife and his growing sons, as family assets whose contributions to the harvest meant stability in the family's life.

As the demand for cotton rose on the world market, the owners of Palto sought to tighten their hold on the fiber produced on their land. They no longer allowed their tenants to arrange for loans with speculators in Pisco, and they developed practices meant to give them control of all the cotton produced at Palto. The most important of these was to insist that tenants give the landowner first option on the remainder of the crop above rent. The most dangerous aspect of this arrangement was the required loan guarantee. The crop itself was not enough; the owners of Palto insisted that the tenant put up his field animals as a hedge against a lost crop.

In effect, tenants were forced to sell to the plantation owners at below the market price. Esquivel resisted this latest intrusion into what he regarded as his independent farmer status. For years he had argued with the manager over the correct interpretation of his contract: Did he owe back debts first to the hacienda, or did the obligation to pay his creditor come first? At times, the manager became so incensed that he used racial epithets rather than rational arguments to counter Esquivel's behavior. "Colored ingrate!" "devilish black!" and "games player!" he thundered more than once, to suggest that the tenant was deceitful. And, on one occasion, the manager subjected Esquivel to the worst possible humiliation by commanding that he spend the day in the plantation stocks, a punishment ordinarily reserved for drunks and brawling field hands.

Despite the conflicts and setbacks, Esquivel remained at Palto. His stubbornness in the face of insults and demands by the manager and owners of the plantation at first seems incredible. But Esquivel survived because he knew farming. As cotton demand fell off after 1910 he increased the number of fields that he planted in vegetables and corn. Yet, to satisfy the owners, he continued to produce cotton, partly by taking on new sharecroppers and partly by extending the size of his loans. At one point, he had as many as three creditors, and, more than once, he used one crop to guarantee another.

A bewildering maze of loans and guarantees began to characterize his activities, but as long as the crops continued to do well, Esquivel was able to pay into his left hand with what he held in his right. All the while, the amount of his indebtedness increased. Between 1910 and 1913 his debts accumulated ominously when flooding again ravaged the fields of Palto and his cotton crops repeatedly fell short of his promises. He was about to give up when the Aspíllagas decided that it was time for the landowners to invest in flood control. However, they accomplished very little. A few more dikes were built along the riverbank, and loan payments were extended, but the plantation system remained intact.

Not long after the owners' halfhearted effort, Esquivel's situation brightened for one final moment. He was, once again, the plantation's most prized tenant farmer. The holder of over thirty-five hectares of land, more than 90 percent of it planted in cotton, he was the most productive and, no doubt, the most influential person at Hacienda Palto aside from the chief administrator. For the first time, however, the manager decided to tell Esquivel what to plant. Astonished and mortified, Esquivel could not let this challenge go unanswered. He now felt comfortable enough to take the steps necessary to protect his contractual rights and ensure his family's security. When he did, the actions he took were a grave threat to the manager's authority. On one occasion, the manager tried to deny him access to the plantation woodlot. Esquivel insisted that he had a contractual right to cut firewood there, and he complained long and loud until the manager, who received no support from the owners for his position, gave in. Years later, the manager notified him that he was required to allow the landowners' cattle to pasture on his fallow fields. Esquivel refused to permit it. If his own oxen did not get enough healthy grasses, would not his cotton production be severely affected? Shortly thereafter, Esquivel and other tenants fenced in their fields with wire. For the moment, the Aspíllagas did not respond to the manager's complaints, and this action went unchallenged. Again, Esquivel's activities had caused him no difficulty with the Aspíllagas. True, the manager was unhappy, but the owners seemed willing to uphold the difficult parts of their contract with him. Perhaps they cared more to honor their agreement with their tenant than to make life easier for their manager.

Calculating that this was so, Esquivel composed a careful letter to the owners the next time he and the manager collided. The moment came in 1918. Of course, it was not possible to come directly to the point. First, he asked after the health of one of the Aspíllaga brothers who had spoken to him on his last visit to Palto. This was Esquivel's way of reminding the owners that it was not a nobody writing to them. On the contrary, he had been singled out in the past as an especially industrious and successful tenant. Surely they must remember him?

Once he had established his credentials, Esquivel explained the discord that had arisen between himself and the administrator, making it clear that the man had no right to insist that Esquivel grow no vegetables at all and that he plant only cotton. Finally, he asked the question that was gnawing at him and that revealed his contempt for the administrator. Juan Esquivel could not contain himself, he had to know: Had the administrator really received such an order, as he claimed, to tell Esquivel to grow only cotton? Esquivel could not believe that the owners, knowing his record, would allow the manager of Palto to treat him, a loyal tenant for so many years, in such a degrading fashion. And, he ended, "If this is true, then I do not understand your patronage very well."*

It was an easy step to the end of the tenant system. That point was reached when the tenants at Palto lost control of their pastures, their last bulwark against being reduced to sharecroppers. In 1919 the Aspíllagas announced that the tenants would no longer be allowed to fence in their gardens and that fixed rents would be abolished. Thereafter, all tenants were in effect reduced to sharecropper status.

Soon the plantation manager was talking about the new machinery the owners had introduced into Palto's fields in 1920, especially the Fordson tractor they had purchased from an American dealer. The plantation had become more independent of its tenants, and Juan Esquivel was a marked man. His name disappears from the records altogether in 1920. The manager had refused to renew his rental contract and "canceled" his debt to Hacienda Palto.

The value of all of Esquivel's assets were totaled against the value of his outstanding debts to the Aspíllagas. Whatever was left over was his to keep when he departed. In fact, he and his wife exited the plantation gates with nothing but the clothes on their backs. While together with their sons they had grown tons of cotton that added significantly to the plantation's coffers, and to its value as a capital asset, their return for such work was hard to see. Even the animals and tools they had brought to Palto had gone to pay off debts. Though Esquivel was a skilled farmer, the plantation system had betrayed his skills, reducing their importance and

*Juan Esquivel to Ramón Aspíllaga y Hermanos, Lima, September 9, 1918, Hacienda Palto, Accounts and Correspondence, 1867–1949, Archivo del Fuero Agrario, Lima.

rewarding only their value as labor rather than as specialized knowledge of farming.

He was not alone. From 1917 to 1925 most of the tenants who had farmed alongside Esquivel at Palto found their debts canceled and their services rejected. None of those still alive show up on the rolls of the hacienda in 1925, and few of them left the plantation with anything but a small amount of cash and an uncertain future. Left on the plantation were about one hundred tenants and their families, a total population of about three hundred fifty or four hundred men, women, and children according to an informal count by one of the Aspíllagas. This labor force of sharecroppers and day laborers was producing an annual cotton crop of roughly 177,000 pounds.

Juan Esquivel's farming success in the Pisco River valley blinded him to the realities of Peruvian society in the early twentieth century. Esquivel expected his skill in cotton farming to be recognized by the owners at least enough to gain respect for his judgment in farming decisions. He forgot that the owners and the manager paid attention to a different set of criteria. This led him to challenge the system of administrative control of tenants, not by striking out violently against the plantation manager but by personally challenging the manager's authority in a discreet manner, through a letter to the owners.

By questioning the manager's views, however, especially by calling attention to the manager's "mistakes" as early as 1909, Esquivel exposed himself to the charge of disobedience. He appeared thereafter to be an unreliable tenant, and only his ability to produce cotton in the face of difficult conditions saved him from eviction before 1919. The plantation owners wanted a clear line maintained between a tenant's working hard to meet the plantation's needs and his challenging the manager's authority. "Silent" hard work was viewed as constructive, while personal challenges, although they might in special circumstances be tolerated for a short time, were seen as ultimately threatening the system of plantation command. If the tenants learned that the manager could be opposed, it would only be a short step to their challenging the authority of the owners. The Aspíllagas were sensitive to such an eventuality. A farm workers' movement was under way in the Pisco Valley, and the Aspíllagas had heard about a strike and demonstrations in Pisco. The workers on some of the plantations had struck for higher salaries, and the demonstrations reportedly had paralyzed commerce in the town for a short time.

Toward the end of his stay at Palto, Esquivel had begun to recognize that there was no room for compromise on the matter of tenant choice and managerial authority on the plantation. Tenants worked under severe tension generated by the competing demands of the export plantation world. On the one hand, they were expected to work in harmony with the overall management goal of achieving greater productivity on the plantation while, on the other hand, they were encouraged to use the land as if it were their own. The explosive mixture of authoritarian management and individual choice overshadowed the tenants' daily lives. Ordinarily, such conflicts were submerged beneath the routines of farming, weeding, feeding of animals, harvesting, and other chores, thus preserving the illusion that the tenant on a commercial cotton plantation was an autonomous farmer. The moments of crises that floods, insect plagues, poor harvests, and similar disasters induced caused great stress on the plantations, disrupting the Pisco Valley countryside and filling the air with the discordant sound of clashes between independence and authority. At these moments, when they were treated like field hands, the tenants came face-to-face with the horrors of the plantation world.

SOURCES

The social and economic activities of Juan Esquivel and his family on the plantation were reconstructed from the letterbooks and accounts of Hacienda San Francisco de Palto that are located in the Archivo del Fuero Agrario, Lima, Peru. Other aids were necessary. Of critical importance were the following collections and studies: Pablo Macera, *Tierra y población en Peru (ss. xviii–xix)*, 4 vols. (Lima, 1972); Jean Piel, "The Place of the Peasantry in the National Life of Peru in the Nineteenth Century," *Past and Present* 46 (February 1970): 108–33; Bill Albert, "Yanaconaje and Cotton Production on the Peruvian Coast: Sharecropping in the Cañete Valley during World War I," *Bulletin of Latin American Research* 2, no. 2 (May 1983): 107–15; Eduardo Arroyo, *La hacienda costeña en el Peru: Mala-Cañete, 1532–1968* (Lima, 1981); Manuel Burga and Alberto Flores Galindo, *Apogeo y crisis de la república aristocrática*, 2d ed. (Lima, 1981); Carlos Samaniego, "Peasant Movements at the Turn of the Century and the Rise of the Independent Farmer," in *Peasant Cooperation and Capitalist Expansion in Central Peru*, edited by N. Long and B. R. Roberts, 45–71 (Austin, TX 1978); W. S. Bell, "An Essay on the Peruvian Cotton Industry, 1825–1920," University of Liverpool, Centre for Latin American Studies, Working Paper 6 (1985); and Rolando Pachas Castilla, *Economía sociedad en el valle de Chincha: 1860–1918* (Lima, 1976).

9

The Rough-and-Tumble Career of Pedro Crespo

Gilbert M. Joseph and Allen Wells

Mexican, and perhaps all Latin American, political culture has been dominated by patron-client relationships that rely on power brokers as the critical links between authorities and the people, individuals who make these webs of hegemony work. One such broker was Pedro Crespo, the subject of the following vignette. Above all, Crespo and others like him negotiated between the state's high-and-mighty words of revolutionary idealism and the needs, interests, and desires of local people. These critical figures, variously motivated by a craving for adventure, envy, revenge, social conscience, or the courage and cursedness typical of ordinary human beings, made the revolution what it was.

Crespo's opportunity came on November 20, 1910. Starting in the northern state of Chihuahua and quickly spreading to other regions, the epic Mexican revolution was made by insurgents who first decapitated the old regime, sending President Porfirio Díaz into exile, and then turned on the military and each other. The fighting lasted the entire decade and cost at least one million lives. The intensity of the fighting and the ferocity of the violence reflected the conflicting views of what the revolution should represent, what kind of nation Mexico should become, and what kind of people should be considered Mexicans. Pedro Crespo's tale is a poignant example of this struggle.

Gilbert M. Joseph and Allen Wells, who teach history at Yale University and Bowdoin College, respectively, have made the Yucatán peninsula their second home. Both men wrote dissertations, since published, on the political and economic development there. They have collaborated on several publications, most recently *Summer of Discontent, Seasons of Upheaval: Elite Politics and Rural Insurgency in Yucatán, 1876–1915* (Stanford, 1997). Their scholarship was recognized by their election to membership in the Academia Yucatanese de Ciencias y Artes.

Temax is at the end of the road. A few blocks north of the weatherbeaten plaza, the paved road from Izamal runs

131

out; further on, *camino blanco* winds for about twenty kilometers through scrub, then mangrove swamp to the Gulf of Mexico. Eighty kilometers west of the town is the state capital, Mérida; en route one travels through the heart of the henequen (sisal) zone, glimpsing remnants of a more affluent past. Poorly tended henequen fields line both sides of the highway, which is crisscrossed here and there by the rusting and twisted rails of imported Decauville narrow-gauge tram tracks. Blackened chimneys and the ruins of once elegant haciendas similarly bear witness to the grandeur of a monoculture now in irreversible decline. To the east of Temax, henequen's bluish-gray spines soon give way to denser scrub and clearings of grazing cattle; beyond the neighboring village of Buctzotz there is little to see for another seventy kilometers, until Tizimin, cattle country's new boomtown. Hot, dusty, and unprepossessing to the casual eye, Temax appears to be just another desperately poor and sleepy municipal seat that time has long since passed by.

Current appearances, however, mask a turbulent and intriguing recent past. Indeed, Temax has figured prominently in Yucatecan history since the apocalyptic Caste War of the mid-nineteenth century. Poised as it is between the dynamic henequen zone and the marginal sparsely populated hinterland, between the settled plantation society and the zone of refuge for the rebellious Maya campesinos who resisted plantation encroachment on their traditional way of life, Temax has been a strategic periphery or frontier. Consequently, its control has posed a significant problem for Yucatán's modern rulers. And, for much of the first half of the twentieth century, Temax's political fortunes were closely linked to the career of an extraordinary rural insurgent and political boss, Pedro Crespo. State authorities came to realize that the price of peace in Temax was a certain degree of autonomy for Don Pedro. Like Carlos Fuentes's archetypal revolutionary cacique (boss), Artemio Cruz, Crespo knew how to survive. And, much like that of Cruz, Crespo's political career came to embody the achievements and contradictions of the larger revolutionary process.

We know relatively little about Crespo's prerevolutionary career, before he burst upon the local political scene in March of 1911. During the presidency of Porfirio Díaz, Temax was overwhelmingly rural—even today, 80 percent of the working population is employed in agriculture—with a small town-based commercial sector catering to nearby hacienda and peasant communities. Born about 1870, of humble village origins, like many campesinos on the fringes of the expanding henequen zone Crespo grew up determined to preserve the family's status as small but free cultivators. Quite likely, he chose to enlist in the state national guard, to avoid the mechanism of debt that tied an ever-increasing number of villagers as peons to the large and powerful henequen estates.

In short order, Crespo demonstrated his prowess as a soldier and was made an officer in the local guard. How did Crespo regard his duties, which included hunting down and returning runaway peons to their masters, quelling worker protests against brutal, slavelike labor conditions, and implementing the hated *leva* (conscription), which dragooned villagers and drifters into the guard? We'll never know. No doubt, Crespo came to know the social world of north-central Yucatán beyond the boundaries of the rural countryside. Temaxeños remember him as a man with a foot in both worlds: "un mestizo de buen hablar"—a Maya campesino who spoke Spanish well and could handle himself in town.[1] Through his work, young Crespo was introduced to the milieu of urban politics, to the ever-shifting layered networks of patronage and clientele, which tied the local *dzules*—powerful rulers of land and men in their own right—to even more powerful patrons in the state capital.

As an officer in the guard, Crespo was compelled to play this exacting, dangerous game of late Porfirian politics. Although he initially flirted with the intrigues of a disenfranchised faction of the planter elite in 1909, by the eve of the 1910 gubernatorial election, Crespo had allied himself with Enrique Muñoz Arístegui, the "official" candidate of the "Divine Caste," an entrenched oligarchy led by the state's most powerful planter, merchant, and politician, Don Olegario Molina.

Don Olegario was a formidable patron. He was a favorite of President Porfirio Díaz, and, following a term as governor of Yucatán, he served as minister of development in Díaz's cabinet (1907–11). Molina's relations and cronies filled the upper echelons of the state's bureaucratic machine. Indeed, the power of the "Divine Caste" radiated outward from the Molina *parentesco* (extended family), which, apart from its national connections, was greatly fortified by its partnership with the principal buyer of raw henequen fiber, the International Harvester Company. Under the terms of a secret arrangement between Molina's import-export house and the North American corporation, large sums of foreign capital were periodically placed at the oligarch's disposal, enabling Molina y Compañía to affect price trends, acquire mortgages, and consolidate its hold on fiber production, communications, the infrastructure, and banking in the region. Despite the fabulous wealth generated by the fin de siècle henequen boom, the first decade of the new century was a veritable summer of discontent for the vast majority of Yucatecan producers, merchants, workers, and campesinos who found themselves personally indebted or subordinated, in one form or another, to the Molina *parentesco.*

Francisco Madero's national political campaign against the Díaz regime emboldened two disgruntled *camarillas* (political factions) of the Yucatecan planter class and their middle-class allies to organize parties for the purpose of challenging Molinista hegemony in the 1910 elections. Formed in 1909, these rather loose political coalitions, the Centro Electoral Independiente and the Partido Antireeleccionista, were known popularly as "Morenistas" and "Pinistas," after their respective standard-bearers, Delio Moreno Cantón and José María Pino Suárez, who were journalists. But they were financed by their planter supporters, and each faction hastily attempted to construct alliances reaching into the urban intelligentsia and small working class, and, perhaps even more tactically, into the large and potentially explosive Maya *campesinado.*

As a rising military leader able to bridge the cultural distance between *dzules* and campesinos, Crespo was a valuable asset in strategic Temax and was wooed by incumbents and dissidents alike. After testing the waters of Morenismo, however, he chose to stay with the Molinistas. Along with Temax's other prominent functionaries, Colonel Antonio Herrera, the *jefe político* (district prefect), and Nazario Aguilar Brito, the municipal tax collector, Crespo joined the local chapter of the Unión Democrática, the political club working for the election of Molina's puppet, Muñoz Arístegui.

It was not long before oligarchical repression foreclosed the electoral road to Maderismo nationwide and to the moderate political reformers in Yucatán who had affiliated with it. When Morenista and Pinista candidates and their supporters were harassed and jailed, these parties entered into a nominal alliance, plotted secretly, and ultimately rebelled against the established order. In June 1910, 1,500 insurgents—mostly peons led by a local property owner, an accountant, and a hacienda foreman—rose prematurely in the eastern city of Valladolid. Fueled chiefly by hatred of the abusive Molinista prefect, who was summarily shot, this rebellion held Valladolid captive for six days but, lacking effective leadership and focus, did not spread to other localities. While campesinos indulged themselves in celebration and *aguardiente* (the cane liquor of the masses), federal and state troops stormed the city. Justice was served in characteristically draconian fashion: public executions of the leaders, stiff jail sentences and penal servitude in the jungles of nearby Quintana Roo for the lesser lights. The oligarchical order stood firm.

Still, Pedro Crespo stood with the establishment. What, then, turned this cautious policeman into a revolutionary? Quite likely he was unable to ignore ties of blood and a claim for vengeance. Like Pancho Villa, whose sister was raped, and countless others who joined Madero's national movement in 1910, a sense of deep personal outrage set Crespo at odds with the Porfirian authorities. Sketchy press accounts and judicial proceedings, which here and there are corroborated by local tradition, shed light on the question of Crespo's motivation. Crespo had been left by Temax's corrupt prefect, Colonel Herrera, who also was Crespo's superior officer in the local guard detachment, to languish for thirty days in the notoriously unfriendly confines of Mérida's Juárez Penitentiary. Crespo would later speak vaguely of "differences he had [had] with the Temax authorities," and his lieutenants would cite the tyrannical abuses of Herrera's local rule. Some old-timers recall that Crespo had been openly critical of the *jefe político*'s high-handed tactics in meetings with Temaxeño campesinos. But for Crespo, much more than *mal gobierno* or perhaps even personal rivalry was at issue here: Herrera had killed Crespo's father, Don Cosme Damían, under shadowy circumstances. Apparently, while Pedro was in jail, Don Cosme had balked at Herrera's arbitrary order that he do *fagina* (unpaid, forced road work), whereupon the *jefe político* had ordered his goons to gun down the old man in broad daylight.

Soon after his release from prison, Crespo sought revenge. He mustered up a small band of his kin and clients—most of them peasant villagers—and exploded into revolt. Operating in the chaotic political climate that was Maderismo in

Yucatán, Crespo elected to burn his bridges behind him, joining his local vendetta to the larger regional movement against Díaz and the Molinistas. On March 4, 1911, he led his column in a lightning predawn raid on the county seat of Temax. The rebels easily overwhelmed the nine-man guard detachment of Temax's central plaza. (Later, the town police commander would charge that the *guardia* had been sleeping on the job.) Crespo immediately rousted Colonel Herrera and the treasury agent Aguilar Brito from their beds and hauled them, clad only in their skivvies (*paños menores*), to the plaza. All the while, as members of his band shouted "Viva Madero!" and "Down with bad government!" Crespo vented his rage on the stunned Herrera: "You bastard, you killed my father! Before you were on top and screwed me, but now it's my turn!"[2]

The tables were indeed turned. Handpicked as district prefect by the great Molinista planters, Colonel Herrera was the dominant figure in Temax's political life, and his physical presence made him even more menacing to local campesinos. Hulking in stature, with his shaved head and long gray beard, Herrera often took on the dimensions of a mad monk or an avenging prophet. Only days before, during the Carnival revels of Shrove Tuesday, although too cowed to make a statement about their *jefe político*, Temaxeños had mocked his subordinate, Aguilar Brito, as "Juan Carnaval," shooting an effigy of the treasury agent in front of the Municipal Palace. Now, in the same central plaza in the wee hours of the morning, Pedro Crespo was cutting the despised prefect down to size. In a final act of humiliation, Crespo strapped Herrera and Aguilar to chairs and riddled them with bullets in the same spot in front of the town hall where Aguilar had been "executed" during Carnival. The bodies were piled into a meat wagon and then dumped at the gates of the town cemetery. (It was ghastly ironic that the treasury agent would later be interred in the same coffin that "Juan Carnaval" had occupied the preceding Shrove Tuesday.)

Before he left town the next morning, Crespo emptied the municipal jail, freeing some campesinos who had been imprisoned for refusing to do *fagina* ordered by the deceased *jefe político*. Crespo armed his new recruits and then, in the manner of the Valladolid rebels, requested food, drink, and "contributions" from local merchants, and took the 300 pesos (one peso equaled fifty U.S. cents) in the municipal treasury. Yet Crespo had learned some valuable lessons from the Valladolid debacle: He made sure that Temax's prominent families were not physically harmed, and he strictly limited his men's intake of *aguardiente*. There would be no premature celebrations in Temax. Crespo saddled up his force—now swollen to about eighty—and divided the men into two mobile bands, one to head west toward Cansahcab, the other east, under his direction, toward Buctzotz. All wore red bands on their hats.

In the weeks and months that followed, Pedro Crespo became Yucatán's most successful insurgent. His hit-and-run tactics, based on an intimate knowledge of the local terrain, were celebrated in the pueblos and hacienda communities of north-central Yucatán, and his ranks continued to multiply. One week after his raid on Temax, his troops mushroomed to 200; by mid-April some estimates placed his strength at 400, in May, close to 1,000. Many free villagers and some hacienda peons joined his campaign willingly, eager to strike a blow against the *dzules*, particularly the despised *jefe políticos* and hacienda overseers who symbolized the encroachments and abuses of the oligarchy. In Buctzotz, a group of villagers rose up upon Crespo's arrival, took the National Guard barracks, and cut out the tongue of the municipal president before executing him. In Dzilám González, dozens of campesinos, including the town's band, defected en masse to the rebellion. The musicians brought their instruments and enlivened the guerrilla campaign in the weeks ahead with a series of impromptu Saturday night *jaranas* (folk dances) in remote backcountry hamlets.

Although many hacienda peons were recruited at gunpoint by the rebels, Crespo sought to erode planter paternalism and social control with clientelist measures of his own. At the Cauacá, Chacmay, and San Francisco Manzanilla haciendas—the estates of the largest henequen planters—he decreed "liberation," canceling all of the peons' debts. Moreover, Crespo provided amply for his recruits, derailing trains, raiding *cuarteles* (barracks) for munitions, and levying forced loans on local planters and merchants. At Cauacá, 150 peons joined Crespo, and suddenly Maya surnames were greatly outnumbering Spanish ones in his ranks. Many planters, hoping to avoid the total loss of their work force, immediately ordered the temporary evacuation of their *sirvientes* to nearby county seats, where they would wait out the rebellion.

Crespo's guerrilla campaign forced the Molinista regime to expend great amounts of time, money, and manpower in a futile effort to pin down the rebels. Soon other risings against government installations and officials—like Crespo's, nominally Maderista—spread throughout the countryside. During the spring of 1911 the Mérida government found itself unable to do more than hold the county seats, leaving the hinterland to the insurgents. Moreover, village-based campesinos increasingly resisted government attempts to recruit them to fight against the rebels, or mutinied following recruitment. Finally, Muñoz Arístegui was compelled to resign, and the new military governor issued an amnesty for all disaffected rebels designed to coax rebel leaders like Crespo to lay down their arms, a desperate move that did little to quell rural unrest throughout the state.

All the while, Crespo moved at will throughout the Temax district and penetrated into neighboring Izamal, Espita, and districts farther east. Early on, he reached an understanding with Juan Campos, a popular insurgent who also had risen against local abuses and later conveniently labeled himself a "Maderista." Campos already was carving out a power base (*cacicazgo*) north of Temax, in the area around Dzidzantún and Dzilám González. In the months and years ahead, Crespo and Campos would wage a number of joint operations and together come to control all of north-central Yucatán for over two decades. *Ancianos* still recall the two chiefs as local instruments through which the revolution put an end to "la época de esclavitud" (the age of slavery). Campos was even more audacious than Crespo in his dealings with the planter class. Local lore has it that he would arrive at an estate, hear the grievances of the peons, and then mete out the appropriate number of lashes to the hacendado or his administrators prior to distributing merchandise from the hacienda's store (*tienda de raya*).

By late May 1911, Díaz had fallen, and Pedro Crespo had disbanded his forces. But, far from being finished, his career was just beginning. For the next thirty years, Crespo arbitrated the political fortunes of Temax, brokering power between elites, villagers, and peons during the most volatile juncture of the revolutionary period.

In the political vacuum that resulted in Yucatán from Díaz's defeat, Morenistas and Pinistas vied for leadership, and rural violence reached dangerous new levels. But, under Crespo's sway, Temax remained relatively calm. The cacique had only contempt for noncombatant civilian politicians like Pino Suárez—soon to become Yucatán's Maderista governor and then vice president of Mexico—who during the insurrection had called upon Yucatecos to join Madero but to avoid acts of vengeance such as those committed at Temax. Unfortunately, once in power, Madero and Pino seemed intent upon employing the same nefarious "bola negra" tactics of political imposition that they had deplored during the Porfiriato. Crespo's sympathies lay with the more popular Morenistas, who now intrigued throughout the state with their former Molinista foes against the ruling Pinistas. At no point, however, during the short-lived Madero regime (1911–13) did the Pinistas feel strong enough to move against Crespo in Temax. Following Díaz's ouster, Crespo had sent his lieutenants to Mérida to serve Pino notice that, although they had been disbanded, his followers remained armed and could be activated at his command on short notice.

Like Maderista liberals, the neo-Porfirian Huertista military leaders who would supplant them (1913–14) saw the wisdom of accommodating the Crespo *cacicazgo*. Nor did the pattern change significantly when the Mexican Revolution in Yucatán moved dramatically left under the socially active administrations of Constitutionalist General Salvador Alvarado (1915–18) and the Marxist Felipe Carrillo Puerto (1921–24). These progressive caudillos also found it wiser to court rather than wrangle with the powerful Crespo as they sought to mobilize campesinos behind their agrarian, labor, and educational reforms between 1915 and 1924. For his part, Crespo was a political pragmatist; he could live with—even actively support—regimes of widely varying ideological coloration, provided that they favored, or at least did not intrude upon, his *cacicazgo*.

Particularly interesting is the nature of Crespo's collaboration during the twenties and thirties with the Socialist Party of the Southeast (PSS), led by Carrillo Puerto (1915–24) and his successors. Whereas General Alvarado had brought the Constitutionalist revolution to Yucatán in March 1915 with eight thousand troops, the civilian governor, Carrillo Puerto, was not always able to count on the support of a loyal, progressive military and, consequently, had to rely more heavily on the muscle of local power brokers like Crespo. Moreover, in case of hacendado-backed insurrection against the socialist revolution (a very real possibility), the geopolitics of Crespo's *cacicazgo* were critical: Temax was located on the rich eastern fringes of the henequen zone, astride the Mérida-Valladolid Railroad. Its proximity to the *comunero* hinterland made it essential that Temax be secure since, if it fell into hostile hands, Valladolid and the southeastern part of the state—the base of rebel operations during the nineteenth-century Caste War—might once again be cut off from the state capital in Mérida.

To ensure Crespo's loyalty, Carrillo Puerto awarded him the plums of civil government and agrarian office, either to hold himself or to dispose of as he saw fit. Like other powerful caciques, Crespo combined the municipal presidency with leadership of the local resistance league (*liga de resistencia*), the PSS's constituent unit in Temax. Upon Crespo's recommendation, his ally, Juan Campos, was chosen as the district's federal deputy. Several years later, Crespo succeeded Campos in the Chamber of Deputies.

Generally speaking, Governor Carrillo Puerto was careful not to impinge upon the establishment of economic preserves by such local bosses. During the early 1920s the socialist government was inundated with petitions from campesinos protesting against abuses that, in most cases, were explicitly linked to individual caciques. A sampling of the complaints registered includes: irregularities in the implementation of agrarian reform, as bosses obtained personal control of the best *ejido* (communal lands); violation of landlord-tenant agreements; the use of unpaid communal labor; and the embezzlement of resistance league dues. Carrillo Puerto's response invariably was to promise redress, and, in many cases, he made good on his promises. Yet the frequency of such petitions suggests either an inability or, in certain situations, an unwillingness to act.

In Crespo's case, irregularities were alleged in the press and in petitions to the governor; indeed, some of them are still heard in Temax. Powerful hacendados like Pastor Castellanos Acevedo, a former *jefe político*, accused Crespo of forcibly removing peons from the large estates and exploiting them as his personal servants. On the other hand, there are some old-timers who claim that Crespo actively colluded with planters to impede the agrarian reform process. In June 1918, Temaxeños petitioned for land, originally belonging to the old Temax *ejido*, which was under the control of neighboring estates. Ordinarily, Carrillo Puerto's PSS was particularly well disposed to requests for *ejidal* grants from the villages of influential chiefs like Crespo. Critics charge, however, that because of Crespo's alliance with the planters, restitution of the traditional lands was delayed until June 1925, after Carrillo Puerto's fall from power. Even then, the size of the grant was thousands of hectares (1 hectare equals 2.47 acres) less than the area to which the Temaxeños were entitled.

Such allegations are difficult to verify; moreover, there is no shortage of partisan advocates on either side of the question. Certainly Crespo's personal land holdings increased during the twenties and thirties, but not excessively, according to most accounts. We know that, in addition to his membership in the Temax *ejido*, he was granted a medium-size plot (*un terrenito*) and one dozen head of livestock by Carrillo's government. In his last years, Don Pedro would donate a piece of this land in Temax for a federal primary school that he named after his father. Despite the charges of economic impropriety, no indictments were lodged, nor was redress ordered by Carrillo's government or by any subsequent PSS administration.

To the day he died, Pedro Crespo lived in much the same manner as his campesino followers: He spoke Maya among friends, wore the collarless white *filipina*, and lived in the *kaxna*, the traditional wattle-and-daub cottage with thatched roof. What interested him most was political power, not wealth. The revolution had offered him a chance and he had seized it. No doubt he viewed himself and came to be regarded in Temax as a *líder nato*—a born local leader, a chief. As such, he did what was necessary to preserve, even extend, his *poderío,* or his local power base. This entailed constant political vigilance and negotiation; deals might be made with powerful planters and bargains struck with the emerging revolutionary state, but it never called upon Crespo to sell out his clientele, to accumulate great wealth and leave Temax for Mérida. Indeed, precisely because he was a *líder nato*, he was incapable of transcending his locality and breaking with the political culture that had produced him.

In return for Carrillo Puerto's preferment and patronage, Crespo performed a variety of services for the PSS. Not only did he selectively bring violence to bear against local opponents of the party to ensure it a political monopoly within the state, but Crespo also doubled as an informal ward boss, guaranteeing, through a variety of incentives, the enrollment of local campesinos in Temax's *liga de resistencia*. Like other loyal party officials, Crespo scheduled weekly cultural events and frequent recreational activities.

Although few in the region appreciate it today, under Carrillo Puerto baseball became a strategic component of the PSS's campaign to mobilize its rural-based revolutionary regime. The sport already was rooted in the regional environment. In addition to its incredible popularity among all classes in Mérida and Progreso, the principal port, campesinos in the larger rural towns had demonstrated a particular fascination with it. Now, the party's goal was to mount a statewide campaign to organize baseball teams "hasta los pueblitos"—in even the most remote interior Maya communities. Such a program would enhance the popularity and morale of the PSS, which might then be parlayed into other programs for social change. It would strike at traditional rural isolation, which impeded the socialist tradition, and would immediately contribute to the party's goal of social integration, even in advance of longer term efforts to improve regional communication and transportation. Carrillo Puerto had no way of knowing it at the time, but his campaign also would have the effect of institutionalizing *béisbol* as the regional pastime, an anomaly in a nation where elsewhere *fútbol* became the people's game.

Pedro Crespo and Juan Campos became energetic promoters of the game in north-central Yucatán. In 1922 these *beisbolistas* petitioned the Liga Central de Resistencia in Mérida for money for gloves, bats, balls, and uniforms, and personally organized ball clubs in Temax, Dzilám González, and surrounding pueblos and hacienda communities. Once this rudimentary infrastructure was in place, Crespo and Campos worked with the presidents of other interior *ligas de resistencia* to schedule country tournaments and leagues and, later, to arrange for tours by the more experienced Mérida and Progreso clubs. To this end, they frequently petitioned Governor Carrillo Puerto for free passes for ballplayers on the state-controlled railroads.

It is not surprising, then, that local nines still bear their names, or that Temax has become synonymous with high-quality baseball, periodically producing bona fide stars for the Mexican League. The backcountry ballgames that these caciques promoted in the twenties and thirties likely echoed with the same patois of Maya and Spanglish that one hears on hacienda and pueblo diamonds today: "¡Conex, conex

jugar béisbol. . . . ten pitcher, tech quecher, tech centerfil!"
("Come on, let's play ball. . . . I'll pitch, you catch, and you
play center field!")

Carrillo Puerto's socialist experiment ended suddenly and
tragically in January 1924, when Yucatán's federal garrison
pronounced in favor of the national de la Huerta rebellion
and toppled the PSS government, which had remained loyal
to President Alvaro Obregón. Carrillo Puerto and many of
his closest supporters in Mérida were hunted down and executed by the insurgent *federales*, who had the financial backing and encouragement of Yucatán's large planters, whom
Carrillo Puerto had threatened with expropriation. When
push came to shove during the de la Huerta revolt, the majority of the irregular bands led by Carrillo Puerto's cacique
allies proved unreliable; in fact, remarkably few of them
mounted even token resistance against the *federales*. The
truth is that few of these local bosses were ideologically
motivated or were organizationally prepared to become dedicated socialist revolutionaries committed to a defense of the
PSS regime.

Pedro Crespo was one cacique who did not desert his
patrón. In Carrillo Puerto's vain attempt to elude the
Delahuertistas in December 1923 and, ultimately, to gain
asylum in Cuba, he stopped in Temax, where he was received
by Don Pedro and his intimates. One eyewitness graphically
recalls the brief, poignant exchange between the two socialist leaders:

Carrillo Puerto: "We're lost."

Crespo: "Where will you go? You can't leave. Wait this
thing out here with us. I held out for months in the bush (*en
la montaña*); I can do it again. We can survive."

Carrillo Puerto: "It's over. I can't compromise you and
your people."[3]

Crespo could not persuade his *patrón,* who continued his
flight eastward across the peninsula, a journey that soon
ended in his capture and execution.

By April 1924 the de la Huerta revolt had been quelled
and the PSS returned to power in Mérida but now with a
social program more in tune with the moderate politics of
national leaders Alvavo Obregón and Plutarco Calles in
Mexico City. The next decade (1924–34) witnessed a decline

in the membership and organization of the resistance leagues, a reconsolidation of the power of the peninsular bourgeoisie, the infiltration of the PSS by that group, and a sharp falloff in the agrarian reform, especially in the henequen zone. As the Yucatecan revolution reached its Thermidor, Crespo, now in the autumn of his years, adjusted with the times. In 1930 he was still president of the local resistance league, but now, more than ever, "Yucatecan socialism" was a matter of form, not substance. Led by their patriarch, Temaxeño socialists wore red shirts, spouted revolutionary slogans, and invoked their martyred Don Felipe Carrillo on appropriate public occasions. Yet few serious agrarian or labor demands emanated from Temax's *liga de resistencia*.

Apart from the revolution's ideological drift to the right, the economics of the period left Don Pedro and the socialists little room to maneuver. The henequen boom had crashed on the rocks of world depression and foreign competition. Temaxeños, like other Yucatecan campesinos, were experiencing severe privation and were glad for even the reduced workload that the henequen estates provided. Like most of the PSS rural chiefs, Crespo was forced to seek an accommodation with the most powerful planters during the Great Depression in order to keep fields in production and minimize layoffs. Indeed, it was his ability to balance and play off the hopes and fears of both *dzules* and campesinos amid the roller-coasterlike political economy of the twenties and thirties that preserved his *cacicazgo* until his death in November 1944.

Even the renewed populist groundswell of Cardenismo, which unleashed a fury of riots and political assassinations throughout the state during the late thirties, could not topple Crespo. Newly formed radical mass organizations like the "Juventudes Socialistas" denounced Crespo and the larger evil of "revolutionary caciquismo," but Don Pedro's alliances within the party and provincial society allowed him to hang on. In fact, it was Melchor Zozaya Raz, perhaps the most vocal of the young firebrands in the Juventudes Socialistas during the late 1930s, who would become Don Pedro's protégé in the early 1940s and ultimately inherit the Temax *cacicazgo* upon Crespo's death.

Now properly reverential of Pedro Crespo's "revolutionary legacy," Don Melchor Zozaya ruled the district into the 1970s, until diabetes and blindness weakened his political grip. Although no powerful individual boss has emerged since, *caciquismo* as an informal institution of power and patronage has endured in Temax. Municipal government, *ejidal* office, and access to work on private sector estates are in large part controlled by a *camarilla*, which corporately functions as a cacique. A favored few are endlessly recycled through the same offices, thereby assuring the Party of the Institutionalized Revolution (PRI) a large majority at all levels of government. And, while the PRI periodically excoriates bossism in the abstract, the national regime seems reluctant to tamper with the political culture of the institutionalized revolution—in Temax or anywhere else. This is because the Mexican state rests upon a multitiered system of patronage and clientele that always finds new aggressive, upwardly mobile elements to sustain it.

In the Temax of the 1980s, Pedro Crespo also has been institutionalized; Yucatán's branch of the PRI has duly incorporated him into the revolutionary pantheon alongside more famous regional icons like Salvador Alvarado and Felipe Carrillo Puerto. Temaxeño popular tradition, however, has reached a more ambiguous verdict regarding Crespo's *actuación revolucionaria*. "Era cacique . . . gran cacique," old timers pronounce, often with raised eyebrows or a wry smile. ("He was a boss . . . a very great boss.") This rather terse depiction reflects admiration for Crespo's courage, resoluteness, and shrewdness but also registers a sardonic appreciation of his surmounting ambition to control and dispense power.

NOTES

1. In Yucatán the term *mestizo* differs from the standard usage. It indicates a person or attribute—that is, style of dress—which is at root Maya but has been influenced over time by Hispanic culture.

2. Archivo General del Estado de Yucatán, Ramo de Justicia, "Cause seguida contra Pedro Crespo y socios por homicidio, rebelión y robo," 1911. Interview with Don Melchor Zozaya Raz, December 31, 1986.

3. Interview with Don Melchor Zozaya Raz, December 31, 1986.

10

Miguel Rostaing: Dodging Blows on and off the Soccer Field

Steve Stein

Miguel Rostaing, much like his compatriot Juan Esquivel (whose biography is also in this volume), sought new opportunities in the Peru of the early twentieth century. While Esquivel went into commercial agriculture, Rostaing turned to the building trades in Lima, the capital city. Here, at the turn of the century, the clash of ethnicity, caste, class, and gender intensified with the burgeoning urban population. Social divisions and boundaries became more visible and grating. Daily life was subject to commercialization as not only food, housing, and health care required cash payments but also the leisure-time pleasures of music, recreation, and sports. Nevertheless, faced with increased tensions caused by congestion and higher cash costs than in the countryside, the urban life for Rostaing offered opportunities for him to find both enjoyment and satisfaction, especially through the release of playing soccer.

Modern organized sports provide—as Rostaing's vignette directly illustrates—the occasion for the blending of individual artistry through physical performance with the cooperation required in team competition. Despite his working long hours each day, Rostaing found the time to play soccer for the newly developing teams. He enjoyed the game, and it gave him the opportunity, when his opponents were white teams, "to settle the score" with at least some members of the elites who dominated his life off the playing field. This biography demonstrates how Rostaing developed skills that served him in both his sport and his life.

Rostaing's biography comes out of extensive oral interviews conducted by Steve Stein during his research on working-class culture in Peru from 1900 to 1930. Stein's interest in this topic developed during graduate study at Stanford University and, in 1980, resulted in his book, *Populism in Peru: The Emergence of the Masses and the Politics of Social Control*. This work was followed in 1985 by a three-volume study *Lima obrera, 1900–1930*, in which Stein examines popular culture, working-class politics, and urban social structure.

Stein is a professor of history at the University of Miami and director of the university's North-South Academic Exchange Program and Programs in Great Britain.

INTRODUCTION

Miguel Rostaing (1900–83) was one of Peru's premier soccer players in the early decades of this century. Playing before the sport was professionalized, Rostaing worked full-time (sometimes twelve to fifteen hours a day) as a bricklayer at the same time as he was a member, for nearly fifteen years, of the first string of Alianza Lima, the most successful and popular of all urban soccer clubs. His life on and off the field was representative of the daily hardships and the occasional joys experienced by Lima's lower classes. Through Rostaing's account, we can begin to understand some of the subjective as well as objective components of the daily experience of the Lima poor. On one level, we are witness to certain common occurrences in the popular-sector family in the period from 1900 to 1930, to the formation of the city's earliest soccer teams, and to the virtual racial warfare between "black" teams such as Alianza Lima and their more white, higher-class adversaries. On another level, we learn how a man like Rostaing felt about his life—about being abandoned at an early age by his father, about the cheers of the crowd that greeted him after an especially good play, and about being black in a society that relegated people of African origin to the lowest rung on the social ladder. And it is in this realm of feeling, in this innermost precinct of human existence, that life histories like that of Miguel Rostaing are most revealing.

I was born in Lima in 1900. All my life I took good care of myself because of soccer. That's why I played for many years, from the year 1914 to 1936.

We really fooled around when we were kids. We had to be home at a certain hour. If we were late, we got it. My mother waited for us with a whip and a belt in her hand, those pointed whips that the milkmen used. That's what she hit us with, and we would run underneath the bed. She stuck us with a broom handle to get us out, and at times we wouldn't let her since we were strong. "Let go! Because I'll get you, get you out if I have to kick you!"

Once we went to the circus. We didn't go to school. And a man who knew us told my mother: "I tell you I've seen Miguel and Juan in the circus." We really got it then. My mother beat us on the naked rear end, and we really got it. If she got distracted, we escaped, because we had a door and windows that faced the street. So we escaped, and we didn't come back until after she went to work.

My mother never liked it when we answered her back, or even looked at her. *Uf!* She gave it to us with whatever she had around, even with big metal and wooden spoons. My mother wouldn't let us look at her when she was bawling us out. At midnight and at two or three in the morning, she hit us on the naked rear end because they had told her about something we had done. She got us then because we couldn't escape, because if she fell asleep we escaped and we didn't come back until after she left for work. Since we knew she had to go, when she came back she had already forgotten, then she didn't hit us.

I say that my mother was really tough, she punished us. If not, we would have come out, well, bad. Because in our neighborhood of La Victoria,[1] a lot of boys came out bad. They became thieves. There were a lot of chicken coops in the *corralones*, all that, because chickens weren't raised in Lima because it wasn't allowed, and when La Victoria grew up, almost everybody in the *corralones* and *callejones*[2] raised their chickens. There is where some got robbed. And there were some guys who didn't just steal chickens. They also robbed clothes from inside of houses. They were robbers but not big ones. And they were our friends out in the streets, and that's what my mother didn't want.

We weren't into stealing chickens. We weren't into anything bad, because my mother wouldn't let us. We tried to obey her because it was good. Because if we hadn't paid attention to her, we would have gone bad. Sometimes we stole a few pieces of fruit or some vegetables, just fooling around. That was different.

My mother had been abandoned. My father left us. He left me when I was two years old and my brother was in my mother's womb. I finally met him when I was twelve years old. He came to see us. He wanted to make up with my mother. She wouldn't go along, and us kids, me, for example, we didn't have any respect for him any more. We didn't act badly towards him, but there was no affection, especially because we never got an education. My father was one of the top typesetters of *El Comercio*.[3] He was really sought after. So he could have given us a good education. He left us without an education. When I got to know him, I told him what I thought. Talking, talking, I told him: "For me, you are not my father anymore."

I only went to school for one year because of my mother's situation. Mother had to be helped. My mother was left, you could say, almost a widow, when we were very young. I had to leave school to go to work. I liked mathematics because it helped you with your jobs. I just didn't have enough school. I couldn't continue because we were in need of a lot of things. Especially clothing was a problem. My mother had to buy it, and she didn't have enough.

My mother worked in the most tiring of jobs. She was a cook and a washerwoman. She worked in various places as a cook, and at home she washed for certain people who knew her. We never went hungry, but we had a hard life because we didn't have a father. She worked for a priest who was a really good man. He gave us all his leftovers. I have never met any priest like him. He had us come in: "Take the meat, let's not have any food left over here." And that's why my buddies used to hang around my house, because there was lots of food.

My mother would do the washing early in the morning. She got up at five and washed from five to nine. Then she went to work and came back at nine or ten at night. That's when we would go to the priest's for the leftovers. She had a terrible life. She just worked and worked and never had a rest. She worked all the time. On Sundays she worked until one in the afternoon.

When my mother was working she left us alone. My older brother heated up our food. Once my face was burned. I was two years old, and when my brother was heating up dinner he burned my face. I was sitting at the table, and my brother poured too much fuel in the stove, and he lit a match to see if it would start, and the cooking fuel fell on me. And since in those times they used to dress you up with girls' clothing, I got all burned. I don't know how my mother revived me because I really got burned, even my hands. Since then I've always had this burn on my face, and that's where I got the nickname *"El Quemado"* [the burned one]. And that was my nickname for soccer.

My mother's situation probably forced me to start working. I started to work at the age of nine in construction, as a peon for a man who was a specialist in floor tile. The man's name was Espinosa. I started making five reales in 1909. The situation was bad, and I wanted to help my mom. Because a pair of shoes cost three-and-a-half soles. I realized that we had food, but we needed money to buy clothing. Sometimes there wasn't enough and besides we played a lot of soccer and we ruined a lot of shoes. Sometimes we had to wear broken shoes, and there you could see that we didn't have enough. My mother considered what I made a help. I gave everything I made to my mother, and she gave me fifty centavos on Sundays as allowance.

To get a job, you went to where there was construction, and you asked if they needed a peon. But my mother knew a Sr. Espinosa, a specialist in floors, so for helping him mix the cement and lay the tiles he paid me five reales. In construction there were kids working but not many, because at that age you aren't so strong. That's why I got an easy job with the tiles where you didn't have to carry that much, and a little mixing too. To carry bricks you have to be bigger, stronger. Sr. Espinosa treated me like family. He gave me five reales like a tip.

You started off as a peon, and then you moved up to bricklayer, master bricklayer. When you're a master bricklayer then you know just about everything. I must have worked six years as a peon, yes, six or seven years. After Sr. Espinosa I carried bricks to the bricklayer. It was hard work because the bricklayers laid the brick fast; I had to keep him supplied. At the beginning, I didn't carry much. You went on helping the bricklayer with two, three bricks. Guys who were strong carried three. And the bricklayers hurried you up. Most of the walls were made of adobes, not of bricks, and you had to carry the mud mixture or the adobe bricks in a tray on your head and dump it out for the bricklayer. The adobes are heavy. You had to hurry up to supply enough to the bricklayer, but the tray couldn't be very big. Us kids had small trays, but you had to hurry up in order to keep the bricklayer happy. He would call you: "Come on, you, bring me the mud!" You had to hurry up. Afterwards, when brickmakers used bricks, it was something else. And it wasn't so dirty either, because the mud was what made it so dirty. Not a day passed when you didn't get your shoes dirty with the mud. The first years were the hardest. I became a brick-layer when I was around sixteen years old. You learned pretty fast. And I said to myself: "How am I going to continue making so little? I have to go about finding out how to earn more."

When I worked as a bricklayer, most of the time I did piecework. The fastest workers made the most. You had to hurry up to lay the most meters. You always had to hurry up to lay more, because there were a lot of engineers who made you work for a daily wage, and then they paid you less. But there were engineers who paid more when they were in a hurry; they paid by the meter when they were in a hurry. The day laborer worked for a daily wage, that's all. When you're young, you don't feel so tired working fast. It's at the end that you feel tired.

I was a bricklayer for forty some years, and that's why I suffer from bronchitis. You were always very cold as a brick-layer. In bricklaying you felt a lot of dampness, because in the old days to work as a bricklayer you had to dig wells in the streets because you didn't have so much water available as you do now. You needed the water to mix the plaster, the mud. You had to dig wells five or six meters down to store the water. So all this water affected the bricklayer, because almost all bricklayers die from their lungs, from asthma, from things you got from having colds. It was a dangerous, a tough job.

All this time I was playing soccer. Hour after hour we played. Some left, and others continued playing until it got dark. When I was nine, I played with a rag ball. When one of my mother's stockings got torn, we would rob it from her to make a ball. We filled it up with rags. The rag ball was common everywhere, because leather balls were pretty expensive. So we made rag balls, we made them good, they even bounced. Now everybody has rubber shoes. Before, the only thing we had were rope-soled shoes, much cheaper, they cost three soles. We used to play in open fields, that's all. We made goals with little sticks dug into the mud or sometimes just with stones. My mother used to watch me sometimes when she was going around where we played. She used to say that they were going to kick me. She said: "Be careful when you're going to play soccer. When I go by where you are playing, it seems to me that they're going to kill you, they're going to give you some bad blows."

My first team was called Huáscar. We formed it in the neighborhood in 1914 among friends. We were players and

founders of Huáscar. Most of us used to train after work.
Between five and seven at night we would run and do calis-
thenics. Some who couldn't go in the afternoon trained in
the morning. Those who could went in the afternoon, and
others trained at night. On Huáscar every team member paid
monthly dues, I think fifty centavos, to maintain the club.
We rented a room for the team to get together. If we hadn't
charged dues, how were we going to pay for our room? Sometimes we had to buy shoes too. There were times that some
players didn't have enough for the shoes, and we had to help
them out. Guys that had enough bought their own shoes. We
had a president whose name was Don Andrés Broche. He
had an Italian name. He was the one who paid the most.
Don't you see, he made chocolates. If there was a player who
couldn't pay, he took care of everything. He was a great guy.
We even helped him wrap the little chocolates, the candies.
They used to wrap them in papers, almost the same as they
do now, but now they make them nicer. But before they
wrapped them in papers and twisted them at each end. Sometimes we also helped him deliver the chocolates. He didn't
pay us, but sometimes he gave us candies. He made a lot of
them to sell. It was like a little factory.

When I played, I played every position. I was like a
one-man orchestra, to be exact. I played right forward, left
forward, left wing, right wing, right half, left half, and once
I even played center half. And I also played defense. They
always changed me around to different positions. I played
them all the same. After all, the ball is round everywhere on
the field.

I started playing on Alianza in 1918.[4] A lot of us came in
that year, and we formed a new Alianza, made up of young
guys, because the guys that had originally founded the team
were going downhill by that time. Alianza had some spon-
sors, and they talked to you, if you wanted to join the team
or not. But since Alianza was a celebrated team, it had its
fans. Any player for them became popular.

When I joined, we had old people on the team, and we
had to renew ourselves. We looked first for José María
Lavalle. I knew José María for a time from the neighborhood. And we saw him play, we went about pulling him on to
the team, and the modern Alianza began to be formed. He
was a guy who played in the street; he made adobe bricks.
So we saw him play and saw that he was good. So we got
him for Alianza. We pulled a couple of players from other

teams—Montellanos from Gálvez, Filomeno García from Peruano, "*el loco*" Quintana from Progreso. Alejandro Villanueva played with a team called Teniente Ruíz, and Dr. Soria too. But they preferred Alianza because it was a famous team, and it was better than any other team. And we convinced them with friendship, through friendship, that's all. We knew every one of them, the guys who you met on the street. So we went out and convinced them with "Come over here, you," until they came, and that's how the modern Alianza was formed.

They called us the *intimos* [intimates], and they also called us the *compadres*. Those names came out sometime after the 1921 Centennial of Peru: '21, '22, '23, '24. They called us that because of the friendship all of us had with each other. We always celebrated our birthdays together at home. We felt like we were related. Somebody's birthday came, everybody went. Another *compadre*'s birthday came, and there we were. It was something else. We were intimate friends. We were always together. None of the other teams were like that, just Alianza. In Atlético Chalaco,[5] our friendship was only at the club, not in the home. On Alianza, on the other hand, no.

Alianza became conceited because of their fame. José María was right wing, and he had a really terrible urge, a really bad habit. When he found a halfback who wasn't too good, who you could easily dribble around, he would have a banquet with him. He laughed at him, and he danced the *marinera* around him. He ran, he stopped, he gave him the ball and took it back. He would spin him around the field. When this happened he wouldn't let go of the ball for anything. Those things hurt the team. He didn't center the ball, and the team couldn't make goals. And he just laughed. Valdivieso [the goalie] had to swear at him to make him pass the ball. He would scream at him from the other end of the field to stop screwing around with the poor halfback: "All right, come on, *negro*, get rid of the ball!" José María just laughed. You had to talk tough to him, threaten him. We had to make him center it. You couldn't score a single goal because he was having a banquet with the halfback. That *negro* was a real sly one. He looked like a mullet, that *negro* José María. *Uf!*

Alianza always had players who drank a lot. Most of them were drinkers. I drank, but very little. At times they played drunk and they lost. When we made our first trip to Chile in

1933, the players came in drunk on Saturday night and played the next day. That's why we lost almost all of the games. My *compadre* Domingo García played drunk. If you took away his liquor in the middle of the week, he couldn't play. Although it might seem a lie, he needed liquor to play. Once we were going to play, I think it was going to be against Universitario: "Let's shut *compadre* Domingo in. Don't let him out to drink." And he almost collapsed while playing. I tell you, he didn't do anything that day. So what were we going to do with him? Starting Friday, we made him his fish soup, and he stayed shut in from Friday before the game. But since we took away his liquor in the middle of the week, he couldn't do anything in the game. He was the best of the Garcías; he would go forward even though he was a half-back. He's still alive. But he still has his drinks. Even now we get together to drink.

We would drink cognac during the games but in a very small quantity. This was only on Alianza. We made a preparation of tea, lemon, and cognac, and we didn't feel tired. It was mostly lemon, a kind of strong tea. Sometimes we took three bottles of that to the games. One little glass of that and you didn't feel tired. We would drink it after the first period, just before going out for the second. You didn't get drunk with it. You didn't feel dizzy either, nothing like that. You could say that we revived with that drink. Now, Segalá [the goalie] was very nervous. So we always gave him a few drops of Valeriana[6] in his tea because we knew all too well about his nervousness. You would see him even change color when he was starting the game. He came onto the field all yellowish until he made his first save. And then he became sure of himself. In the second period, three more drops of Valeriana in his tea.

Alianza was always a team of the people, to a certain point, of the blacks. That was the idea of Alianza. Alianza's players were working people. The majority worked in construction, and one or another of us had [a] different kind of job. Sometimes they said to us: "There come the bricklayers," and sometimes, "There come the blacks."

Our fans were from different neighborhoods. Of course, the largest quantity from La Victoria, from Abajo el Puente, from Malambo,[7] from all those places. I used to think: "I'm a player; I'm not making any money at this." I guess I played, at least in part, because the people applauded me. Ah, the fans loved you! The fans would start to buzz, and as you were playing you would start faking out your opponent, dribbling around him. They would call you, for example, "*Quemado* Rostaing!" "Villanueva!" "Lavalle!" They would call to us, and we would dribble by the other guy. *Uf!* We would pass to somebody else. Sometimes he would let the ball go to another teammate. The game opened up there. It was, in fact, the fans who made us do that.

It was there that the olés came. For example, there were a lot of olés when you made a good play; in those times there was a lot of that with the goals. That's where the olé of Alianza came from. Because when Alianza scored one, two goals, then they started screaming: "*Titán, titán,* olé, olé!" That came from Alianza. There was a kind of friendship. For example, you were leaving the stadium and you would always go and have a glass of beer with two or three friends. And since most of Alianza were big drinkers, they liked being treated by the fans. They would stay until they were pretty drunk. The fans paid for the beers.

After every game, that's when the celebrations began, the applause, the cries. The wives and *compadres* and *comadres* went too. We had a rooting section of women. And, later on, Alianza came to have a women's club to put on the fiestas of the team. But most of them were dark. But the fiestas were nice, well set up. All of those ladies were maids, and they even knew about the fiestas of the rich. And when Alianza had a fiesta, it was like a rich people's fiesta. It was just the same.

There was a special section of the stadium where our fans sat. Sometimes our fans got into fights. If there was an argument, you fought, the women too, everybody. A lot of women went, and even they fought with other women there. But the toughest fans were from Callao, from Atlético Chalaco. They were fishermen. They were fierce, the people from Callao, a lot of bad people, those fishermen. They came with dynamite, and the Lima fans couldn't stand up to them. What did you defend yourself with? You had to get out of there on the run.

They almost blew up a back that we had. He was going to throw in the ball, and they threw a stick of dynamite at him, and they almost blew him up, ball and all. We were playing in those times [1922] for a gold medal. They beat us when some fans cut Segalá in the behind [*el potingo*]. They were in back of the net, the fans on that side. Somebody stuck a knife through the net and cut him. Segalá turned around, and the ball went in the net. They had to take Segalá out and give him five stitches. Chalaco was ferocious. Against Chalaco it was terrible. Their fans were scary. *Uf!* You had to run out of there with your pants in your hands because those fishermen threw dynamite.

There was this rivalry, in terms of sports, with the Universitario de Deportes team. Any team could beat us, and it wasn't so bad, but not Universitario. Universitario was made up of students, and you could be sure that there wasn't anyone on that team who wasn't a student. They were all students. Such is the case that all of them have university degrees now. That was the difference. To be on Universitario you had to be from the university, only little white boys. And Alianza's players, blacks, poor, bricklayers, all of us. Maybe stronger, better players.

Alianza was popular, the team of the workers. Those who supported Universitario were university students. Alianza represented the poor people, and Universitario the rich people. That's why they called them black and white. You could say that this rivalry came from the whites. There was this rivalry between blacks and whites, and, well, Universitario was the team that most upset us. There was this rivalry, no, according to my mother, since the blacks got their freedom from Castilla,[8] that the blacks and the whites didn't rub shoulders. Yes, instead, they stuck to their own race, above all the whites.

The blacks don't want to be blacks. The black doesn't want to be a black. The black, for a woman he looks for a lighter one. Because they themselves have been brought up in this rivalry of the black and the white. The black wants to improve the race. Naturally, that's why he looks for a lighter woman. If not, how do you explain José María? His wife is a light *zambita*.[9] The majority of the blacks look for whites. Those who look for a black woman are rare unless you go to Cañete, which is filled with blacks. There you see black men with black women, very few whites. In Lima, we've always looked to cross our race. Well, I think that the black doesn't want to be black up to this day—this from the moment that the blacks themselves imply that the black is detestable, from the moment that they want to cross their race. But it's very rare to find somebody who wants to cross with a black. What blacks have looked for, yes, is to improve their race. I have seen blacks here who look for light women. And, of course, if they get a white woman, they take up with her. It depends on the woman, no?

In soccer I always took pride in being a *pícaro* [sly] player. They call a *pícaro* a sharp person. To be sharp as a player means not letting yourself get kicked by anyone. You could say that you were sharp if you were quick and didn't let yourself be kicked much. Jumping here, jumping there, and sometimes give back a little so that the other player is afraid of you, too. You jumped when a player came after you to cut you down. You had to jump, and then you kicked him, too, with your foot. When you are a *pícaro,* when you fall and are on the ground, you give it to the other player with your foot so that he doesn't jump on you. Once, I got kicked in the ankle by a guy, and he left me limping for two months. Don't you see I was with my head up, looking at the ball, and crack! I even swore at him. "I'm going to get you!" But he wouldn't let himself be caught, and I couldn't do much because I was like a limping rooster. It was then that I learned to give this special blow in a moment that nobody saw you.

You're born a *pícaro,* born that way. I didn't learn it from anybody. It's something I have. I was always that way since I was very young, since I was fourteen when I played on Huáscar and then when I was eighteen and started on Alianza. To face life you have to be that way. Because life is like a soccer game. You have to be quick so that they don't knock you around like that in your daily life. It's like in work. You have to protect your job because they're always trying to sabotage you, to take your job away from you, and you have to be careful.

You played because you liked soccer. There was no material gain. The gold medal, the diplomas, those are the most pleasant memories. We played two times for the gold medal; one of them Chalaco beat us when they cut Segalá in the behind. But the other time, yes, we won. But when times got bad, we had to pawn the medals and they were lost. And the diplomas, now it's just too expensive to frame them.

NOTES

1. A lower-class neighborhood on the edge of central Lima established in the early twentieth century.

2. Two of the most common forms of lower-class urban housing.

3. Lima's most important daily newspaper at the time.

4. Alianza Lima, Peru's first, and most famous, popular-sector soccer team. It was founded in 1901 in Lima.

5. An early popular-sector soccer team from Lima's port city of Callao for which Rostaing played in 1930.

6. A mild tranquilizer.

7. A working-class neighborhood with a large black population.

8. The Peruvian president who freed the slaves in the 1850s.

9. A racial mixture of black and Indian.

V

Midcentury
Generations, 1920–1959

World War I disrupted Atlantic trade patterns, shattering established European and North American markets, and set the stage for
the Russian Revolution of 1917. These developments created new
strains in Latin America as politicians, churchmen, industrialists, workers, peasants, and university faculty divided—some looking to a Marxist solution to national problems, and others turning to corporatist
parties in the hope of blocking class organizations that might encourage Marxism. The Catholic corporatist groups found models and inspiration in Italian fascism and Spanish corporatism. Moreover, a rising
popular tide of concern about ethnicity (indigenous and African
peoples) in several nations compounded these stresses in politics
and society. The adoption of dance crazes like the Tango, new mass
media such as radio and the movies, and increased public activities
of women brought even more change to the intense politics of the
era.
     The Bolshevik success in Russia created both hope and despair
among Latin Americans. It resulted in a flurry of Marxist revolutionary
activity matched by counterrevolutionary political organization aimed
at preempting the possibility of radical change. Even the Mexican
revolutionaries cast a wary eye on the Soviet model as a threat to
their regime. Both the Great Depression and the Spanish Civil War
added to the fears of universal revolution. Many conservative Latin
Americans turned to conservative Catholic organizations such as
Mexico's Sinarquistas (the name expressing the goal "without anar-
chism"), or to protofascist or at least highly corporate political groups
such as the followers of Getúlio Vargas in Brazil and the *descamisados*
(shirtless ones) of Juan Domingo Perón in Argentina. The stresses
and strains on politics would surface again after World War II but
were redefined in the terms of the Cold War.
     Roman Catholic lay organizations and conservative groups re-
sponded to what they perceived as the Bolshevik political threat that
fed on the prospect of social breakdown. The latter seemed to them

to be epitomized in the audacity of the flappers, called *pelonas* (baldies) in Mexico and elsewhere because of their daringly bobbed hair (Chapter 11). These women and others who became more visible in public were accused of threatening to disrupt family and religious values, codes of social propriety, and standards of feminine virtue (Chapter 13). Many women reacted with a simple, "So what?" Others turned to politics, especially to left-wing campaigns to create unprecedented opportunities for women and social justice for the entire nation (Chapter 12).

The U.S. government responded to both the new economic and political circumstances of this period. The Good Neighbor policy, announced by President Franklin D. Roosevelt, was intended to strengthen political, economic, and social bonds in the hemisphere. Washington dropped its most outrageous demands for the right to intervene in Latin America, abandoning the Platt Amendment to the Cuban constitution, for example, and working to expand trade and security assistance. Latin Americans generally supported the effort to destroy the Nazi Germany of Adolf Hitler. Brazilian soldiers in Italy and sailors in the South Atlantic as well as Mexican pilots in the Philippines served in combat, while others in the region worked on the home front against the Axis powers. Some Latin Americans, especially the Peruvian Japanese, suffered arrest and incarceration in detention camps (in this case, the camps were located in the United States). For the most part, World War II provided an occasion of cooperation and mutual respect throughout the hemisphere. The goodwill and financial benefits largely ended at the conclusion of the war, as the Truman administration turned its attention back to Europe and the Far East.

Postwar military dictators seized governmental power and justified repressive actions against any opposition as anti-Communist campaigns. This rationalization was supported with financial and military aid from Washington and linked the U.S. government to such repulsive dictators as Rafael Trujillo in the Dominican Republic and Marcos Pérez Jiménez in Venezuela. Moreover, the United States remained oblivious to emerging social revolutionary movements despite rumblings in the region. In fact, the Central Intelligence Agency worked to eliminate any regime that threatened social and economic reforms harmful to U.S. corporate or political interests.

The most dramatic example came in the CIA-assisted military revolt in 1954 in Guatemala against the government of Juan José Arévalo (it had undertaken agrarian reforms that threatened transnational corporations, primarily United Fruit Company) and the installation as president of Carlos Castillo Armas, whose regime was propped up by the State Department and United Fruit. The 1958 tour of South America by Vice President Richard Nixon faced constant disruption from demonstrators, who at one point forced him and his party into hiding at the American embassy in Caracas. The U.S. Senate investigation into the vice president's ordeal determined that the cause was not Communist-inspired rioting, but rather individual Latin Americans intent on bringing the need for social change to the attention of Washington. Their efforts failed. World attention finally focused on Latin America in 1959 with Fidel Castro's dramatic and successful takeover in Cuba. Castro ushered in a new era in the hemisphere.

11

Pagu: Patrícia Galvão—Rebel

Susan K. Besse

The impact of industrial capitalism on the lives and values of Brazilian women in São Paulo has fascinated Susan Besse since she began her dissertation at Yale University. She has brought her studies of gender, capitalism, and modernism together in *Restructuring Patriarchy: The Modernization of Gender Inequality in Brazil, 1914–1940* (Chapel Hill, 1996). The following essay is one of the earliest results of her research.

Between the world wars, women seemed abruptly to threaten the social order. In some countries armed with the vote, in others only determined to participate more actively in public life, they became more visible. Some women defied boundaries for propriety of dress (flappers in the United States and England and *pelonas* in Mexico) and of dance, adopting the Tango and the Charleston from Buenos Aires to Moscow. Others moved into politics to challenge governmental and economic elites and, on occasion, Liberal and capitalistic regimes.

In this era of greater liberation of behavior, described as decadence by many,* one of the most intriguing of the Brazilian participants was Patrícia Galvão. Popularly known as Pagu, Galvão flaunted the rules of Brazil's polite society and established herself in the 1920s, while still a teenager, as a flamboyant crusader for women's rights, workers' causes, and libertine culture. Eventually jailed by Brazilian authorities and abandoned by the Communist party, she grew disillusioned and frustrated.

Besse, now a professor of history at the City College of New York, has studied in Switzerland, in Chile (as a United Nations intern), and in Brazil. At Yale University and at City College she has taught courses in Latin American studies.

In Brazil's most modern city, São Paulo, the "modernists" pronounced Patrícia Galvão the "ultimate product" of the late 1920s. She was a rebel who broke all the rules, who

---

*See A. J. P. Taylor, *English History, 1914–1945* (New York: Oxford University Press, 1965); and Anne E. Gorsuch, *Enthusiasts, Bohemians, and Delinquents: Soviet Youth Cultures, 1921–1928* (Bloomington: Indiana University Press, forthcoming).

declared war against the status quo. Startlingly free of inhibitions, she used her mind and body to subvert the social, economic, political, and gender order. Infamous for her scandalous behavior and free thinking, she became the quintessential symbol of all that was new, revolutionary, and dangerous. Patrícia was the child of a period of social and intellectual fragmentation, a period when rapid urbanization and industrialization were eroding the restraints imposed by São Paulo's old agrarian-commercial economy. She seized the opportunity provided by this historical moment of "crisis" to experiment with redefining the categories of acceptable thought and behavior and altering the structures of power. As a woman, she assaulted the boundaries imposed by the patriarchal order, prying open new social arenas and assuming roles that had been previously denied to members of her sex. As an artist, writer, and critic, she struck blows at worn-out conventions, helping to pave the way for daring new forms of creative expression. As a member of the middle class, she sided with the proletariat, advocating social revolution to topple São Paulo's exploitative industrial-capitalist economy. Patrícia (like most rebels who fight battles doomed to lose in the short run) was ultimately shunned by the society she so viciously attacked and is barely mentioned in the historical record. But the story of her intense engagement in the great social, intellectual, and political conflicts of her time is a part of the larger story of the Brazilian and Latin American peoples' prolonged struggle to destroy old hierarchical arrangements and make way for a more just social order.

Born in 1910, Patrícia grew up during a period of tremendous ferment in the city that was the catalyst of Brazil's economic growth. São Paulo's coffee economy produced fabulous wealth, transforming the state's capital from a commercial outpost of 64,934 people in 1890 to a thriving metropolis of 579,033 people in 1920. Within a period of little over a generation, São Paulo was propelled into the modern age. European immigrants who flooded into São Paulo after 1890 swelled the ranks of the urban proletariat working in the mushrooming textile mills, food-processing plants, and small enterprises. Economic boom also fostered the growth of the middle classes, made up of bureaucrats, civil servants, professionals, merchants, small businessmen, and military personnel. Political conflicts exploded between the old rural oligarchy, which was losing its monopoly of power, and the new urban middle and working classes, which were struggling under precarious conditions to achieve social mobility. Politics, which had been the prerogative of a small elite of literate men who negotiated deals behind closed doors, moved into the streets. Successful labor organization by anarchist and anarcho-syndicalist trade unions led to waves of strikes during the 1910s and 1920s, which were met by brutal police repression. The middle classes expressed their restlessness over exclusion from political power in campaigns against political corruption and in the formation of the middle-class Democratic party. Young military officers staged a series of barracks revolts during the 1920s, vaguely calling for honest government and social legislation. To contemporaries, the forces of radical economic change and social upheaval seemed to be tearing the social fabric asunder.

Paulistas reacted to modernization with ambivalence. On the one hand, they were fascinated by "progress," took enormous pride in the newly acquired status and power of their city, and pushed for institutional reforms to meet the new needs of the rising industrial economy and the complex social order it had produced. On the other hand, the rapidity of change undermined old certainties and created profound anxieties about the supposedly "corrupting" influences of "progress."

Among the most conspicuous of changes, and one that was considered extremely dangerous, was the seemingly radical transformation of women. In Patrícia's grandmother's generation, women's roles had been narrowly circumscribed. The majority of women from middle- and upper-class families married as teenagers, raised an average of six children each, and devoted their lives to preparing food, sewing clothing and household linens, and providing health care and education for their families. Not until 1890 did Brazilian law forbid forced marriages, and even after that it was common for parents to play a decisive role in selecting spouses for their daughters. Alternatives to marriage were few and unattractive. In 1893 only 146 Brazilian women and 64 foreign women found jobs as schoolteachers, which provided a meager living. Apart from schoolteaching, little respectable employment was available for middle- and upper-class women, leaving those who remained unmarried in a position of humiliating economic dependence on parents and siblings who typically maintained constant surveillance over these "spinsters'" personal lives.

In a society where concubinage and "free love" were considered little different from prostitution, families zealously guarded the virginity of their unmarried female members. "Respectable" women had little to no opportunity to escape the narrow physical and mental confines of the household. Rarely did they venture into public spaces, and when they did so they were always accompanied. Peddlers and merchants sold their goods from door to door, entertainment was still provided by family members and friends, women's social and charitable organizations were nonexistent, and low literacy rates delayed the rise of the popular press, which only later provided women access to the outside world. Nineteenth-century fashion emphasized the separateness of gender roles. Whereas men cut figures of aggressive public actors with their dark suits, beards, and canes, women projected the image of submissive and sheltered domestic ornaments in their highly elaborate and cumbersome dresses. The public silence of women further testified to overwhelming male dominance.

Patrícia was born into a new age when the old social and sexual proprieties appeared to be no longer binding. São Paulo's booming economy gradually commercialized household production, drawing women into the marketplace as consumers of ready-made clothing and household linens, modern appliances, and processed food products. Shopping became both a daily necessity and a social institution; alluring advertisements, glittering window displays, chic department stores, money-saving sales, and the availability of credit drew in ever larger numbers of female customers.

Technological innovations in communications further encouraged women's entrance into the sphere of the marketplace. Hollywood films arrived in Brazil the year Patrícia was born and quickly captured the popular imagination. Female moviegoers gained as role models the sexy flappers and independent "working girls" portrayed on the screen. At home, radios provided women with daily exposure to new information and ideas. And the spectacular boom in glossy magazines (spurred by the soaring female literacy rates in São Paulo, from 22 percent to 52 percent between 1890 and 1920) also helped promote new values and aspirations for economic independence and social freedom.

Women of Patrícia's generation enjoyed a formerly undreamed-of range of options. Middle-class families, straining to make ends meet in face of inflation and rising pressures of conspicuous consumption, educated daughters to be economically independent in case they failed to marry. Daughters, absorbing bourgeois society's emphasis on independence and taking advantage of new educational opportunities, sometimes prepared themselves for professional careers. Although marriage remained the most secure and the preferred female "career," women delayed marriage, bore many fewer children, and boldly protested their subjugation in marriage. At the same time, more and more middle-class women filled the new respectable white-collar jobs in social services, commerce, finance, and government administration. Even wives who chose not to take paid employment could find an independent source of social identity in one of São Paulo's new female voluntary associations. As middle-class women moved into the male world of work, they also began to move into the male world of politics. A small group of "feminists" organized in the 1920s to fight for legal and educational reforms and won female suffrage in 1932. The "new woman"—independent, active, and sexually provocative— became the symbol of the new age.

The image of the "new woman" figured prominently on the covers of glossy magazines, but critics were terrified by the prospect of a revolution in women's consciousness that could profoundly disrupt traditional gender relations and family organization—leading, in the worst of scenarios, to a "tremendous cataclysm." The flood of cartoons satirizing women who usurped traditionally male roles and the barrage of normative literature instructing women on how to create stable but modern families revealed deep social anxieties. During this period of social disorder, the Brazilian state, the liberal professions, and the Church all struggled to reconcile modernity with traditional values. The result was a confusing mix of contradictory messages. Women were called upon to cultivate an outward appearance of modern sophistication while carefully preserving the qualities of female modesty and simplicity. They were to be enlightened, resourceful, and independent on the one hand and satisfied with the restrictions of the role of housewife on the other hand. In short, women were somehow supposed to be both symbols of modernity and bastions of traditional family life.

In the context of the deep anxiety over threats to the gender order, Patrícia's adolescent rebelliousness attracted enormous attention and comment. As was typical for daughters of middle-class families, she attended normal school; there, girls received a high-school education designed to prepare them to be good wives and competent mothers, and, if necessary, to earn a living through schoolteaching. But Patrícia flaunted her disdain for the traditional canons of proper behavior by adopting the most modern and extravagant fashions. She wore the shortest skirts, daringly low necklines, transparent blouses, false eyelashes, heavy black eye make-up, and bright red lipstick. She let her hair frizz out of control and carried a conspicuous, furry puppy-dog purse. More shocking was her smoking in public, which had traditionally been the prerogative of men only. Even worse, her brazen flirtation with students at the law school and her outspoken, uninhibited responses to their wisecracks were considered to be scandalously aggressive behavior for a woman. Patrícia's wholesale embrace of the fashions and styles of the Jazz Age was an initial outward sign of defiance, which (as those she scandalized probably feared) was to run much deeper later in her life.

In 1927, at seventeen, Patrícia began to cultivate contacts with São Paulo's artistic and intellectual community. Filmmaker Olympio Guilherme became interested in the writings Patrícia submitted for publication in his newspaper column, and they had a short love affair before he left for Hollywood. Her flirtation with the young, flashy Reis, Jr., led to another brief affair. Within the circle of São Paulo's artists, these affairs led not to Patrícia's disrepute and doom but rather provided her an entry into the elite community of the Brazilian avant-garde. In October 1928 poet Raul Bopp, playing around with the syllables of her name, dubbed Patrícia "Pagu" and published a poem in a popular weekly magazine that extolled her seductiveness. The first verse read:

> Pagu has soft eyes
> Eyes like I don't know what
> When you're near them
> Your heart begins to ache
>   Ah, Pagu, hey!
>   It aches because it's good to cause pain.[1]

By this time, Pagu had come under the wing of novelist Oswald de Andrade and his wife, the painter Tarsila do Amaral, gurus of the Brazilian modernist movement that was launched in São Paulo in 1922. Adamantly rejecting stale nineteenth-century European formulas, they sought inspi-

ration in Brazil's primitive, indigenous past. From this retreat to "primitivism," Oswald went on to launch the radical
"Antropofagía Movement." His May 1928 manifesto advocated a ritual, symbolic "devouring" of European values in
order to wipe out patriarchal and capitalist society with its
rigid social and psychological boundaries. In March 1929,
Pagu's drawings began to appear in the second phase of the
Revista de antropofagía, the movement's magazine.

It was Pagu's public debut at a fund-raising event at the
São Paulo municipal theater in June, however, that caused
the greatest stir. Dressed by Tarsila in an extravagant white
dress and red-lined black cape, she recited three poems, including Bopp's poem on her seductiveness and her own poem
about her lewd cat who had a long tail and imagined she
was a serpent. If the audience was stunned by Pagu's daring, they were also captivated. Thunderous applause was
followed by reviews that proclaimed her appearance a "total
success." For the next few months, Pagu occupied the spot-
light as the person who more than anyone else embodied the
antropofagista creed: "[to] constantly and directly consume
the taboo," or "[to transform the] taboo into totem." Her ad-
mirers, in awe of her shocking and audacious defiance of
social conventions, pronounced: "Pagu abolished the gram-
mar of life." "She would be capable of devouring various ven-
omous bishops."[2]

Irreverent and liberated, Pagu went on to scandalize even
the avant-garde community that had so eagerly embraced
her. On the one hand, she lavished praise on her mentor and
friend, Tarsila. In a newspaper interview given on the occasion of Tarsila's August 1929 exhibit in Rio de Janeiro, Pagu
identified Tarsila as her greatest hero. "I'm in love with
Tarsila. I would give her the last drop of my blood. As an
artist, I admire her superiority."[3] She noted that she had
entrusted Tarsila with her autobiography, the "Album de
Pagu," which consisted of a series of free-spirited drawings
and "sixty uncensored poems" dedicated to the Brazilian director of film censorship. But several months earlier, Pagu
and Oswald had already begun their "romance of the anarchist epoch." Oswald, captivated by Pagu's irreverence and
drawn to her for inspiration in his search for revolutionary
paths, betrayed Tarsila. "If Tarsila's home totters," he
scribbled on a napkin at a fancy dinner party, "it is because
of Pagu's intrigue."[4] In September, Oswald arranged a farcical marriage between Pagu and the painter Waldemar

Belisário do Amaral, who had been raised by Tarsila's family. So secret was the real plan that Oswald and Tarsila were the best man and bridesmaid at the wedding. Tarsila gave Pagu a painting as a wedding present, and Pagu's family was delighted by the marriage. But as the couple was driving to the coast for a honeymoon, Oswald met them on the highway and took Waldemar's place. The marriage was officially annulled the following February. By that time, Oswald and Pagu had already consummated their "romance of the anarchist epoch" by "marrying" in front of his family's tomb in the city cemetery—in Oswald's words, "the ultimate defiance." And Pagu was pregnant with a son, Rudá, who was born in September 1930.

Wifehood and motherhood occupied little of Pagu's time and energy. She probably never considered retiring to the "secluded charm of her home" as middle-class wives were supposed to do, or submitting to the routine demands of housewifery. But her refusal to do so was highly deviant at a time when a barrage of articles in women's magazines was trying to convince women that the sole path to true happiness and personal fulfillment lay in accepting the "important and difficult task" of building "happy and fragrant homes." Instead of dedicating her life to overseeing the intellectual and moral development of her child (which her own education, the medical profession, and the normative literature of the period insisted was women's God-given "primordial mission"), Pagu hired a nurse to care for Rudá. She summed up her attitude toward marriage in an article written later in her life:

> Women in all civilized times have only known one goal—
> marriage. Her place in the sun [is] sheltered by the virile
> and protecting shadow of a man who takes upon himself
> all the initiative. All [women's] longings and needs are cut
> off at this point, with the consequent suffering implicit in
> the contract.[5]

Exactly one month after giving birth, Pagu participated in the political demonstrations that erupted around the "revolution" of 1930. The stock market crash in 1929 had devastated the Brazilian economy, thus eroding the power base of São Paulo's coffee-exporting oligarchy and throwing the country into political crisis. In the face of the fierce political battles that ensued and the intense radicalization to the right and the left, members of the artistic avant-garde were forced to choose sides. With Oswald, Pagu joined the Brazilian Communist party (PCB) in 1931, followed its orders to "become a member of the proletariat," and took up the cause of socialist revolution. She immersed herself in the lives of the proletariat, working at the worst of jobs to the point of becoming sick. Having experienced firsthand the arrogance of bosses and the humiliation and rage of women workers, she participated in strikes and fought in the front lines of the PCB to bring about the revolution. In August 1931 she became the first woman political prisoner in Brazil, held for a short time for being an "agitator" in a demonstration that became violent. But it was this period of total commitment to the cause of social revolution that Pagu later remembered as the "happiest time of [her] life, during which [she] had faith."[6]

Pagu's unshakable faith in Marxist ideology and her vision of a future utopia achieved through political struggle changed the focus of her writing. With Oswald, she published an irreverent, satirical, aggressively polemical pamphlet called *O homen do povo* (The Man of the People). (It was closed down by the police in April 1931 after only eight numbers, following rioting by law students who were insulted by Oswald's denunciation of the São Paulo law school as a "cancer.") Pagu's column, "A Mulher do Povo" (The Woman of the People), commented on the behavior and values of São Paulo's female population. It viciously attacked the hypocritical, sterile bourgeois (and Catholic) morality that prevented women from using their minds and bodies freely, thus fostering triviality and neurotic perversions rather than healthy sensuality. Pagu's condemnation of the bourgeois feminist movement was especially ardent. She mocked the notion that Brazil's feminists, a small group of professional women, were in any sense a "vanguard" or had anything "revolutionary" to propose. Pagu scornfully dismissed their campaigns for sexual liberation, "conscientious maternity," and female suffrage as elitist and naive. Instead of fighting for female suffrage that was irrelevant to the majority of women (who would be excluded because they were illiterate), Pagu proposed that they should fight to transform radically the social and economic structure of Brazil. According to Pagu's vision, women could only achieve equality and sexual liberation after poverty and class exploitation had been eliminated.

The theme of female oppression and liberation was taken up again in Pagu's "proletarian novel," *Parque industrial*, written in 1931–32, but only published in 1933 at Oswald's expense. It describes the lives of the Paulista female proletariat with a frankness that was shocking at the time. Pagu openly discusses the sexual exploitation of female factory workers by bosses and the tragedy of working-class women who were seduced by bourgeois men with promises of marriage, impregnated, and abandoned to a life of prostitution. The villains of the novel are the morally corrupt and decadent bourgeois "parasites," among whom are feminists whose "freedom" depended on their exploitation of maids, and members of São Paulo's modernist movement who were ideologically co-opted by continued economic dependence on the rich aristocracy. The victims are the politically unconscious proletariat. The heroes are two women who join the ranks of the Communist party and struggle to raise working-class women's class consciousness in an attempt to help bring about the revolution. The novel uses the modern literary technique of piecing together short cinemalike scenes, and it pioneers the movement toward social realism of the 1930s. But its concern for artistic innovation is subordinated to heavy doses of doctrinaire political propaganda and a call for revolution as the solution to the human problems created by São Paulo's booming capitalist economy.

If the biting satire and vulgar street language of *Parque industrial* made it offensive to bourgeois society, the sexual explicitness and radical feminist perspective that underlay its Marxist analysis made the novel unpalatable to the puritanical Brazilian Communist party. At the insistence of the party (which did not consider women's exploitation to be an urgent political issue), Pagu published her novel under the pseudonym Mara Lobo. In the memoirs of two activists are other hints of Pagu's conflicts with the party hierarchy over her nonconformity. Octavio Brandão held up his wife Laura as a model; in addition to organizing female workers, Laura worked behind the scenes of the PCB to keep morale high, she performed administrative tasks, and she raised children. Octavio praised his loyal wife for having "protected [his] life, health, and liberty" and for having helped to uphold socially acceptable sexual behavior. Perhaps partly in reference to Pagu's deviant behavior, he wrote: "In the Brazilian Communist Party between 1922 and 1929 mutual respect and 'revolutionary ideology' always prevailed. Laura contributed much to this. There was never any case of an amorous adventure or a sexual scandal."[7] Another activist, Leôncio

Basbaum, attacked Pagu directly as a "pernicious" influence, who, he claimed, like other middle-class intellectuals, approached her activism in the ranks of the PCB as "supremely entertaining and exciting."[8]

Gradually, the physical exhaustion of daily political work, combined with the emotional exhaustion of confronting not only police harassment but also condemnation by party members, wore Pagu down. Between December 1933 and November 1935 she traveled through the United States, Japan, China, Germany, and France, working as a foreign correspondent for three Brazilian newspapers. Years later, Pagu revealed the motivation for her trip abroad:

> From the age of twenty to thirty, I obeyed the orders of the Party. I signed the declaration that they gave me to sign without reading it. This happened for the first time [during the 1931 demonstration in commemoration of the execution of Sacco and Vanzetti] when I guarded the dying body of the black dock worker Herculano de Souza, when I stood up to the military cavalry in the Government Square in Santos, when I was imprisoned as an agitator—taken to Jail 3, the worst jail in the continent.
>
> Then, when I regained my freedom, the Party condemned me; they made me sign a document that exonerated the Party from all responsibility [for the demonstration]. All of that, the conflict and the bloodshed, was the work of a "provoker," of an "individual agitator, [who was] sensationalist and inexperienced." I signed. I signed with my eyes closed without sensing the collapse that was occurring within me.
>
> Why not?
>
> The Party was "right."
>
> Step by step I descended the stairs of degradation, because the Party needed those who had no scruples, those who had no personality, those who did not argue, those who simply ACCEPTED. They reduced me to a rag that left one day for distant places, because the Party grew tired of using me as a scapegoat. They could no longer use me for anything; I was too stained.[9]

On the surface, Pagu's around-the-world trip was glamorous. She was offered a contract in Hollywood, which she turned down, declaring: "My goal is much larger and more difficult to achieve." In China she attended the coronation of the last emperor, gained access to his palace, and accompanied him on bicycle rides through the palace grounds. Through the emperor, she arranged for the first soybeans to be sent to Brazil. In China, she also met Sigmund Freud. And in Paris, she became friendly with the most famous surrealist poets and attended courses of the leading Marxist professors at the Popular University.

Pagu's trip abroad also marked the beginning of her profound disillusionment with political activism. She wrote to Oswald from Moscow: "This here is a cold dinner without imagination." Later, she recounted in greater detail the shock she suffered in Stalinist Russia:

> My ideal collapsed, in Russia, in face of the miserable children of the gutters, the bare feet, and the eyes full of hunger. In Moscow, a large luxurious hotel for high bureaucrats, tourists of communism, and rich foreigners. In the street, children dying of hunger; this was the Communist regime.
>
> So when an enormous banner pronounced in the streets of Paris "Stalin is right," I knew this was not true.[10]

Nevertheless, when she arrived in Paris, Pagu obtained a false identification and enlisted in the youth wing of the Communist party. A bad injury suffered at a demonstration landed her in the hospital for three months. Then, after three detentions, Pagu was imprisoned as a foreign Communist agitator. But the Brazilian ambassador protected her from being tried in France and saved her from being deported to fascist Italy or Nazi Germany by arranging instead for her repatriation to Brazil.

Pagu returned to Brazil in November 1935, separated definitively from Oswald (who by that time was living with another woman), and moved into her sister Sidéria's apartment. Once again, she quickly became embroiled in politics. Bitter ideological conflict between the right-wing Integralist movement, which in many ways resembled European fascist parties, and the left-wing National Liberation Alliance (ALN), which was run from behind the scenes by the Brazilian Communist party, exploded in street battles. Finally, in November 1935, the ALN launched a poorly planned insurrection, a desperate last-ditch attempt to capture power. Pagu's participation in this fiasco led to her imprisonment for four and a half years. In jail, Pagu still refused to submit despite periods of solitary confinement and torture. She went on hunger strikes which seriously damaged her health, escaped on one occasion only to be captured and sent back to prison, and delayed her release for several months by refusing to pay homage to the authorities.

Pagu left jail in July 1940 in miserable physical condition, weighing eighty-eight pounds. More serious, perhaps, was her existential crisis. Profoundly disillusioned and embittered, she resigned from the Communist party. Although she never renounced her socialist ideology, she did discard her utopian vision of the inevitable and liberating revolution and abandoned political activism. Her experience had taught her to distrust the dogmatic left wing as much as she despised the reactionary right wing. Later, Pagu explained that her worst experience in jail was the psychological torment she was subjected to by fellow political prisoners. In her words, they "had nails to drive into my head, and on the point of each nail, was the word YES. To which I responded NO. They affirmed that the Party was right, that I had to yield, that I ought to submit to orders: YES. 'Yes, because you are wrong.' And I always responded: NO."[11] She was relieved to be transferred to a jail for common criminals, where she escaped from the "nails" of the party.

For the rest of her life, Patrícia (the name she used after her release from jail) waged a continual struggle against sickness, exhaustion, and massive depression. She survived several suicide attempts, one soon after her release from prison, another in 1949, and another in 1962, a few months before she died of cancer. Initially, she refused to speak to even the people she loved, and always remained withdrawn in public. But ultimately, she found consolation in a stable private life and in art, literature, and theater. She went to live with literary critic Geraldo Ferraz, by whom she had a son in June 1941 and with whom she remained until the end of her life. Despite the stigma attached to her name, she was gradually able to obtain work as a journalist. She redirected her energies into writing polemical columns on the world of art and literature. She introduced European avant-garde authors to Brazilian audiences. And finally, she led a campaign to promote theater in Brazil.

Patrícia's second and final novel, *A famosa revista*, which she coauthored with Ferraz in 1945, was born of her struggle to find a substitute for political activism. Its message inverts the message of her first novel. Whereas *Parque industrial* had been an apology for the party, *A famosa revista* denounces the evils of the monolithic party: bureaucratization, corruption, opportunism, and debasement of human values. The first sentence of the novel announced: "This is a love story between Rosa and Mosci: a protest and a blow against the vortex that outlaws love." The plot follows Rosa and Mosci's transcendence of the pettiness and corruption of the party to their refuge in art, intellectual life, love, and an insistence on an absolute moral purity that admits no compromise. Patrícia's concern for developing a "poetic" literary style signaled her rejection of the subordination of literature to immediate partisan political goals. Having been betrayed by politics, she returned to literature as a means of liberating mankind through the expansion of mental horizons and the fostering of the imagination.

Patrícia died at home in 1962 at the age of fifty-two, her body riddled with cancer. She had paid a high price for the many heresies she committed: abandonment by friends, political persecution and years of imprisonment by the establishment she threatened, betrayal and condemnation by her comrades in the Brazilian Communist party, physical sickness, and tremendous disillusionment, anguish, and pain. But she never shrank from the inevitable consequences of her idealism, intellectual honesty, and personal integrity. Upon her death, her husband Geraldo Ferraz wrote that "she considered her setbacks and defeats, the blows of destiny, attacks by police, prison, and the scandal that shrouded her name and her actions to be the crosses of a struggle that would bring her face-to-face with death."[12]

Patrícia, being too far ahead of her time, was gradually but systematically marginalized. Her revolutionary vision never fit within the project of the PCB, within the program of Brazil's feminists, or within the narrow confines of the country's intellectual life. Moreover, by the mid-1930s, it was apparent that the social and intellectual space opened up by the disruptive forces of economic revolution was closing. With the imposition of the authoritarian Estado Novo in 1937, a new bourgeois economic and cultural hegemony emerged. Dissident voices were repressed, and the threats to the hierarchical order that had been posed by women and the working class were safely contained. Women's domestic roles were reenshrined (for the good of the patriarchal family and public order) through protective legislation that kept women out of higher-paying "male" jobs, through female education that continued to prepare women to be competent housewives, and through propaganda issued by the Church and the medical profession insisting on the "naturalness" of women's role as wives and mothers. The working class was incorporated into political life, but not as a source of social renovation.

Social legislation, a new labor code, and unionization carefully controlled by the state undermined working-class autonomy and militancy. The period of "creative disorder" that fostered the relative freedom Patrícia experienced as an adolescent and young adult proved to be temporary.

Following her release from prison in 1940, Patrícia's continuing attacks on the new (but still hierarchical) social structure and power dynamic in Brazil passed largely unnoticed. Only in the late 1970s was she rediscovered and resurrected from oblivion by a new generation of Brazilian intellectuals struggling to overcome the legacies of a decade and a half of military dictatorship. The example of Patrícia's lifelong search for intellectual, social, political, and sexual freedom has inspired those resisting authoritarian mentalities and political control today. And her unwillingness to compromise, even in defeat, stands as a proclamation of her conviction that no social order is immutable—that people, thinking and acting, can change their world for the better and have the responsibility to try to do so.

NOTES

1. Raúl Bopp, "Coco de Pagu," in *Pagu: Patrícia Galvão: Vida-obra*, ed. Augusto de Campos (São Paulo, 1982), 38.
2. Campos, *Pagu*, 321–23.
3. Clovis de Gusmão, "Na exposição de Tarsila," in Campos, *Pagu*, 60.
4. Campos, *Pagu*, 324.
5. Quoted in Antonio Risério, "Pagu: Vida-obra, obravida, vida," in Campos, *Pagu*, 18.
6. Campos, *Pagu*, 325.
7. Octavio Brandão, *Combates e batalhas: Memórias* (São Paulo, 1978), 303.
8. Leôncio Basbaum, *Uma vida em seus tempos (memórias)*, 2d ed. (São Paulo, 1978), 119.
9. Patrícia Galvão, "Verdade e liberdade," in Campos, *Pagu*, 188–89.
10. Ibid., 189.
11. Ibid., 188.
12. Geraldo Ferraz, "Patrícia Galvão: Militante do ideal," in Campos, *Pagu*, 263.

SOURCES

Mystery still shrouds many of the intimate details of Patrícia Galvão's life. But the persistent efforts of Augusto de Campos, who spent years searching for lost pieces of Patrícia's life and assembling her widely scattered writings, resulted in the publication of his invaluable anthology, *Pagu: Patrícia Galvão: Vida-obra* (São Paulo, 1982). It includes several essays on her life and work; facsimiles of two manuscripts, Pagu's 1929 autobiography, "O álbum de Pagu," and Oswald and Pagu's diary, "O romance da época anarquista"; autobiographical passages from Patrícia's 1950 political pamphlet "Verdade e liberdade"; Patrícia's poems, a selection of her articles published in the press, and excerpts from her novels; contemporary reviews of her writings; testimonies by Patrícia's last husband, Geraldo Ferraz, and her sister, Sidéria, as well as by others who knew her; homages to her; photographs; a detailed itinerary of her life (which constitutes an outline of a biography); and the most complete bibliography of works by and about her. Facsimile editions are available of Patrícia Galvão's *Parque industrial, romance proletario* (São Paulo, 1981), as well as of the journals *Revista de antropofagía* (São Paulo, 1975) and *O homen do povo* (São Paulo, 1985). The first is now available in translation by Elizabeth K. and David Jackson as *Industrial Park* (Lincoln, NE, 1992). Background information on women in early twentieth-century São Paulo is taken from Susan Kent Besse, "Freedom and Bondage: The Impact of Capitalism on Women in São Paulo, Brazil, 1917–1937," Ph.D. diss., Yale University, 1983.

12

Ofelia Domínguez Navarro: The Making of a Cuban Socialist Feminist

K. Lynn Stoner

Lynn Stoner, professor of history and director of the Latin American Studies Center at Arizona State University, has become the leading voice in the United States on the status of women in Cuba since its independence from Spain in 1898. Her investigation of this subject began at Indiana University and resulted in her dissertation on the Cuban women's movement. Before going to Arizona State, Stoner was a consultant at the World Bank, worked for the National Endowment for the Humanities, and taught at Kansas State University. During a 1986 research trip to Havana, she had the opportunity to lead seminars at the Federation of Cuban Women.

In writing about Ofelia Domínguez Navarro, Stoner explores the role of women in Cuba against the background of that nation's history before Fidel Castro's revolution in 1959. For the three decades from 1920 to 1959, Cubans endured life in an off-shore appendage of the United States. Tourists eager for hard liquor (because of Prohibition at home), gambling, bordellos, and luxury vacations streamed to the island. The rise of leisure activities that were illegal in the States brought additional graft and introduced racketeering to Cuba. For Cubans their island became a poorhouse run by scoundrels, first under General Gerardo Machado (1925–1933) and then Army commander Fulgencio Batista, who manipulated puppet presidents (1933–1940), then ruled in person as president (1940–1944) and as dictator (1952–1959). This political charade was played out in concert with economic domination and political oversight from Washington. The great majority of Cubans lived on the margins of their own nation. Generally ignored, women, workers, and Afro-Cubans appeared only as entertainers or quaint characters for tourists or as mobs to be disciplined by the ruling plutocrats.

A number of themes emerge in Ofelia's story that invite comparison with those seen in the experiences of other individuals, especially other women, found in this volume. Her political attitudes, for example, should be compared with those of her Brazilian contemporary Pagu, the erstwhile Communist.

181

Radicalization in Cuba during the 1930s was a response to thirty years of frustrated democratic aspirations and political corruption. Following independence in 1898, Cuba's military and economic weakness in the face of U.S. domination deprived Cubans of their sovereignty. A series of presidents depended upon Washington's approval to govern and, consequently, put U.S. interests above national needs. In 1930 worldwide depression exacerbated Cuban frustrations and led students and workers to rebel. The repressive tactics of President Gerardo Machado incited the opposition of students, workers, middle-class businessmen, politicians, and women who took to the streets to protest his alleged dictatorship.

Ofelia Domínguez Navarro joined this opposition. Instead of choosing the predictable avenues of protest open to middle-class women and feminists, she became a socialist feminist. As a lawyer, she defended radical students, socialists, and Communists against government-ordered arrests and imprisonment. She was jailed and endured exile for her beliefs in democracy and broad-reaching social change. Incarceration, rather than discouraging her socialist principles, hardened her commitment to revolution.

Ofelia was in her prime between 1923 and 1946. During this time she suffered the trauma of cutting herself off from her friends who were not radical enough to see imperialism, economic disadvantage, and male dominance as the causes of injustice. Her direct experience with political and social inequity took an otherwise privileged lady and created a revolutionary.

Ofelia's high ideals, courage, and intellect came from both sides of her family. Born on December 9, 1894, in Matagua, a suburb of Seibabo, Las Villas, she could recall the last years of the Cuban War of Independence, in which her parents were active participants. Ofelia's father, Florentino Domínguez, joined a revolutionary group in 1895 and moved to San Juan de los Yeras, where his parents lived. It was a dangerous time for rebels, whom the Spanish imprisoned, exiled, or executed. Ofelia's mother, Paula Navarro, aided rebel forces by smuggling arms to them and making them hammocks. When she drove her cart into the countryside, the contraband strapped to her body, she told Spanish soldiers that she was showing off her child to relatives. She carried along Ofelia, her firstborn, to convince the soldiers of her mission.

In 1895, Florentino was arrested after a member of his revolutionary group informed the Spanish government of his sympathy with the revolutionary forces. Florentino and his co-conspirators were sentenced to exile in Chafarinas, a penal colony near Algiers. There he worked in a rock quarry, yet he held stubbornly to his revolutionary activities. He and other prisoners printed a newspaper, *The Exile*, in which they demanded Cuban independence. Upon his return to Cuba, Florentino again became involved in the revolution. The Spaniards rearrested him and this time sentenced him to a lengthy exile in Mexico. His family accompanied him.

As a child, Ofelia experienced the harsh realities of the independence struggle. She and her mother lived briefly in one of Cuba's infamous concentration camps, which were rife with disease and hunger. An aunt who had married a Spaniard watched her four children starve to death while her husband flourished in the Spanish army. Another aunt watched helplessly as her son, caught aiding the patriots, was tied behind a horse and dragged. In desperation she tried to yank him free, but instead she had to witness his body broken on the rocks, his brains and body parts left on the streets.

These experiences contributed to the development of Ofelia's principles and courage. Exile and imprisonment, rather than being shameful punishments, signified stalwart adherence to the principles of independence. While this alone did not make Ofelia a revolutionary, the example of her parents made radical action in the name of nationalism acceptable to her.

Peace and stability did not automatically follow Cuban independence. Political disruption and violence characterized the early republican period, and misgovernment, corruption, and U.S. manipulation of national affairs soon alienated Cuban nationalists. In the first decade and a half of the republic, white Cuban elites vied for the administrative power abandoned by the departing Spaniards. National parties were merely launching pads for political careers and had no ideological bases. Politicians used assassination to remove opponents from office, and those who ordered assassinations were immune from arrest. Political campaigns were carried out in the streets, not in the polling booths.

Ofelia learned what political immunity meant as a young adult, first in 1911 when she took a teaching job in Jorobada, a small rural community outside Aguas Bonitas in Las

Villas, and later in Havana where she practiced law. Her teaching experience brought her into direct contact with people who had little hope of escaping poverty, illness, drudgery, superstition, hunger, and premature death.

There was no school building in Jorobada, and the few children who attended classes met in the house of Lao Pérez, an old friend of the Domínguez family. Nineteen-year-old Ofelia had to jerry-build a schoolroom: each day she carried a bench from the park for seats, used an oilcloth as a blackboard, and turned a piece of wood and a barrel into a desk.

Offering the students a modern curriculum threatened the peasants' religious understanding and principles. Some parents were ambivalent about bringing their children to school. They objected to Ofelia's curriculum, which included reading, writing, arithmetic, singing, and physical education. In the P.E. class, the boys marched and jumped hurdles while the girls jumped rope and marched. Some parents complained that their children were being sent to school to learn to read and write and not to ruin their shoes. "For that," one said, "the children could join the circus."

Other parents eagerly brought their children. One father, dragging in his kicking and screaming son, told Ofelia, "I have brought this kid so you can learn him . . . so that between his ears letters will flow along with the blood."

After school, Ofelia read newspapers to the townspeople, who commented on and interpreted national and international news according to their own experiences. She also read their letters to them and then wrote replies. As her life became intertwined with those of the campesinos, she came to respect their essential integrity and honesty, and she began to understand how difficult was their struggle for dignity and the necessities of life.

The principal arm of the government in Jorobada was the *rurales*, a rural police force that "kept the peace" in the countryside. Young peasant males clamored to join the *rurales* because by serving in the force, by donning its well-known yellow uniform, they could earn a steady salary, hold power, and achieve status. Repression and corruption were unconcealed facts of life in Jorobada, and bribes were the modus operandi in local politics. Anyone could become the victim of police extortion. Victims had no recourse because such actions were not regarded as crimes.

Torture was a common means of extracting information about local discontent, theft, and anything else the police wanted to know. The police station opened onto an alleyway beside Ofelia's makeshift school, and she and her students could hear the screams of tortured prisoners.

One day, a local officer, Sergeant Nardo, came to the window that faced Ofelia's desk. In front of the class he challenged her to approve of his activities. "Can you hear it, teacher? We are beginning the torture again. Any man leaving this jail leaves in tatters."

Heedless of the consequences, Ofelia exploded with indignation. "Students," she said to the class, "corporal punishment is prohibited by our constitution, and the first time a uniformed bandit lifts his whip or machete against you, kill him and do not tolerate the affront."

"Teacher! Teacher!" the sergeant roared while the students applauded, "you don't know what you are doing!"

"Yes," she answered, "I am doing what I should do."[1]

Ofelia was not exempt from political exploitation simply because she was a teacher. During her first year of teaching, she earned forty pesos per month, just enough to cover food and clothing, yet she also had to donate money to build a school. When the people of Jorobada learned of the arrangement, they built the schoolroom and paid her rent for one year. She used what extra money she earned to defray the expenses of her younger sisters' and brothers' educations.

Sometime later, the government raised teacher salaries to eighty pesos per month, but the teachers had to donate half of their pay to build a house for the minister of education. Incensed, Ofelia went into action and refused to pay for the home of a man who had wealth and lucrative businesses. Although Ofelia thought she was alone in her protest, teachers at the normal school, most of whom were women, demonstrated publicly.

While Ofelia taught in Jorobada, she also was studying for her *bachillerato* (high-school diploma). After completing the degree, she decided to attend law school. Her father wanted her to study for a doctorate in pharmacology because it was a popular degree among educated, elite women in Havana. Ofelia prevailed. She completed law school, mostly through correspondence courses, and moved from Jorobada to Santa Clara and then to Havana to practice law.

Ofelia learned about the seamier side of life through her experience as a criminal attorney. She defended murderers, prostitutes, and thieves. She also saw how public office could be used to subvert the legal system and how legal power often benefited the privileged class. Ofelia could have become cynical about the legal profession and human misery, but she did not. Although she was repelled by crime, she often felt compassion for the victims and the accused. A delinquent, to her way of thinking, was the product of an exploitative system, and ignorance and desperation were the real motivations for crime. Ofelia was most compassionate toward prostitutes. Without denying the immorality of the occupation, Ofelia felt that prostitutes were made to suffer for the transgressions of the men who were their customers. She argued that jurists, who often saw prostitution as a "necessary evil," never considered the women's destitution, which, in Ofelia's opinion, was the fundamental cause of this activity. It was through her defense of these women that Ofelia became a feminist.

Ofelia was not the first to raise the question of women's rights in newly independent Cuba. Women of her mother's generation had fought for independence alongside their husbands and brothers, and they had won respect and recognition for their efforts. Yet, after the signing of the Cuban constitution in 1902, these same heroines found themselves disenfranchised and sent home with nothing more than monuments and poems as rewards for their sacrifices. The principles of independence apparently did not include equality between men and women. Women's rights did not receive attention until women took up the cause for themselves. In 1917 women of good education and high breeding challenged male politicians to reform the laws so that women would have the same rights as men.

Middle- and upper-class women who became leaders in women's organizations were the first to connect women's legal and political disadvantages with the promises of independence. They demanded universal suffrage, representation in court, government welfare programs, and control of their own and their children's lives. They believed that the freedoms they sought for themselves would benefit all women regardless of race or class. These early feminists became self-appointed leaders of a women's civil and legal rights movement. They were part of a ruling class that expected to lead and to define new rights in terms of their own understanding of freedom and justice, but they were reluctant to give power to women of the laboring classes so that they might articulate their own notions of justice.

On the surface, Ofelia Domínguez Navarro appeared to be a typical member of Havana's highly educated, cosmopolitan middle class. She was a lawyer and a founder of the Club Femenino de Santa Clara and the Alianza Nacional Feminista, two feminist organizations. Ofelia's colleagues were progressive women of property and influence, who traveled in Europe and the United States. Yet Ofelia's background also included struggle and hardship, and she was sympathetic to the needs of the poor. She supported the women's movement, but she opposed its philanthropic programs for disadvantaged women. In time, she broke with the middle-class women's organizations over the question of poverty, the rights of illegitimate children, and political activism.

Ofelia first became nationally known as an advocate of women's rights in 1923, when she attended the First National Women's Congress. The Club Femenino de Cuba, one of several women's organizations, had called the congress to assess the state of Cuban feminism and set directions for the women's movement. Delegates from thirty-one organizations and all seven of Cuba's provinces attended. Advocates for change spoke about women's comparative legal disadvantages, and the delegates enthusiastically passed reform resolutions. The harmonious atmosphere was disturbed when Ofelia, Dulce María Borrero de Luján, Hortensia Lamar, and others proposed a resolution to correct the unequal status of legitimate and illegitimate children. At this point, the congress erupted into pandemonium. For many feminists, Ofelia's resolution, that illegitimate children receive the same assurances of care, shelter, and love as legitimate children, was scandalous. According to many conservative delegates, the protection of unwed mothers was not a feminist matter but a moral question that revealed a woman's, not a man's, immoral character. The delegates, many of them also influenced by Catholic Church directives, defeated Ofelia's resolution, although they did put it on the agenda for the next national women's congress, scheduled for 1925.

If Ofelia was disgruntled by the conservatives at the first congress, she must have been appalled at the Second National Congress in April 1925. She again addressed the issue of equal rights for all children, regardless of their parents' marital status. Since the last congress, she had gathered evidence about the living conditions of unwed mothers and the hopelessness of their children. But rather than consider the plight of these women and children, the conservative faction accused Ofelia of being a Communist. They argued that she, as a single and childless woman, could not understand mothers and children, and that in her arguments she was merely espousing Communist ideology, which sought to destroy the family by supporting divorce, free love, and concubinage. The kindest criticism called her a stupid sentimentalist.

What had been pandemonium over the issue in 1923 turned into a near riot in 1925. Women pounded tables with their shoes as they vied for the floor. The conservatives threatened to walk out, but Ofelia and her supporters upstaged them and left first. After the progressives' departure, the reactionary Catholic elements met in secret sessions so that they could control the voting on all issues. As a result, the congress passed nothing more radical than a suffrage resolution.

After this congress, Ofelia increased her activity in the Club Femenino, one of the more radical groups within the women's movement. The Club differed from philanthropic organizations in its demand that the state take more responsibility for the poor and that women have the same civil and political status as men. The Club joined student militants who were fighting in the streets for the release of Julio Antonio Mella, the founder of the Cuban Communist party, who was being held in jail without bond. Although the women in the Club were not Communists, they did sympathize with the students' protest against corruption and gangster politics.

The Mella incident was crucial in Ofelia's political development, for Julio Antonio Mella was a friend with whom Ofelia shared some ideological ties. She had been his guest at the Popular University when she gave a talk about the equality of children.

Mella went on a hunger strike, protesting his arbitrary arrest and harsh treatment in prison. Many Cubans thought his arrest was unjust, and they feared that Mella would be allowed to die. The Club Femenino, led by Ofelia, supported the nationwide demonstration. Together with the students of Santa Clara, she planned a massive protest. Sánchez Arango and Gómez Guimeranez organized factory workers, and Ofelia brought out the students from the institute, the normal school, and the law school. In less than three hours, the students, workers, and others marched peacefully on the provincial government. They held a meeting in Santa Clara's central park and then dispersed.

But Ofelia was not through. She led a contingent of delegates to the home of President Machado's parents, who lived in Santa Clara. Ofelia told them of the arrest, the hunger strike, and the misuse of the law. Señora Lutgarda Morales was visibly moved by Ofelia's description of Mella's fragile condition. She immediately telegraphed her son, asking him to release Mella. "We beg you as your parents who have loved their children to order the release of the poor young prisoner."[2] In Havana even larger demonstrations had been held to demand Mella's release. At the eleventh hour, Machado released Mella, thus sparing his life.

Ofelia's association with students and workers broadened her understanding of oppression and of how to organize against government retaliation. Her interest in reform was no longer defined solely in terms of the women's movement. Despite her enlarged perception of what constituted social injustice, she remained loyal to women's issues. Between 1915 and 1928 she participated in national and international women's meetings to which she carried her message about the rights of illegitimate children. She met other Latin American feminists, such as Paulina Luissi of Uruguay. She also encountered the North American feminists who proved that they were no friends of Latin American women at the 1926 Interamerican Women's Congress in Panama. The delegates from the United States abstained in the vote for a resolution that Latin American nations grant women their civil and political rights. These delegates said that they were not convinced that Latin American women were ready to exercise their rights. This episode reinforced Ofelia's anti-U.S. sentiments.

Women's suffrage turned out to be a political issue inextricably linked to the overthrow of the Machado government. As such, it initially pulled together the conservative and radical elements of the feminist movement. General Gerardo Machado became Cuba's fifth president in 1924, and some hoped his administration would be different from previous, corrupt regimes. Machado acknowledged the need for improved public works and for the elimination of corruption. Many of his projects, especially the trans-Cuban railroad, were popular. At the urging of his supporters, he appointed a constitutional assembly in 1927 to rewrite the 1902 constitution to extend the presidential term from four to six years, thus allowing him to succeed himself. To deflect allegations that he was a dictator, Machado declared his support for women's suffrage. He wanted to convince Cuban dissidents that he was broadening the electoral base and favoring democratic rule, despite his consecutive terms in office, abolition of certain parties, and repressive tactics.

By 1927 essentially all feminists, regardless of their political leanings, supported universal suffrage, since that had been their cause for ten years. Even Ofelia spoke before the constitutional assembly in favor of Machado's resolution. She argued that votes for women would dignify the electoral process and give women the same rights as men, which they should have had immediately after independence.

The constitutional congress's decision to reject universal suffrage sharply disappointed the feminists, many of whom had stood vigil outside the capital to await the decision. Although the delegates had felt free to tinker with the constitution and provide for an irregular presidency, they claimed they did not have the authority to grant women the vote.

Outraged feminists formed a group called the Committee for the Defense of Women's Suffrage. They interviewed the most prominent men of the constitutional assembly, made declarations to the press, and presented a petition to Dr. Antonio Sánchez de Bustamante, president of the convention, demanding that the assembly write women's suffrage into the constitution. The members of the committee knew they would be unable to convince the assembly, but they wanted to keep the issue alive and before the public. Ofelia, along with Hortensia Lamar, Pilar Jorge de Tella, Rosaria Guillaume, and Rosa Arredondo de Vega, carried the petition to Dr. Sánchez during an assembly meeting. She and her associates also denounced the claims made by some of the delegates and medical doctors that women were physically and mentally inferior to men.

In the wake of the setback, a group of women decided to create a united feminist front with members from all social sectors of the republic to fight for the civil and political rights of women. In 1928, Pilar Jorge de Tella and Ofelia invited feminists to an organizational meeting. Pilar urged them to continue the feminist struggle, stating that women's rights were necessary for the well-being of the nation and world peace. Ofelia spoke about the legal status of women, reminding those present that laws included problems of criminality and the economic subjugation of women. Upper-class women such as Elena Mederos de González initially supported Ofelia.

Within days of the meeting, Ofelia invited women working in tobacco factories to become part of the organization. Working-class women, teachers, factory workers, professional women, and the wealthy formed the Alianza Nacional Feminista on September 6, 1928, in the Salón de Actos of the Reporters' Association of Havana. The women called themselves the *"mambisas* for the new army of justice, ideals, and rights."

On behalf of the Alianza, Ofelia sent a letter to President Machado demanding that women have the vote and full citizenship. She argued her case not only in terms of women's rights but also in terms of the rights of the poor. The president promised only to send a message to congress supporting women's suffrage. Whether he fulfilled his promise is not known, but no resolution came before the assembly.

Popular opposition to the Machado government was in its infancy in 1928, and Ofelia was in its vanguard. She wrote for opposition journals and newspapers, several of which were published by the Communist party. She also did regular radio editorials on Havana stations. Fascism was rising in Europe, and some of its repressive tactics were being adopted by its supporters in Latin America, whom Ofelia strongly criticized. But she differed from many of her *compañeros* in the Communist and Socialist parties because of her feminist views that women must advance both as members of the proletariat and as women.

Ofelia's radical leanings were not lost on the moderate feminists in the Alianza. Although their stated purpose was to include women of all classes in the fight for women's rights, their vision for change would primarily benefit the middle class. The Alianza focused on legal changes to improve the civil status of women and labor laws. Many members of the Alianza, rather than tailor their program to include prostitutes, peasant women, tobacco workers, domestic servants, blacks, and mulattos, believed that discipline, education, and better health standards would improve the poor's standard of living. Until poor women could become respectable women, the moderates thought, feminists could aid them only through philanthropy and educational programs.

Ofelia broke with the Alianza in 1930 after losing the organization's presidential election. The membership had tolerated her radical views as labor vice president, but it would not accept her as its leader. María Collado, the leader of the Suffrage party and a vigorous opponent of Ofelia's views, claimed that Ofelia lost the election because she was egotistical and tyrannical. Ofelia's memoirs offer another explanation:

> Because of the heterogeneous composition of the Alianza, we could not do any more than act for civil and political rights for women. We could not incorporate poor women and address their needs. Since rich women predominated, they could not reconcile their interests with those of tobacco workers, sales clerks, or teachers, etc.
>
> For my part, I confess that in spite of the high intellectual and moral values represented in the Alianza, they were skewed enough to make me feel uncomfortable because I had to limit my activities which favored the social rights of working women. . . .
>
> The Alianza had a number of issues and activities. I eventually left this group for no other reason than ideological convictions. The group did not address the needs of people outside their economic and social class.[3]

On May 30, 1930, Ofelia and Bertha Darder Bebé formed the Unión Laborista de Mujeres, which was intended to attract women of all classes to fight for a broad program of reform. The new group focused on women's issues, but it also was anti-imperialist and nationalistic. It differed from the Alianza by identifying poverty, gender exploitation, and North American capitalist imperialism as the sources of women's oppression. It called for collaboration between women and men to create new economic bases and opportunities for all Cubans, especially for those who worked. Ofelia insisted that the Unión be free of Church interference and the influence of members' husbands. Women of prestige and status filled the administrative positions, but they were women whose loyalty to socialist values was unquestionable. The Unión soon had the support of many progressives in the press, among the veterans of the wars of independence, and from the international feminist community.

At this point in her life, Ofelia was a socialist feminist, not a Marxist-Leninist. She did not advocate the destruction of democracy through revolution, nor did she support a totalitarian state or communism. She also refused to let women's issues be subsumed by the proletarian struggle. She worked within the democratic system, and she argued for reform in democratic terms. Because her organization called for major economic and social changes and because of her alliance with other political groups, Ofelia was swept into the political turmoil that erupted between 1930 and 1934.

Four months after the founding of the Unión, Rafael Trejo, a student at the University of Havana, was assassinated. His murder by police during a demonstration galvanized opposition to Machado's regime. Until then the targets of Machado's repression had been striking workers and outspoken opponents of his administration. When Trejo, a student who had had no previous association with revolutionary groups, died, Machado was serving notice that he would use indiscriminate violence to preserve his presidency.

Trejo's death prompted accusations of police misconduct. Students rushed to newspaper offices to publish their denunciations. Trejo's friends, defying repression, carried his body first to the emergency room of a nearby hospital and then to his parents' home where it lay for public viewing. Ofelia and the women in the Unión stood vigil all night.

President Machado declared a state of siege until after Trejo's funeral. He ordered that only family members could accompany the body to the cemetery, but women from the Unión and other prominent radicals marched at the head of the funeral procession. Unión members were pallbearers and carried the casket on their shoulders from the chapel to the grave site. For once, being female had an advantage, for soldiers stationed along the route were reluctant to shoot women who were doing what women do after outbreaks of violence—mourn the dead. Ofelia delivered the eulogy, intended to unify everyone who objected to Machado's repressive tactics.

The Unión did not stop with its participation in Trejo's burial. Its members demanded the firing of the university's rector, who had called for police intervention, and insisted that the police be brought to justice. For those efforts, the Unión became the target of police investigation. Occasionally, policemen interrupted Unión meetings and disrupted the recruitment of new members. They also searched Unión offices for evidence of seditious activities.

Undaunted, the Unión leadership kept up public protest, but they always conducted themselves like ladies and avoided violence. On one occasion, the executive committee of the Unión, along with Dr. Candida Gómez Cala, the niece of

Maximo Gómez, one of the greatest generals to survive the wars of Cuban independence, visited Camp Columbia, the military headquarters in Havana, to protest police brutality. The police, who were used to society ladies visiting police headquarters to see that prisoners were clean and well fed, cordially received Gómez and the delegation. When Colonel Castillo, the commander, realized that their purpose was to criticize police behavior, he stiffened and asked that his staff members leave the room. Gómez humiliated Castillo by impugning his nationalism and accusing him of betraying the objectives of independence by repressing Cubans as the Spanish had done. Castillo, chastised, only mumbled that he had no answer to their accusations. The women left unharmed and returned to their homes.

As his administration came under increasing fire from opposition groups, Machado searched for a way to appease some of his opponents. An obvious ploy was to offer votes to women. As proof of his support for suffrage, he reminded the public of his 1927 constitutional resolution, blaming the congress for rejecting the measure. Although few feminists believed Machado, his maneuver succeeded to some extent in dividing the movement.

Most of the women's groups—the Alianza Nacional Feminista, the Partido Sufragista, the Club Femenino, and even the Lyceum—called for an end to the dictatorship and for women's suffrage, but they did not insist upon major political or economic changes. The Unión, on the other hand, was a more radical feminist organization. Ofelia and the executive council accused the government of trying to dilute the strength of the women's movement by using the vote to draw feminists' attention away from more difficult problems. Ofelia called on feminists to forget about suffrage for the time being and concentrate on economic, racial, and gender issues. She went so far as to say that, by paying exclusive attention to suffrage, the feminists demonstrated that women were a retarding force in revolutionary movements.

Machado's desperate attempts to appease opposition elements were unsuccessful, and 1930 marked the beginning of three years of bloody repression. The president outlawed public gatherings during the November by-elections. Newspapers threatened with censorship closed. Police hunted down and killed students because they were members of the Directorio Estudiantil, and they shot and killed protesters and suspected conspirators with their infamous "shots into the air." Violence only begat violence, and groups such as the ABC, a middle-class organization that advocated the violent overthrow of Machado, joined the fray.

At first, the Unión did not endorse violence as a means of ousting Machado. The women became radical only after helping families search for fathers, sons, and brothers who had disappeared. The experience taught them the lengths to which Machado and his supporters would go to crush rebellion. After they had visited prisons as defense attorneys for jailed students and workers, Ofelia and the women of the Unión openly advocated revolution, although they would not bear arms themselves.

Ofelia was first arrested on January 3, 1931, when she and others were recruiting students from the normal school for the Directorio Estudiantil. The meetings were always secret, but the special police (the "Porra," or experts) learned that the students were meeting at 106 Linea. There were two such addresses, and the Porra went to the wrong one. By chance, Ofelia and Dulce María Escalona de Rodríguez, another celebrated female activist of the time, happened past and recognized two police lieutenants. The women knew it was only a matter of time before the police found the correct address, so they drove quickly to Teté Suárez Solís's house, where the meeting was being held. By the time they convinced the students of the danger, the police arrived. Ofelia and several other women pretended they were celebrating Teté's birthday. The police found them listening to the Victrola, with no students in evidence. When the police demanded that they be allowed to search the house, Ofelia collapsed on the bed as if she were ill, for she did not want the police to enter the bedroom where many of the students were hiding.

Her efforts failed. The Porra arrested everyone in the house and packed them off to jail. At first, Ofelia thought she would be spared because she was not put in the wagons with the students. However, one of the policemen invited her, in the name of Lieutenant Calvo, the most infamous of the Porra, to join him in the police car. She suspected that the policeman was taunting her, so she refused and went to one of the wagons with the students. The route to the jail, located downtown at the base of the Prado, meandered through the business center and colonial quarter. Along the way, the prisoners shouted, "Down with tyranny! Down with assassination! Down with Yankee imperialism!" Ofelia recalled

Torriente Brau's strong voice calling out, "Who killed Mella?" The answering chorus rang out from the other wagon, "Machado, Machado!"

All gaiety ended at the prison. It was a cold January afternoon, and the prison had no heat. Ofelia's cell, which was ten to twelve meters long and four meters wide, was dark when her jailers opened the barred door. The cell's only fresh air came in through a duct, too high to serve as a window, that faced a bracken marsh. The duct's bars and metal mesh limited the amount of air that could enter, and the only light came in through two windows in the ceiling. The cell was so dank that it took Ofelia two days to dry her handkerchief. The cold and dampness chilled to the bone. The cell had eighteen narrow beds, a few steel chairs, one wooden table, and some small boxes nailed to the walls for storing personal possessions. The prisoners had to share one toilet. On each side of the entryway were small dungeons reserved for solitary confinement.

Ofelia, Dulce María, and Teté found Carmen Gil, a Venezuelan poet, in one of the solitary confinement chambers. She was burning with fever, and she told the women of her terror over the previous seven days. She had been tied to her bed and subjected to the grossest kinds of sexual abuse, all this when she was essentially postpartum, having had a baby only three months earlier. She was suffering from internal infections.

The women hardly slept that night. From down the stairway, they could hear sounds coming from the men's quarters, so they knew who had been arrested and who was being tortured. Dulce María could hardly contain herself at first because of worry over her two small children and then because she could hear the voices of her husband and brother in the adjoining male prison of the Castillo Príncipe.

Two days later, Ofelia and the women were released. Still enraged by Carmen Gil's plight, Ofelia went directly to the offices of *El País*, the Communist newspaper, where she reported what had happened to Carmen and her husband. The following day, Ofelia protested to the secretary of government, Dr. Vivanco, who threatened repressive measures if she did not keep quiet. But threats of reprisal did not intimidate Ofelia; if anything, they ignited her defiance.

Police arrested Ofelia four more times on manufactured charges, for she never violated the law. In her first arrest, the allegation was conspiracy, although the government never prosecuted Ofelia. Future imprisonments followed charges of conspiracy and inciting riots, but she was never convicted, even in the one case that came to trial.

Another common characteristic of Ofelia's arrests was that the police offered her preferential treatment because of her class, status, and occupation. On one occasion when the police arrested her at the Unión office, they realized that she was not well, and they offered to put her under house arrest. She refused. On another occasion, Ofelia had a broken leg and was running a high fever. Again the police wanted to put her under house arrest, and again she refused. Preferential treatment saved Ofelia's life on two occasions. In 1933 and 1937 she fled Cuba after receiving warnings from people who were close to her family that she would be assassinated if she did not flee.

Until March 1931, when Ofelia served her second prison term, she was a socialist feminist with a commitment to democracy and to radical social reform. She sympathized with the Communists, but she had not joined the party. She was a defender of the right to political dissent, a principle of the independence movement but not necessarily one of communism. The isolation of her cell, the contact with prostitutes and thieves, the filth and the bad treatment made her despair. Her only support came from Communist women who befriended her and offered some reason to endure the suffering. They taught her to hope. The final break with her old allies, the progressive feminists, came as she found stronger bonds of compassion and support behind prison walls. Prison made her a revolutionary.

When Ofelia went to prison in 1931, she became both a prisoner and a reporter. She wrote graphically about her arrests, her treatment, and her relationships with common and political prisoners. She experienced firsthand what people on the outside could never know: the smells, the tastes, the sights, and the feel of prison. She knew of the prisoners' hopelessness, despair, ignorance, illness, and suffering. Stripped of her social and political protection, she stood defenseless before the abusive wardens and officers. She lived alongside prisoners who could be violent and duplicitous. She suffered physical illness and mental anguish. With nothing but her intellect as a tool, Ofelia identified her moral convictions, and she deepened her commitment to revolutionary socialism without forgetting her allegiance to feminism. Only socialism, she resolved, considered the motivating factors for crime, and only feminism helped women assume a new consciousness about their victimization in a patriarchal society.

When Ofelia entered Guanabacoa prison in March 1931, nearly all of its 140 female inmates were serving sentences for prostitution. Most of them were disease ridden, and they knew how to steal, swindle, and cheat. Most probably would die a premature death by murder or from venereal disease. Ofelia had understood before she entered prison that a lack of skills and education limited women's chances of obtaining gainful employment, but prison showed her other cultural factors that contributed to women's entrapment in prostitution. Hopelessness and superstition ruled their lives. Santerías, Afro-Cuban rituals, were the sources for supernatural cures, curses, and hoaxes. The women wore red colors in their clothing, patted out rhythms with their feet, used cleansing ceremonies, concocted special drinks, and fulfilled promises to Santa Bárbara to cure themselves. During these ceremonies they often shrieked and fell into trances. The women used rituals to reduce their sexual passions, and they also took out curses against their enemies in prison or against the clients and pimps who were exploiting them. Ofelia saw the tragedy in the santería, for it was an artificial cure for the profound problems that confronted these women. Their minds were darkened by confusion and supernatural forces, leaving them helpless in the face of their oppression.

With no effective outlet for anger, shame, or desperation, the prisoners frequently fought among themselves. A fight might begin between two persons but it usually ended in a brawl between gangs. The issue might be insignificant or a facade for deep resentments between a homosexual couple. No one was exempt from the violence. The women's snarling and cursing, often consisting of racial slurs and taunts about what sort of beast another woman was screwing, shocked and horrified Ofelia.

Soon Ofelia felt some of her fellow prisoners' passions. She, too, experienced intense hatred, especially toward the jailers, whose authority was represented by the huge key used to open and close her cell door. The key became an icon of her contempt for her oppressors. She despised the stooges who went to the wardens with stories of prisoner disobedience. She hated the warden, who was stealing prison provisions and selling them for profit. Ofelia used her own alienation to understand the self-destructive behavior of the women with whom she lived.

Nothing shielded Ofelia from the horrors of drug addiction and homosexual and heterosexual rape. Many of the prisoners were alcoholics and marijuana smokers whose pimps brought them drugs on visiting days. Without their chemical means of escape, the prisoners often became mean and abusive. Prisoners and guards both were involved in perverted sexual adventures, such as rape and bestiality, violations that occurred between prisoners and between prisoners and guards. Homosexuality seemed almost normal. Some of the women pointed out their lovers to Ofelia and told her they were engaged.

Ofelia despaired for these women, but was especially distressed by problems of venereal disease. Mothers arrested for prostitution were allowed to bring their youngest children to prison with them, and since the mothers were often syphilitic, their children also carried the disease. None of the prisoners understood hygiene, and, even if they had, cleanliness in the prison was impossible. Only prisoners who could afford private medical treatment received it, and even they depended on the prison officials to notify a doctor. Venereal disease was so prevalent that Ofelia learned to recognize it by its appearance and smell. Yet prison officials took no precautions to prevent its spread. The prisoners used everything in common: cups, soap, sheets, towels, and spoons. They shared three showers and three toilets.

Nothing sickened Ofelia more than the syphilitic children who were mentally and physically defective. Children who entered the prison healthy stood little chance of leaving it that way. Healthy and sick children played together in one corner of the prison and shared food and toys that they put in their mouths. Their mothers would pick up their children and kiss them with mouths full of syphilitic sores. During the night, children screamed from the pain of the disease, and one girl had to be restrained from tearing at herself where lesions had appeared. The adult women often used drinking utensils and common water supply for santerías intended to cure their disease, a practice that exposed everyone to contact with syphilis and gonorrhea.

Desperate to contain the spread of disease, Ofelia encouraged the prisoners to take precautions and sent letters of protest through the Unión Radical de Mujeres (the new name of the Unión Laborista de Mujeres) to the secretary of health. She was unable to convince the prisoners that there were "bugs" in the water, and they saw no reason to separate the sick from the healthy children. Worse yet, the doctor sent by the secretary of health to investigate Ofelia's complaints never entered the prison, though he did write a letter denying her charges.

Perhaps Ofelia's greatest accomplishment while in prison was the effort she made to understand the psychological composition of her jailers, who brutalized and mistreated prisoners. They not only forced the prisoners to follow arbitrary orders but also insisted upon humiliating them. The guards' actions demonstrated to Ofelia that they were no better than the "criminals" who were prisoners. She discovered that most guards were frightened or embittered widows and single women. Life had been hard for them, and so they channeled their fury against the only people whom they could control, the prisoners. Nothing stopped them from taunting or accusing a prisoner, and on occasion, a prisoner committed suicide following cruel encounters with the guards.

In her darkest moments, Ofelia drew strength from the more seasoned revolutionaries around. Prisoners who were members of the Communist party tried to organize the others so they could protect themselves from abuse. They also got news from the outside and kept in touch with the revolutionary movement. They paid the price for their actions, though, for they were constantly under surveillance and subjected to harassment by the guards.

One evening, a nurse who was their contact informed them that some would be taken to the Isle of Pines. Ofelia was marked to go, and the news was nearly more than she could bear. She had endured this imprisonment with a broken leg, and she was ill and depressed. Her Communist *compañeras* helped her pack her few things and hide her notes. Her misery increased with the knowledge that most of the other prisoners would not know about her move until after she had gone. When the guards came at midnight to take her away, the political prisoners shouted, "Down with tyranny! Long live the revolution!," and sang the "Marseillaise" and other revolutionary songs. As Ofelia followed the guards out of the prison and into the waiting police wagon, she heard from the highest prison galleries the boisterous voices of her *compañeras* singing the "Internationale."

At that moment, Ofelia made the spiritual conversion from an intellectual socialist to a revolutionary whose identity originated in socialist values and community. She ceased to identify primarily with middle- and upper-class intellectuals, choosing instead the solidarity of revolutionaries, for they were at her side during her moments of need.

Although Ofelia thought she was going to the Isle of Pines, she in fact went to the Calixto García Hospital where doctors treated her broken leg and fever. From the hospital, she returned to prison for another two months. She was released in September 1931, after a total of seven months in prison.

From 1931 through the overthrow of President Machado in 1933, Ofelia was a militant defender of the rights of student and labor dissidents. Wherever there was a crisis or a demonstration, Ofelia was present, either as a lawyer or a public speaker. When Communist newspaper reporters were jailed, she took over the editorship of their newspapers. She was jailed again, although briefly, and after her release received a tip from Machado's brother that she was on the Porra's assassination list for speaking at the funeral of a fallen revolutionary, Mirto Miliam, which the government correctly viewed as inciting rebellion.

If Ofelia were to survive, she had to flee. In January 1933 she left for Mexico, the home of her parents, where she remained until Machado's overthrow in September. It was a crucial moment for the anti-Machado forces, and Ofelia wanted to help direct the Unión but to do so meant certain death. In Mexico she spoke to revolutionary student groups and to Cubans in exile, hoping to build support for the revolution and to oppose U.S. mediation and control of Machado's ouster.

From 1933 to 1940 no less than seven men occupied Cuba's presidential palace—men who were essentially appointed and replaced by the new commander in chief of the military, Fulgencio Batista. Batista's abandonment of social reform issues and his groveling for U.S. support repelled Ofelia. She sided with the dedicated revolutionaries who were demanding socialist reform. She was a member of the delegation that brought back Julio Antonio Mella's ashes and buried them in Cuba. She demanded amnesty for all political prisoners. She denounced labor practices and the subsistence wages paid to workers, in particular the female workers at the ten-cent stores. She protested Cuba's continued subservience to the United States. She encouraged tobacco union members to stiffen their armed resistance to police control, reminding them that they were more numerous and powerful than the rural police. She also encouraged other organizations, such as the needleworkers' union, to join international workers' shops to protect themselves against capital and labor exploitation. Her most continuous battle was with the Emergency Courts originally set up by Machado, and continued by subsequent governments, to try revolutionaries immediately after their arrest. They used no juries, and the judges were political appointees with questionable legal training. In effect, the courts were the government's tool for disposing of political dissidents.

Ofelia went to jail two more times before 1937 for her continued opposition and in 1937 fled again to Mexico. There she observed the reform government of Lázaro Cárdenas. In Mexico, she concluded that reform was possible without armed revolt, but only if socialists and Communists could organize the workers' movement and only if the labor movement had significant access to political power. From 1937 to 1939 she worked in a legal and organizational capacity in Mexico to secure the nationalization of U.S. oil interests and to organize Mexican workers. Throughout her exile, Ofelia wrote for radical Cuban journals, denouncing Nazism and fascism.

Upon her return to Cuba, Ofelia maintained her Communist affiliations, but she also took part in the 1939 Third National Women's Congress. Again she raised the issue of women's rights and of equality for children regardless of the legitimacy of their birth. She published her opinions about women's rights in newspapers and discussed them on a ten-minute radio program on Radio Salas. She also spoke out against Hitler's aggression and the coming world war. And in 1940, only a few days after the death of Leon Trotsky in Mexico, she offered to defend the murderer, Jacques Monnard. Although she could not act as a lawyer in Mexican courts, she helped the defense lawyer prepare the case.

The pinnacle of her international influence came in 1946, when Cuba organized its delegation to the United Nations planning meetings in San Francisco. Ofelia was the secretary-general of the Cuban delegation, a post she held for sixteen years. While a part of the Cuban delegation, Ofelia involved herself in programs for children affected by war devastation. She also created programs for improved international education.

Ofelia earned international recognition for her work at the United Nations. She also continued her opposition to the United States, a position that was not without consequences. In 1950, while traveling to New York as the Cuban delegate to the United Nations, she was detained, searched, and interrogated by FBI agents at the Miami airport. It was at the height of the McCarthy period, and the U.S. government was taking no chances with spies or Communists visiting the country. The FBI kept Ofelia in Miami for ten days without her luggage or lodgings. She protested her detention to the president of the Cuban delegation, who finally gained her release.

In 1952, when Batista took over the government in a coup d'état, Ofelia protested. But she was no longer a young and vigorous woman, and her actions were not militant. Rather than participate in guerrilla movements, she concentrated on her work in the United Nations. When the 1959 Cuban revolution succeeded, however, she worked with the local block organizations, called the Committees for the Defense of the Revolution. In 1962 she resigned her post at the United Nations due to severe arthritis.

Ofelia was a woman of awesome courage, tremendous insight, and honesty. In 1971, when she published her autobiography, she described herself as old but basically at peace with herself. She neither cheered nor mourned the outcome of her struggles. She was grateful that she had maintained the strength to withstand imprisonment, and she knew that hardship had shaped her ideals. In the end, Ofelia rejoiced in a socialist Cuba because her and her nation's struggles had drawn her into international solidarity with other socialists and given her a commitment to humanity. She felt no remorse for losing the wealth that might have been hers nor bitterness for the planned austerity in Cuba's economy that she endured in her later years. She believed that she had lived well. She had been a socialist feminist and a revolutionary, but she was also a bit of a Quixote whose dreams reached beyond ideology.

NOTES

1. Ofelia Domínguez Navarro, *50 años de una vida* (Havana, 1971), 49–50.

2. Ibid., 84.
3. Ibid., 118.

SOURCES

This sketch is based on Ofelia Domínguez Navarro's autobiography, *50 años de una vida* (Havana: Instituto Cubana del Libro, 1971), her book about her imprisonments, *De seis a seis* (Mexico City, 1937), and newspapers and feminist publications from the period. To obtain these materials required my traveling to Cuba as well as the assistance of a number of Cubans. I would like to express my deepest appreciation to Tomás Fernández Robaina at the José Martí Library in Havana for his support and interest. His excellent bibliography on Cuban women facilitated my research. Margy Delgado, Rita Perrera, and Marta Alberti from the Federation of Cuban Women invited me to Cuba and aided me with my work. Their trust and good faith have made this project possible; I remain in their debt.

13

Ligia Parra Jahn:
The Blonde with the Revolver

Judith Ewell

Judith Ewell first encountered the story of Ligia Parra Jahn as she thumbed through Venezuelan newspapers of the 1940s in search of news of the Venezuelan military dictator Marcos Pérez Jiménez. For Ewell, reading about Ligia's struggles with the traditional concepts of honor and *vergüenza* (shame) proved a welcome relief from Pérez's reorganization of the General Staff. Finally, Ligia's turn has come.

On one level Ligia's story belonged on a newspaper's last page, the one reserved for tawdry crimes and gory traffic accidents. Yet her respectability, her beauty, and her argument that a woman should be allowed to defend her own honor, vigilante-style, struck a chord among many of her compatriots. Women recognized some of their own dilemmas and humiliations in Ligia's plight. Venezuelan men often felt protective toward the young blonde and resentment toward the Basque adventurer who had disgraced her. Traditionalists believed that Ligia's freedom not only caused her tragedy but also threatened the web of custom and decency that binds society together.

This account of Ligia forms part of the mosaic of Venezuela's history during a time of flux that affected politics, economics, and, above all, society. As in much of Latin America, post-World War II Venezuela experienced the rapid growth of cities, a renewed rise of raw material exports, and the reversion to dictatorial regimes. The capital boomed in the late 1940s, flush with economic success, for the few at least, resulting from the well-established oil industry and the new export of iron ore from Ciudad Bolívar. The country experimented with reforms through the government of the Acción Democrática party led by Rómulo Betancourt, which tried to use oil income for national improvements. These reforms included a new constitution in 1947 and the election of novelist Rómulo Gallegos as president in 1948. The program to improve the wages of urban workers and to give land to rural laborers and plans to balance the military with militias resulted in a military coup after only nine months. New provisional president Carlos Delgado Chalbaud had to answer to the military and business leaders. When he was kidnapped and murdered in 1950, he was replaced by Marcos Pérez Jiménez, who established an iron-fisted dictatorship. It was during this swirl of social change, reform, reaction, democratic elections, and military intervention that Ligia fell in love.

Newton Family Professor of History at the College of William and Mary, Ewell has published *The Indictment of a Dictator: The Extradition and Trial of Marcos Pérez Jiménez* (College Station, TX, 1981); *Venezuela: A Century of Change* (Stanford, 1984); and *Venezuela and the United States: From Monroe's Hemisphere to Petroleum's Empire* (Athens, GA, 1996). She received the prestigious Governor of Virginia's Commonwealth Award for Outstanding Teaching in 1991.

L igia Parra Jahn was born in 1927 at the moment when youthful challenges to the dictatorship of Juan Vicente Gómez (1908–35) indicated that the "autumn of the patriarch" had begun in Venezuela. Yet traditional cultural values lingered longer than did the caudillo system and filled the emerging modern political and economic system with contradictions. Women's roles and attitudes illustrate the tensions inherent in a system undergoing rapid political change. Women accepted jobs outside the home and responsibilities in the nascent political parties. The new political generations lauded women's political and economic participation without fully recognizing the challenge that it brought to the lingering cultural definitions of honor and *vergüenza*.

Hispanic custom dictated that a family's honor was intertwined with the chastity of its women. Legal codes granted the father of the family, or its oldest male, the exclusive right to guide and protect his family. If he attacked or killed another male who threatened his family, the law usually exonerated him. In particular, the patriarch of the family could not overlook the affront if another male had sexual relations with any of the women—his wife, sister, daughters—under his protection. The offense was compounded if others knew of the slip and ridiculed the man who had been unable to defend his family. Even though the suggestion of a woman's sexual activity shamed the entire family, women played an essentially passive role in the honor-*vergüenza* drama. Women, traditionally and legally considered weak, depended on male family members to protect them and their family's honor. What was to become of this network of traditions when women left the shelter of the family patio for the business office?

The beginning of commercial oil exploitation in Venezuela in the 1920s affected the nation and women's lives in unanticipated ways. The foreign companies, and the service economy they spawned, required a host of literate Venezuelan white-collar and clerical workers. Increased government revenues also supported the expansion of the Venezuelan government bureaucracy, especially after 1936 when the government put in place a minimal system of social services. Women became nurses for the oil camp hospitals, secretaries, receptionists, and file clerks for the foreign companies and the new government offices, office workers for the burgeoning group of lawyers and other professionals who dealt with the companies, teachers for the schools in the camps and elsewhere, and clerks in the new commercial establishments which sprang up in the cities. Venezuelans did not immediately recognize the implications of these changes, but there came to be a small space in female society between the idle and respectable—and bored—upper-class women and their poorer sisters who enjoyed neither the luxury of male protection nor the social accolade of honor as they labored in fields, kitchens, bars, and bedrooms. Subtly, the changes in the labor market would challenge the rather Manichaean way of viewing women as virgins or whores. Was a woman from a respectable family less respectable if she worked in public with men? Should she follow the behavior patterns and values of the sheltered upper-class or those of the less sheltered, more independent working-class women?

Like most children, Ligia Parra Jahn was oblivious to such weighty issues as she grew up in the 1930s. She lived near the colonial core of Caracas (population of 264,400 in 1936) and close to the Pantheon, the monument that sheltered the remains of Simón Bolívar and of other national heroes. The modest middle-class neighborhood evoked the sleepy past of the "City of the Red Roofs." It also lay near the new commercial and government offices that the petroleum wealth had spawned.

Ligia adored active games and romping about the neighboring plazas, but she also absorbed the Hispanic traditions of her neighborhood. She especially liked baseball and was one of the few girls who played the game with the neighborhood boys. She attended Amelia Cocking primary school for girls, where she organized a basketball team and played enthusiastically. She also enjoyed bicycling. Even her youthful dreams turned around becoming a sports star, and she fantasized about sports where few women had achieved fame. The ritual drama of bullfighting drew her even more than the methodical game of baseball. Her imagination had been fired by seeing the famous bullfighter, Conchita Cintrón, and Ligia pleaded to be allowed to take lessons. Her indulgent parents engaged the matador, Mario Núñez, who lived nearby, to tutor her, and she practiced faithfully on the flat roof of her house. Núñez later told a journalist that Ligia had shown promise as a bullfighter, but he must also have cautioned the young girl that the fraternity of *matadores* did not welcome women.

Ligia's love of activity and sports, and her fantasies, continued into her teens. If she had dreamed of a rather traditional Hispanic hero's career—that of bullfighter—she also turned her eyes to some of the newest heroes: airplane pilots. She knew of Amelia Earhart's exploits and determined to become the first woman pilot in Venezuela. The small Venezuelan air force had a training school in the nearby town of Maracay. One day, Ligia set out for Maracay to enlist in the school. On the way, she called home to tell her parents what she was about to do. Her father remonstrated that aviation was not a good career for a *hija de familia* (daughter of good family), for there would be no one to protect her. Señor Parra convinced Ligia that she should return home and prepare for an occupation more suitable to her gender and family position.

Denied the most active and iconoclastic of her fantasies, Ligia still insisted that she could not accept the boring and sheltered life of most middle- and upper-class young women. She dreamed of becoming a writer or a poet or an artist. Perhaps she thought of the romantic life of Venezuelan novelist Teresa de la Parra, who had lived in Paris and Madrid from 1923 until her death from tuberculosis in 1936. Ligia enrolled in painting and sculpture courses at the Escuela de Artes Plastícos, but, more pragmatically, she also completed a secretarial course at one of the new business academies that had sprung up in Caracas. In 1947, at age nineteen, Ligia became one of the first secretaries of the dental division of the Social Security office. Her job had not existed a decade earlier, for there had been no social security system or state health care in Venezuela until after Gómez's death. Her parents were not enthusiastic about her job, but they may have decided that headstrong Ligia was better off as an office worker than as a bullfighter or an aviator. At least she still lived at home where her parents could protect her. While employed, Ligia enrolled in night school to work toward a high-school diploma, a mildly unusual ambition in a country in which only 16 percent of the high-school graduates were women. By 1948 she had successfully completed two years of high school.

Ligia's training and education set her apart from many of her contemporaries. She also could have confidently applied for any job that required that the employee be *de buena presencia* (attractive). Ligia was a striking blonde, fair skinned and slender, a younger edition of Evita Perón, who was then the First Lady of Argentina. Ligia enjoyed buying new clothes with her earnings, and photographs of her in 1948 show a stylishly dressed and attractive young woman.

After a few months, Ligia left her job with the Social Security office and began to work at a wholesale drug firm owned by Pedro Penzini Hernández. She liked the job and her coworkers, and, by all accounts, she was a capable and responsible employee. Ligia still enjoyed being active, and she balanced the sedentary life of her clerical job by exercising at a Swedish gymnasium on Saturdays.

Although iconoclastic and restless in some ways, Ligia apparently paid little attention to the swirl of political activity about her. A joint military and civilian conspiracy had unseated General and President Isaías Medina Angarita on October 18, 1945. A civilian government headed by Rómulo Betancourt initiated the three years of unprecedented democratic government known as the *trienio*. Ligia's parents were not politically active, and perhaps they suggested to her, as some parents did, that attendance at political rallies and night meetings could compromise a young girl's reputation.

Women had played a larger role in politics since Gómez's death, both in women's organizations and newly legalized political parties, especially Acción Democrática (AD) and the Partido Comunista de Venezuela (PCV). President Isaías Medina Angarita (1941–45) had allowed women to vote in municipal elections in 1945, and the *trienio* government decreed that women could vote for and hold office as delegates to the 1946 constituent assembly. Sixteen women won seats in the assembly. The new constitution, promulgated in 1947, granted the right of suffrage to all Venezuelans over the age of eighteen. Many women activists considered that their goals had been achieved with suffrage, and several women's groups dissolved. Other women, such as journalist and activist Carmen Clemente Travieso, complained that more important issues of women's economic and civil rights still needed to be addressed.

The male leadership of the two major political parties, AD and the PCV, paid little heed to their women colleagues' tentative proposals to revise the civil and penal codes. Constituent delegates Mercedes Carvajal de Arocha (who wrote under the pen name Lucila Palacios), Panchita Soublette, and Mercedes Fermín, among others, had argued that the state, through a modern constitution and legal codes, should guarantee the civil and social rights of women and children. No longer should women have to rely on the goodwill and wisdom of the family patriarch for protection. When the female delegates offered specific resolutions to transfer to the state the protection of women's rights, their male colleagues sometimes refused even to second or to debate the proposals. More extreme proposals for economic equity also failed: equal pay for equal work, workplace protections for women workers, an eight-hour working day for women domestic servants, day-care centers in factories where women workers could nurse their babies, rural women's rights to the land they worked, and social security for women. In spite of the government's commitment to investment in Venezuela's human resources, none of these proposals received serious consideration. Journalist Elba Isabel Arráiz concluded that women also contributed to the social climate that blinded the legislators to the dangers of patriarchical control:

> I believe that, in the depth of our souls, we all feel a kind of respectful veneration for the strong man, for the man who dictates the life of all the members of his family and demands that his decisions be respected. We have been brought up that way and most of us have not even thought of rebelling against that imposition.

Some of the female representatives to the constituent assembly also pondered ambiguities of social attitudes toward women. A lawyer with a doctorate in political science, Panchita Soublette Saluzzo, could debate a male colleague in the constituent assembly, but propriety dictated that she could not attend a dance alone with that same colleague. Communist Inés Labrador de Lara could go with fellow party member Gustavo Machado to Caracas jails to gather information about the treatment of prisoners, but she could not eat alone with him in a restaurant without being criticized and embarrassed. Obviously, more than legal codes affected women's behavior in this era of uneasy coexistence between modern and traditional values.

While well-educated and elite women struggled with the issues raised by a patriarchical legal and social system, some simpler women sought autonomy in more traditional ways. *El Nacional* reported the case of María Cristina Arguinzones, whose lover, José Angel Aponte, had left her when he got a good job in the nearby town of Los Teques. Angered and hurt by the abandonment, María Cristina prepared a spell in which she lit a candle, which had been stuck full of pins doused in sugar, in front of José's picture and next to one of his old shoes and some of her underwear. The spell was designed to compel José to return. José's mother, Julia, concerned about her son and his new job, denounced the young woman to the Jefe Civil. The authorities detained María Cristina for practicing witchcraft. Despite her detention, María Cristina must have had the satisfaction of knowing that she had not simply resigned herself to José's abandonment.

Meanwhile, Ligia Parra Jahn had discovered men. In spite of her attractiveness, she had had no *novios*, or boyfriends, before she went to work for Dr. Penzini in 1947. There she met the twenty-five-year-old José María—or Joseba, as he was called—Olasagasti, an accountant who worked in the same firm. Joseba was a Basque who had fought with Francisco Franco's Legión Blanca in Spain and had come to Venezuela in early 1947. Joseba became a well-known and popular member of the Basque community in Caracas, in part because of his skills at the game of jai alai. Charming, attractive, ambitious, foreign, athletic, Joseba attracted women easily, and Ligia was smitten.

The courtship of Ligia and Joseba followed the still traditional patterns of old Caracas. As members of the respectable middle class, Ligia and her family guarded her reputation and family honor as carefully as the more prominent political women of the constituent assembly did theirs. Ligia might have railed at some of the restrictions, but she too realized that eligible bachelors valued propriety—and virginity—highly for their wives, if not for their mistresses. For all of her heroic youthful fantasies, Ligia also dreamed of a happy marriage and children.

Ligia and Joseba saw each other at Dr. Penzini's shop, but they did not go out together alone. Caracas bustled with new nightclubs and excitement in the years following the war, but respectable people considered such "boîtes" as little more than covers for prostitution, as indeed many were. A couple might attend a movie, usually accompanied by family or friends. Most entertainment still revolved around the home and family.

It is worth stressing, however, how small a sector of the Venezuelan population actively shared, or lived by, many of the Parra Jahn family's notions of honor and shame with respect to sexual matters. Venezuela had not had the opulent colonial past that could have spawned a large number of elite families. Economic insecurity, civil wars, and disease conspired to keep the population small, poor, and scattered in the nineteenth century. Changes wrought by oil income, which had come in since the 1920s, and by the rush of foreigners, both those with the oil companies and the immigrants who followed World War II, further encouraged shifts and changes in the economic landscape. A father-patriarch who could not support an extended family often gave way to a household headed by a woman, at least for part of the year. Insecurity of life and income, and the comparatively weak hold of the Catholic Church, meant that relatively few unions were consecrated by matrimony, either ecclesiastical or civil. The case of María Cristina, the spell-caster, is illustrative; when her lover found a better job in a nearby town, he left her. The job may have been better than his Caracas one but perhaps not secure enough to support a family. In the 1940s over half of all births were illegitimate.

Thus, the old values of honor and shame with respect to sexual purity had eroded considerably by 1948. Indeed, some would argue that they always had reflected the ideal more than the reality in Latin America. Only those families who had social status to preserve—or those who wished to climb up the social scale—could afford the luxury of protecting their women and family honor. Ligia Parra Jahn's virtue and attractiveness might improve her family's status through a successful match with a wealthier or more prominent family. In any case, public possession of honor would ensure that she would at least marry, unlike the less fortunate women who had no family to protect them or who had to work in more compromising situations.

Felipe Parra Barrios initially opposed Joseba's courtship of his daughter. Joseba was a worldly foreigner with no real roots in Caracas. Moreover, many Venezuelans retained a residual resentment of Basques dating from the eighteenth century when a Basque mercantile company had had a monopoly of Venezuelan trade; the Basque traders and governors had prompted hatred and rebellion because of their high-handedness and arrogance. The post-World War II flood of European immigrants in general also met with mixed reactions from Venezuelans.

Headstrong as always, Ligia pleaded for Joseba to be allowed to visit her. In August 1947, Sr. Parra allowed his reservations to be overcome and told Joseba that he was welcome as a guest in the Parra home. The paternal permission was tantamount to accepting him as a prospective son-in-law, a status of "engaged to be engaged." Ligia was radiant, forgetting all of her earlier heroic ambitions in favor of the more traditional one of marriage to the man she loved. Having won his case, Joseba probably paid little heed to Sr. Parra Barrios's admonition, "Be careful what you do in my home. . . . Be careful!"

After a few months, Joseba became restless, and he stopped visiting Ligia. She became despondent and depressed, causing her parents and friends to ask what was wrong. She finally confessed to her parents that Joseba had told her that he would not see her anymore, that his father opposed his getting married. More seriously, Ligia told her parents that she and Joseba had had sexual relations. Ligia's parents acted promptly, consulted a lawyer, and threatened Joseba that they would take legal action if he did not keep the pledge that had been implicit—but public—in his frequent visits to the Parra Jahn home. Cornered by Ligia's parents, Joseba returned and formalized his engagement to Ligia before parish officials. The lovers also exchanged rings. Ligia and her family accepted the young Basque back into the home, perhaps judging that he had just gotten nervous at the thought of marriage. In any case, Ligia's reputation and honor were safe if she married Joseba. Ligia even agreed to give up her job at the Penzini firm when Joseba said he did not want his future wife to continue working.

Joseba's promises and concern proved short-lived. In mid-July 1948, Joseba wrote Ligia:

> I have to confess to you that I have been acting out a role before your father. . . . I love you, that is true, but not enough to marry you. You deserve a better partner than I. It is best that you forget me. Forget me! I will not marry you now or ever.

Ligia did not tell her parents or her lawyer about Joseba's new treachery. She devised her own plan to try to save her honor and perhaps the man she loved. She wrote Joseba that she thought that she was pregnant. Desperately, she begged him in the name of their child to marry her just for a few days in a civil ceremony. She would release him later. If he would not, she told him that she was considering suicide, since life without honor would hold no future for her.

His veneer of patience and chivalry worn thin, Joseba wrote back that he had decided to break off with her definitively. Rubbing salt in her emotional wounds, he added that he did not care if she was the most disgraced, unhappy woman on earth.

Ligia heard rumors that Joseba was courting other women. He also gossiped with his friends about her. In the relatively small Caracas middle class, and with Joseba's prominence as a jai alai player, Ligia's reputation would be ruined. She was not only rejected but also humiliated by a man who had used her, thrown her aside, and then laughed about her to his friends. Joseba's father, who was also in Caracas, had referred to Ligia as a *mulata* and said that his son must marry someone of his own "race."

Ligia waited. Did she hope that Joseba would repent and return to her? Was she deciding whether again to ask her parents to have the lawyer threaten Joseba? Or was she simply hoping that her menstrual period would start and at least she would not have to suffer through a pregnancy? When she went to a clinic on August 4 for a pregnancy test, she was so nervous that a nurse prescribed a tranquilizer for her. Ligia had received a number of anonymous phone calls telling her about Joseba's activities. The one she received on Thursday, August 5, was different. The male voice taunted Ligia with the news that she would never win Joseba. He had booked passage back to Spain and would leave Venezuela in a few days. Then, humiliation again, the voice gave a loud laugh and hung up. The phone call ended Ligia's hope and her indecision. Recalling the moment later, she said that she had thought of a sports metaphor: "A player who risks nothing, neither wins nor loses."

The next day, Friday morning, Ligia dressed carefully in a gray cashmere suit with red trim, put on matching red shoes, picked up her red purse, and told her parents that she was going to visit a friend. She went to Penzini's office and entered to chat with some of her former colleagues at 9:15 A.M. Joseba was in an inner office with Dr. Penzini. He came to the outer office to fetch something, and Ligia greeted him. He didn't speak to her, only shrugging his shoulders disparagingly as he returned to Penzini's office. Ligia entered the inner office and nodded to Dr. Penzini. She stopped about six feet away from Joseba, drew a Smith and Wesson revolver from an inner pocket of her jacket, and shot Joseba twice before he had a chance to move. The bullets entered Joseba's neck and chest, and he died an hour and a half later at the Córdoba Clinic.

Ligia calmly walked out of the inner office, revolver in hand, and headed toward the street. When Adrian Urarte, a colleague of Joseba's, tried to take the revolver from her, she fired two more shots, which buzzed harmlessly about the office. Penzini's stupefied staff let her leave the building. The poised young blonde hailed a cab and told the driver to take her to the police station, for she had just killed a man.

The cab driver obediently drove her to the police station where she gave herself up. Her father and brother then met her at the judge's chambers where she rendered her first official statement. Her father asked her, "Ligia, why didn't you leave that job to me?" Ligia replied, "You are old and my mother needs you." She had not called on her brother to avenge her honor, because his career would have been ruined if he had had to go to jail. After all of her suffering and disgrace, Ligia said, going to jail meant nothing to her.

Word traveled quickly in Caracas, and Ligia faced a crowd of over one thousand curious *caraqueños* when she left Dr. Jesús Enrique González's courtroom at one o'clock. Dr. Panchita Soublette Saluzzo was in the crowd and one of the first to shake Ligia's hand and offer her sympathy.

The following day, Ligia again was closeted with judges and lawyers for seven hours to explain her actions. Ligia told the authorities that her love for Joseba had turned to hatred when she had been humiliated and taunted so publicly. She realized that her future was bleak, that Joseba had ruined her chances for a happy marriage and family. Only his death could compensate for the dishonor she had suffered. She concluded, "And let it be known that women too know how to defend their honor."

Ligia provided several challenges to the Venezuelan penal system. The most immediate dilemma was where to detain her during the long trial process. There was no jail for women, and only recently had the first female warden been

appointed to supervise and discipline female prisoners. Ironically, the warden, twenty-one-year-old Delia Alemán, had
been a school chum of Ligia's. Delia allowed Ligia to stay in
her own apartment at the Cárcel Modelo (Model Jail).

Journalists avidly followed the sensational case and were
fascinated by Ligia's apparent serenity and lack of tears. With
her brother and sister and the warden and another friend,
Ligia received reporters in the warden's office on August 7.
She told the press that she had lived a happy and tranquil
life until Joseba had publicly humiliated her, her family, and
even the authorities before whom he had promised to marry
her.

> What hope do I have now? To marry immediately, or never
> to marry. I had always dreamed of what all women dream
> of: a man to love me, an upright and virtuous home, chil-
> dren. If I had not dreamed so much of this, I believe that I
> would never have done what I did . . . but I was a dead
> woman morally. At least, that's how I felt.

Reporters, and Venezuelans, disagreed on what the real
crime had been, who had committed it, who should be punished, and how. Part of the ambiguity lay with the
seventy-six-year-old penal code, which retained much of the
Mediterranean interpretation of honor and the patriarchical
value system. A man who killed in order to defend, or repair,
his own or his family's honor explicitly was exempted from
punishment. The traditional code, however, did not recognize that a woman had honor that she could avenge on her
own. Could Ligia, then, legitimately plead self-defense, or
defense of her honor, as an extenuating circumstance?

Strict constructionists and traditionalists said that Ligia
had shamed herself and her family by surrendering herself
sexually to Joseba. She then compounded her offense by killing Joseba, in effect punishing him for her own weakness.
The prosecuting attorney presented the strongest statement
of the traditional argument. Poet and essayist Rafael
Olivares Figueroa elaborated on the value of women's chastity when he wrote in *El País* that society had a responsibility to promulgate traditional moral and sexual education.
Satisfaction of all desires did not bring happiness, he argued, especially for women. If women were allowed excessive sexual freedom, he believed that home and children
would suffer. Those who had slipped, like single mothers,
needed special guidance and rehabilitation.

In contrast, Ligia's defenders compared her to Joan of Arc and quoted from the seventeenth-century Mexican poet, Sor Juana Inés de la Cruz. "Hombres necios, que acusáis a la mujer sin razón, sin ver que sois la ocasión de lo mismo que culpáis." ("Ignorant men, who accuse woman unjustly, without seeing that you are the cause of the crime that you reproach her for.") They argued that the penal code had not kept up with women's changing roles in society. Women journalists such as Juana de Avila, Teresa Troconis, Peregrino Pérez, Isabel Jiménez Arráiz de Díaz, and Ana Mercedes Pérez made the case that Ligia had been forced to act because the judicial system provided no protection for her. Women no longer remained at home where male relatives could defend them. The state should take on the patriarchical role and enact severe penalties for the breach of a prenuptial contract. Juana de Avila argued that the tribunals did not recognize male sexual irresponsibility as a crime, even when a respectable woman had been publicly disgraced. Ligia Parra Jahn had taken justice into her own hands to punish a crime that men committed with impunity against women every day.

Isabel Jiménez Arráiz de Díaz added that Joseba had acted as if he had thought that a feudal, colonial right of conquest still existed. Ligia's action was especially justified against a foreigner who had abused Venezuelan hospitality. If men could defend their honor, then why couldn't women?

Teresa Troconis gave a popular reason for the state to intervene to protect women from Don Juans—at least until men became accustomed enough to the new social rules so that they could restrain themselves. She wrote:

> The feminine soul is made of passion; woman more than man lives for love; love is both an end and a means, since through it she achieves the realization of her destiny: motherhood. Thus, woman puts all in love, her heart, her honor and her courage. To deceive her when she has wholly given herself destroys all her strength, all her moral aspirations and all her emotional balance.

Male jurist Luis Cova García agreed that the legal system must give special consideration to women's nature. "In women to think and to feel are two inseparable actions, a thing which does not occur in men." Women's biological role so affects their psychology and their will that they should not be held fully accountable for crimes they commit. Women can vote, hold public offices, enter the liberal professions, compete with men, but their social salvation still is in love and marriage.

Juana de Avila touched another chord when she asserted that many women saw Ligia as an avenging angel, a symbol of "just vengeance which has collected for all the pain and suffering that thousands of women have had to endure for their whole lives." Spokespersons for women's associations expressed a kinship with Ligia. Sra. Caridad de Novel, president of the Asociación Venezolana de Mujeres, said, "As a woman . . . it is my duty to be on the side of Ligia Parra Jahn, through a natural sense of fellowship not only feminine, but eminently human." Ana Senior de Delgado, of the Agrupación Cultural Femenina, said that she did not condone violence, but she thought that Ligia's action was a natural consequence of the omissions in the legal codes with regard to the rights of women. She hoped that the legislators would be encouraged to pass laws that are "more just and humane for those eternal social slaves that we women are."

Ligia's defense attorney, Dr. Juan Antonio Gonzalo Patrizi, in Ligia's October 13 court audience, confirmed some of the women's arguments when he said that he was acting not only for Ligia but also for all women. Ligia symbolized women who found that man-made laws did not aid them and those who had cried in silence or turned to prostitution when they had been dishonored by a man.

A few perceptive observers found the real root of the tragedy beyond the penal code, men's perfidy, or women's weakness. Cultural traditions and values, often nurtured by gossip, limited modern women as much as the laws did. Juana de Avila concluded that society must bear some of the responsibility. Society had instituted marriage for women's protection, and a woman who engaged in sex prior to marriage might be guilty of foolishly stepping beyond the boundaries of a shelter that was provided for her. But the same society that admired a man who had an active sex life punished a woman for her entire life for the same behavior. Why should it be a crime for a woman to give herself for love or to have a child without a father? Teresa Troconis agreed. Society, as well as the law, retained anachronistic whiffs of the past. Single mothers frequently could not even secure respectable jobs. Troconis pointed out that Ligia had killed Joseba not because he had left her but because he had left her in an unbearable social position. Avila and Troconis suggested that all those who ostracized single mothers bore some responsibility for actions like Ligia's.

While the debate continued about her, Ligia's body betrayed the surface calm with which she had handled the affair. She took tranquilizers to ward off nervous depression and to be able to sleep. Some of Joseba's Basque friends heightened her anguish. On August 8 an anonymous telephone call to the jail threatened, "You know that you have caused the death of a Basque and there are several of us who are ready to avenge his death. You will die to pay for your crime." Friends had told her brother Luis that they had heard of various people who had sworn to punish Ligia for her action. Her health continued to deteriorate during the long trial, especially when she had been moved from the relative comfort of the warden's apartment to a small, dark, and cold cell far in the back of the Cárcel Modelo. Her pregnancy had either been a false alarm, or her nervous state and poor health caused a miscarriage.

A hearing on October 13 established the defense arguments that Ligia had acted in self-defense to save her honor and thus should not be penalized. The prosecuting attorney rejected the plea of self-defense and asked for a five-to-six-year sentence. Lengthy court proceedings were normal, but the November 24 military revolt that terminated the democratic government may have been bad luck for Ligia. Her defenders had been more closely identified with the democratic opening than with the old caudillo system. The military junta headed by Carlos Delgado Chalbaud hardly represented a return to the caudillo past, but they did have more sympathy with the authoritarian and patriarchical codes. They quickly outlawed political parties and labor unions. In April 1949 they reestablished relations with Spain, not a good omen for a person charged with killing a Spaniard.

In January 1949, Ligia's defense attorney tested the waters. He asked the president of the junta to allow Ligia to transfer to a hospital or some similar institution, under full security. The penal code allowed such treatment for women prisoners who had already been sentenced. Since Ligia had not even been sentenced—and, of course, ultimately would be absolved because her action had been in defense of honor— she should be allowed to leave the Cárcel Modelo, not a good environment for a refined young woman.

Delgado Chalbaud turned a deaf ear to Ligia's plea, and she remained in jail while the process dragged on. Her lawyer died, and she secured a new one. On November 13, 1950, some thugs kidnapped and murdered Delgado Chalbaud. Marcos Pérez Jiménez became the obvious strong man, although he refrained from having himself named president. The political climate became more oppressive.

Two weeks after Delgado's assassination, the judge finally handed down Ligia's sentence. Reporters and an interested public packed the courtroom on November 30 to hear the judge read the sentence for two and one-half hours. Ana Mercedes Pérez heard gasps of disbelief when Ligia was sentenced to seven and one-half years in jail. The two years, three months, and twenty-four days that the trial had lasted would be subtracted from the sentence. The judge reasoned that Joseba had done nothing more serious than break a prenuptial contract, a privilege that a person might take with any contract. Joseba's friends had testified that he was not sexually promiscuous. On the other hand, Ligia could not argue that Joseba had publicly shamed her; she had been the one to confess their relations when she had hired the first lawyer to force Joseba to honor his pledge. Ligia's plea of self-defense had no basis in law.

Ana Mercedes Pérez began lobbying in earnest to have the young woman released. In 1951, Pérez published an account of Ligia's tragedy entitled *Yo acuso a un muerto*. The book was a commercial success, but it also brought the journalist some hate mail and threats, especially from Basques and Spaniards. She followed up her first book with a second one, dedicated to Ligia's parents, which annotated and commented on Judge Monsalve's sentence. She hoped that her book might have some effect on any appeals. Pérez concluded that Judge Monsalve had "acted in favor of those of his own sex" and that he did Venezuela a great disservice to rule that, in effect, it did not matter if men did not keep their word.

The appeals fell on deaf ears until December 1952 when Ligia's sentence was reduced. She was allowed to leave jail after having served four years and four months of her sentence. She dropped from sight after her time in the limelight. Newspapers devoted only a few lines to her quiet marriage to José Rafael Alfaro Ucero on March 21, 1953.

Venezuelans, however, did not forget Ligia Parra Jahn. In 1984 the Venezuelan essayist and playwright Elisa Lerner published "The Dangerous Criminality of Blondes." Lerner compared Ligia with the blonde Hollywood vamps of the 1940s or the gun molls in a Raymond Chandler novel, but with a Hispanic twist:

> The love story of the blonde Venezuelan girl was depressing. When she killed the boyfriend who had *dishonored her*—throughout masculine centuries the term has been used: female virginity was a sealed trunk that only the respectable key of matrimony could open—and had promised her eternal love (read: *legal love*), in part, she was killing herself.

Lerner continued, stating that "any society where blondes emerge sets in motion ill-omened threads of catastrophe. . . . Blonde hair—cooked up at the mischievous hairdresser's—in essence, is a strong warning that a country is going through an ambiguous or agonizing time."

SOURCES

For material directly pertaining to Ligia Parra Jahn, see two books by the journalist Ana Mercedes Pérez: *Yo acuso a un muerto* (Caracas, 1951) and *La sentencia "Ligia Parra Jahn"* (Caracas, 1951). Elisa Lerner's "La criminal peligrosidad de las rubias," in *Crónicas ginecológicas* (Caracas, 1984), is an evocative essay by a contemporary Venezuelan feminist. The newspaper *El Nacional* followed the Parra Jahn case closely in late 1948 and also devoted considerable attention to women's issues during the *trienio*. Other newspapers, such as *El Universal*, *El País*, *La Esfera*, *Ultimas Noticias*, and *Tribuna Popular*, also covered the Parra Jahn case. The more conservative papers, such as *El Universal*, gave minimal, rather matter-of-fact coverage to the case, whereas the papers with more leftist sympathies (the Communist *Tribuna Popular*, *El Nacional*, the Acción Democrática's *El País*) covered the case extensively and openly sided with the young woman.

J. G. Peristiany and others discuss the concepts of honor and shame in J. G. Peristiany, ed., *Honour and Shame: The Values of Mediterranean Society* (London, 1966); and José Ramón López Gómez's *El culto a la virginidad* (Valencia, Venezuela, 1984) explores historical attitudes toward virginity.

Two novels by Venezuelan authors are useful for catching a glimpse of the lives of Venezuelan women: Teresa de la

Parra, *Ifigenia: Diario de una señorita que escribió porque se fastidiaba* (originally published in 1924); and Antonia Palacios, *Ana Isabel, una niña decente* (originally published in 1949).

VI

Contemporary Generations, 1959 to the Present

Fidel Castro and his bearded rebels ushered in a new era in Latin America when they won power in Cuba on January 1, 1959. They brought hope for social justice, political participation, and economic opportunity to the downtrodden, the disinherited, and the poor across the hemisphere. "Revolution" was on the lips of nearly everyone, either in anticipation or in fear of it. As the Cubans and, in particular, Che Guevara began to export revolution to rural backlands of the region, the U.S. government and entrenched regimes initiated countermovements. The Kennedy administration tried at first to smash the Havana government with the Bay of Pigs invasion and then to undermine its appeal with programs of social and economic reform through the Alliance for Progress.

The United States attempted to eliminate the Cuban appeal and the revolutionary conditions throughout Latin America by supplying financial, technical, and military assistance. The step forward by the U.S. government was its recognition that major social changes were necessary in the region. This change led to political support for "preferred social revolutions" in Mexico and Bolivia and tremendous aid to "showcase programs of social change" in Chile during the administration of Eduardo Frei as well as in Colombia and Brazil.

Both Cuban and U.S. programs—the export of revolution and the Alliance for Progress—to influence Latin America had largely run their course with the death of Che in Bolivia in 1967 and the escalation of the war in Vietnam, which was demanding more of Washington's attention. An exception was the 1970 election in Chile, in which voters chose Marxist candidate Salvador Allende. Elsewhere, Latin America entered the bloody phase of urban guerrillas (known as the second wave) who resorted to indiscriminate violence, kidnappings, and assassinations, and of the reaction from official government death squads in what they termed the Dirty War. With a wave of armed takeovers, military governments determined to eliminate—to "disappear"—all radicals, sympathizers, and dissidents. In this brutal, disgraceful period, it was the mothers and wives of the disappeared who challenged authorities throughout the region (Chapter 14). In their efforts, these courageous women found support from within the Catholic Church, particularly from those persons associated with the liberation theology movement and from those lay people who had developed Christian base communities (Chapter 15).

The revolutionary movement, despite the guerrilla terrorism and military-inspired murders, continued primarily in Central America. It found expression in the success of the Sandinistas, who seized power in Nicaragua (Chapter 16). Against overwhelming international opposition, Daniel Ortega and the revolutionaries built a regime in Managua that worked toward an equitable social and economic society despite a Washington-supported invasion from Honduras by the so-called Contras.

Starting in the 1980s, a new period of democratization or at least demilitarization of national governments began. Often these new governments introduced neoliberal economic policies, slashing spending on national services, even education, and shifting responsibility for many federal programs to the public sector. These neoliberal policies to some extent reflected the economic austerity demands of the World Bank and the Inter-American Bank as prerequisites for financial assistance. In other cases, they represented domestic efforts to reduce the authority of the central government and restore initiative to the local municipal ones. The results are too recent to be assessed objectively. Nevertheless, the twists and turns of hemispheric developments have caused shifts in local governments such as in Nicaragua, and the meaning of these programs—their effects and consequences—can best be seen in the lives of individuals such as Leticia.

The end of the Cold War and the collapse of the Soviet Union and Communist Eastern Europe have brought changes to most of the Western Hemisphere. Castro, however, still remains in power in Cuba. The U.S. government, for its part, has shifted its primary concern in Latin America from anticommunism to antidrug wars with little success, while contributing to social and economic dislocation. Meanwhile, as the followers of *subcomandante* Marcos of the Zapatista Liberation Army in Chiapas, Mexico, so clearly express, Latin Americans as individuals—Mexicans, Paraguayans, Bolivians, Dominicans, and all the others—insist on not simply sequaciously responding to great movements, macroeconomics, or international politics but also on taking action to make life better for themselves and their community.

14

Irma Muller

Marjorie Agosin
Edited and Translated by Nina M. Scott

The horror of the ordinary and the unexplained characterizes the chilling repression of society by Chile's military regime. The simple, terrible act of making someone disappear without elaborate, ghastly techniques or Nazi-inspired pogroms—just an abrupt, complete disappearance of someone from everyday life—numbs the sensibilities. This strategy of terrorism was adopted by military regimes, beginning in 1966, in Guatemala, Brazil, Uruguay, and Argentina as well as in Chile during the so-called Dirty War against revolutionaries, Leftists, and even moderates. In fact, the military's death squads turned on anyone who was not a vigorous advocate of its authority. The Chilean military launched its war against revolutionaries in 1973 with the overthrow of the government of Marxist President Salvador Allende. The ruling junta and then its successor, General Augusto Pinochet, carried out a vicious program to eliminate Marxists, reformers, and moderates that continued until 1990. The scars of this era will endure on the nation's history.

In these paralyzing circumstances, women such as Irma Muller came forward. Mothers, grandmothers, wives, and sisters refused to be intimidated by repressive dictatorships. They were determined to learn the fate of their loved ones. Especially mothers challenged the silence of governments and made the technique of "disappearing" into not only a national but also an international issue. These mothers protested in the central plazas in the capitals of their nations where they became the symbols of resistance to military rule.*

Marjorie Agosin has published her volumes of poetry, including *Witches and Other Things*, both in Latin America and in the United States, where she is often called upon to give public readings of her poems. She also publishes extensively in the fields of literary criticism and women's studies. After visiting her native Santiago, Agosin described her reaction to Chile under the rule of General Augusto

---

*For the story of the Mothers' campaign against the military rulers in Argentina, see Marguerite Guzmán Bouvard, *Revolutionizing Motherhood: The Mothers of the Plaza de Mayo* (Wilmington, DE: Scholarly Resources, 1994).

Pinochet in *Wellesley Magazine* (Winter 1986). Currently, she teaches in the Spanish department at Wellesley College and continues to write poetry.

Nina Scott is a professor of Spanish at the University of Massachusetts. Her publications include criticism of both Latin American and peninsular literature and studies of women authors, including Sor Juana Inéz de la Cruz. A veteran of visiting professorships in Germany and Ecuador, Scott is a champion of the Fulbright exchange program. Recently, her research has been in the area of humor in literature.

INTRODUCTION

"To disappear is to vanish, to cease to be, to be lost forever." This is how Amnesty International defines this sinister invention, designed by repressive governments so that all opposition may cease to be, stop existing, or, better yet, so that those who are "missing" are swallowed up into the void of the inexplicable, the irrevocable, the uncertainty that someone has really been absolutely lost. To die is infinitely easier. Life comes to an end with the act of burial; there is a specific resting place for the remains of the loved one. However, for the relatives of those who have disappeared there is no one who knows where they are, in which prisons they have been tortured, and, above all, whether they are alive or dead.

When someone disappears, no one knows anything at all. There is only the indelible memory of the day on which that person disappeared, perhaps the street in which he or she was apprehended, the clothes worn. To disappear, then, becomes that inexplicable amalgam of the real—the act of vanishing—and the unreal. Where has that person gone?

In 1966 the term *desaparecidos* was used to describe a specific practice of the Guatemalan government; this practice has been applied on a massive scale in Chile from 1973 to 1990 and in Argentina from 1976 to 1982. According to the governments involved, their practice of making people disappear has been implemented to safeguard order in their respective countries. However, it seems difficult to believe that order can be maintained in a country by means of repression, violence, and torture.

The story of Irma Muller, the mother of a missing person in Chile, is perhaps among the most concrete examples of what it means to have a member of one's family disappear. Statistics are utterly unable to transmit such a message or to express the pain felt by a mother, a sister, or other relatives when they discover that from one day to the next a loved one has passed to that feared and inexplicable category of "missing person."

Irma Muller is a middle-aged, middle-class woman. Ironically, she lived just half a block from my home in Santiago, but we never met until many years later, after our lives had taken different paths and acquired significantly different meanings.

As she recounts in her testimony, Irma Muller's life was transformed from one day to the next when her only son and his fiancée disappeared. Ever since their relatives disappeared, Irma and other women in similar situations have never ceased to search in jails, concentration camps, and ministries. They have appealed to international organizations for any answer at all, yet up to this time the whereabouts of her son and of the others is as uncertain and as indefinite as the very term "missing person" itself.

I met Irma Muller in the early 1980s, when I was working for the Vicariate of Solidarity and was writing a book on the *arpilleras. Arpilleras* are a kind of small tapestry or wall hanging consisting of scraps of material appliquéd to a larger backing cloth made out of burlap; they are also a direct product of the problem of the missing persons and form a part of Irma's story.

In 1974, when all means of aid for the needy and all of the channels of the protection of human rights were cut off, the Catholic Church assumed a leadership role in creating an organization which, under its stewardship, would help the relatives, especially the wives, of missing persons. This is the Vicariate of Solidarity, an exemplary institution in the history of human rights in Chile. Through the Vicariate, the first *arpillera* workshops were organized in 1975.* The participants, who are known as *arpilleristas*, were given a chance to fight the specific economic problem of hunger as well as other problems of a sociopolitical nature. Spurred on by their desire to denounce the country's political situation, they began to create the tapestries whose small scraps of material speak of torture, of missing persons, of the lack of schools for children. The tapestries became internationally famous

*Bosnia refugee women in 1995 undertook a similar program knitting woolen goods. See Pamela J. Petro, "A Common Thread," *American Way Magazine* (October 15, 1995).

and were more eloquent than any statistics about the number of tortured or missing persons in General Pinochet's Chile.

I got to know Irma in one of the twenty-five *arpillerista* workshops that exist in the poor neighborhoods of Santiago. Within the totality of these workshops, she belongs to the one that is both the oldest and involved in one of the most noteworthy activities in authoritarian Chile, the Association of Relatives of Detained-Missing Persons (Agrupación de Familiares de Detenidos-Desaparecidos). Irma is one of the principal founders and a leader of this group, which was started in 1974 and the majority of whose members are women. Among the association's numerous activities, including specific demands for information on the whereabouts of the approximately ten thousand persons reported missing between 1973 and 1986, this group manufactures *arpilleras* in order to protest political oppression as well as help alleviate the sorrow that comes from the loss of a loved one.

Irma is a quiet woman, but when she tells her story an enormous silence ensues. She says that her own destiny is linked to that of the women in her group as well as to the women in the country as a whole. It is impressive to hear the certainty with which she says, "I will find a way and I will find my son because of it." She describes an *arpillera* she is making that shows a mother and a little boy running freely on a beach. This child is Irma's, but the image is also a metaphor in order to strengthen the morale and the spirit of solidarity within her group.

Most of all, one is impressed by her accounts of the many times when, in search of her loved ones, she went to the different prisoner detention centers. Even though she knew that torture and murder were the norm in these places, she makes it a point of maintaining, "I never let the jailers see me cry."

When one hears Irma speak to her companions, one understands immediately that no one is immune from the threat of exile, of torture, of also becoming a missing person. Because of the awareness of this constant threat, group solidarity is essential both for survival itself and for the ability to deal with the deep wounds caused by their latent grief.

In order to bear witness to her suffering, Irma Muller has dedicated herself for almost fourteen years to the production of *arpilleras*. She feels that her pain moves beyond individual boundaries when it is shared not only by the others who are engaged in making *arpilleras* but also by those who see and buy the finished tapestries and who imagine the life stories behind what is truly an art form born of resistance.

The group's activities are endless, ranging from constant letters to numerous international organizations to nonviolent protests held in the corridors of the legislature, on the plazas, or at the detention centers. Aside from these activities, Irma organizes handicraft classes for students who come from the disadvantaged sectors of the population; she is convinced that Chilean young people have been morally betrayed and emotionally crippled and need encouragement to reform their moral conscience. She maintains that, as grandmother to her daughter's children, it is her duty to tell them and show them what their country's history has been during the years of the dictatorship.

For about six years, during my trips to Chile, I have visited Irma Muller periodically and always find a smile and a kind voice. We sit and have tea, talk a great deal, and laugh together, but we always return to the same obsessive theme: the disappearance of her son and of so many others like him. I asked her to write an account in which she would relate what had happened, and, although it was exceedingly painful for her to re-create the horror of what she had been through, she agreed, saying, "Of course, I will do it because my story must be known and because silence is our worst enemy." This is her testimony.

After having lived for so many years under a dictatorship and having endured for almost all those years the disappearance of a loved one, one almost forgets how to write; so numerous are the thoughts of pain, anguish, rage, and impotence that the senses seem unable to do anything but to focus on all of that. I ask myself constantly, what can I do? How can I escape from the black well which is Chile? It seems that all I do is useless—as though one tries to keep a drop of water from slipping through one's fingers. I don't know where to begin to tell all that has happened to me since my son was arrested and made to disappear. I think there is not enough paper in the world to record what these years have been like.

My son Jorge was a movie cameraman. He studied at the School of Film at the Viña de Mar branch of the University of Chile and began to make films even before he finished his studies. He made documentaries about political events during the time of the Popular Unity government (Unidad Popular) of President Salvador Allende Gossens [1970–73]. In 1970 he toured various European countries to film the trip of the erstwhile minister, Clodomiro Almeyda. His work was steady even after the military coup. Early in 1974 he made his last picture, "In the Shadow of the Sun," in northern Chile. On November 28, 1974, this film premiered in the Las Condes Theater, in an exclusive neighborhood in Santiago. Even those in uniform attended. When I saw the film, I was so proud of what my son had done and said to my husband, "Jorge has a great future ahead of him," little realizing that [that] would be the last time we would see him. When the show was over, we met on the way out and he said, "I'm not coming home tonight because we're going to celebrate the film's success." We didn't ask him where he was going but later, when I began to look for him, we found out that the whole group had gone to the house of a woman friend of theirs and had stayed there all night. The next morning, when he and Carmen were going to Chile Film, that's when they were arrested. The same morning two men came to my home to ask where he was, and when I asked them who they were, they said friends from work; subsequently, I found out that they weren't colleagues at all, but that was a lot later, when I had gotten to know in general what types of men made the arrests—especially one of them who arrested many young people in those years and whose name is Romo . . . at this moment I can't remember his exact name, because it's as though part of me wants to blot him out of my mind, and on the other hand, I know how important it is not to forget him.

On November 29, 1974, when my son Jorge and Carmen should have gone to Chile Film and didn't get there, the office began to call and ask me where he was. I really didn't get too worried, because I spoke with a friend of his, and he told me that he thought that the whole group had gone to the beach, but in spite of that I had my doubts. Personally, I knew nothing about people who were detained; it was Jorge who always told me everything that went on. Actually, at times I didn't want to believe everything he told me. I thought that I had always been partial to the military, all the more so because I have two half-brothers who are retired *carabineros* [Chilean national police] with the rank of captain; back then I thought that if someone had detained Jorge just because he thought differently from them, surely that person would be tried because, after all, that's what the courts are there for. Besides, we're pretty well off economically, and I have a brother-in-law who is a high United Nations functionary in Chile, so I thought nothing serious would come of the whole thing. So many relatives thought and believed just as I did, because nothing like this had ever happened in Chile before.

When there was no doubt as to his arrest, a friend advised me to go to the Committee for Peace [Comité pro Paz] that had been in operation since the military coup of 1973, giving legal advice to those who had been arrested. From that instant on, this whole awful thing began. Every day I visited Los Alamos concentration camp, asking if he were being held there. Sometimes the guards said yes, he was there and could have visitors, and then when the time came to go into the camp they would tell me that he wasn't there, that he had never been arrested. Naturally, the camp was full of armed police; and whenever you got closer than you were allowed to, they'd put a rifle to your forehead as though they were going to shoot. In the camp, I was once able to speak with a lieutenant whose last name was Azbaleta; he was a military lieutenant, and I didn't find out his first name. This man made me think he was nice and said, I'll go in to ask if your son has been arrested; naturally, he came back with the answer that he wasn't there. I kept going to Los Alamos more or less half a year until July or August 1975, in the hopes that they might tell me where they had taken him.

I went to the office where they were supposed to give out information about people who had been arrested. I went every day to ask about my son. The four branches of the military were in this office, and you had to sign in and leave your identity card; afterwards they went through all this farce of going to look at some lists their superiors had and naturally always came back with the same answer. In this office they also had a social assistant called Raquel Lois, who, according to them, was there to help the women who were imprisoned get freed. There was also a soldier named Jorge Espinosa Ulloa, who at one point saw me and told me that my son had not been arrested, that perhaps he, like so many others, had left the country, and then, right in the midst of everything he was telling me, said, "The act justifies the means." How can I ever forget it? And when he was leaving, he held out his hand and I didn't know whether to take it or spit on it.

Another time I went to the Ministry of Defense. I already knew that the head of DINA [Directorate of National Investigations] was General Manuel Contreras Sepulveda, but the Contreras who appeared was very old and had absolutely nothing to do with DINA. Then he said, "I'm not the one you're looking for but go one floor down and ask to speak to General _____"; I can't remember his name right now, but I have it written down somewhere, because I remember very clearly what this general told me. After waiting for him a long time in a big lobby, I watched very attentively as military men went in and out; then they took me to a small room so I couldn't watch any more. Later on, this general comes, and I explain to him what I am looking for; then he says that he isn't from DINA but from the military secret service, which is for the military only. He asks my son's age, and I tell him that he's twenty-six. Whereon he says, why are you so worried? Seems like your kid's a mama's boy. Then I got furious and asked him if he had any sons and if he planned to classify them as mama's boys when they got older. I asked him what kind of a father he was that led him to think that children reached a point where they didn't need their parents any more. I spoke to him of the pain of the Virgin Mary when she saw her son crucified, and I know that morally I shamed him at that moment, but I got nowhere.

I sent letters to all the members of the junta, to any general who was in charge of anything at all. I got answers, but they were always the same ones: he has not been arrested by this ministry. I even sent a letter to that Lucía person [the wife of General Augusto Pinochet], appealing to her love as a mother, and the reply she sent me said, "Submit all details to the appropriate agencies," and that's all I ever heard. Afterwards, I got so angry and the hurt was so dreadful that I didn't want to write anymore, except abroad, letting them know everything that had happened. I wrote to the United Nations, to Amnesty International, and so forth; each time I got a reply which said that they had reported the particulars of the case history to Pinochet but had so far received no answer.

My husband is German, in spite of having lived in Chile for forty years now. He never wanted to change his citizenship and I never asked him to because, after all, a piece of paper doesn't make you a citizen. Because of this my son had the possibility of going to Germany if he wanted to. We went to the German Embassy to ask for a residence permit in Germany in the event that he might turn up again and they gave it to me, saying that he could reside there when he was freed. I think the embassy knew perfectly well that my son was imprisoned, but they didn't do anything either, just gave me the permit. Or did they already know the fate of the people who were detained or missing? I always wondered about that.

In 1976, Pinochet sent the case histories of the prisoners we were looking for to the United Nations. In these case histories it says that the one hundred fifty prisoners we were searching for had no legal status and were fictitious names. Jorge's name was on this list, and in light of this we went to the embassy and told them what monstrous things they were saying about these cases. Then the embassy sent a letter of inquiry to the Ministry of Foreign Affairs. They got a reply on letterhead stationery from the Ministry of Foreign Affairs and, among the other things they were answering for the embassy, [it] said that "because of an unfortunate error the name of Jorge Muller had been put on the list and they would check into it." The signature was a scrawl; nobody was responsible, and no one could be in any way identified. Those cowards, who from the beginning have hidden their evil faces!

The search for my son Jorge sent me on a road I never thought I would take. When I used to talk to my son, I always told him I was too old to begin to do new things. I wasn't even fifty years old then, and I thought that when you got to that stage in life you deserved a little peace and quiet and would wait for the grandchildren. Then he'd say to me, "Mama, at your age how can you possibly think you're too old to learn things? Look at Clotario Blest [founder of the Chilean labor movement in the 1930s]—he was already in his fifties." I had to go through my son's loss to realize that there's no age limit on being able to fight for something. Naturally, I wouldn't be able to go out and fire a gun, but, thank God, one has been given a brain and the ability to think in order to get things done. All the things I've accomplished these past years. . . . But I could never have just stayed home with my hands in my lap. The best memorial I can give my son is to take up his standard and fight, and in a way that's what I've done. I'm an active member of the Association of Relatives of Detained-Missing Persons and have been an officer in that same organization. I make *arpilleras* and use the embroideries as a method of denouncing the human-rights abuses, and this I've done practically from the moment my son disappeared. In the Committee for Peace, they taught us how to make *arpilleras*; they were always looking for ways to lessen the anguish we were living with. You could also do silk screening and knitting. As I said, for some women it was a means of easing their sorrow and for others, for those who were very hard up, it meant a way to earn a little money, because many of their menfolk were among the detained.

Another activity which helped me cope with my suffering has been teaching Chilean folk music, which I knew something about but never actually did anything with. In 1978, I was working in the eastern zone where the Vicariate of Solidarity had assigned us because we were from that area. I made contact with unemployed workers and their wives [who also made *arpilleras*] and with people from the slums who always come to the vicariate in search of solutions to many of their problems. Anyway, lots of people. Then I thought, why not make my knowledge of folk music available to them? People need so much to take their minds off their troubles in order to make them more bearable, and that goes as much for my own grief as for that of these good people. Many times I saw them faint with hunger and thought that perhaps it was sacrilege to put on something as festive as singing and dancing with all that was going on, but I gave myself the courage to do it. I spoke to a young man who is a very good musician so that he'd be in charge of the music and I of the rest, and that's how we got this group of regional music and dance from the area of Chiloé [a large island off the southern coast] going.

That was in August 1978, and in September we were already being asked to put on a show, and that's how it has continued until today, not only doing shows but also teaching youth groups in the villages. We've done all this alone, and it's been an uphill battle. This last year we got a contribution from a foreign organization that liked what we were doing, and the money allowed us to buy the instruments we needed. There's a great deal of solidarity in the group. We do shows in children's cafeterias, in villages, for striking syndicates, anywhere our presence is needed, only charging for transportation. The majority of the people who make up this group are unemployed, but their spirits are totally committed. Having gotten involved in this activity has been good for me in that it keeps me physically and morally strong to keep up the fight, because I know what happened to the people who were arrested and are missing.

The tasks of the association [Association of Relatives of Detained-Missing Persons] are numerous, for every day there is something to do. The morale of each and every relative is high, and everyone agrees that the fight must continue. We are constantly looking for ways to keep our cause alive, and for us the pressure that can be brought to bear from abroad by having them ask about our relatives is very important. We know that for Pinochet we are the crazy old women who stir things up, but he has no idea of the strength of spirit of each one of us. And this in spite of having been arrested, in spite of spending time in jail, as has happened to various of my companions; just recently one of the association's members was freed after having been under arrest for several months. Dictators may think that all this can frighten us, but they're totally wrong. They murder people who are supportive of our continual struggle and mean to frighten us as well, but what they don't realize is the groundswell of indignation that comes when people look at whose hands our poor country is in.

I am a believing Christian, and I pray that God will let me live a little longer, because I don't think I can die in peace if I don't know what has happened to my son. The years I have lived weigh on me as though they were millennia. I wrote a poem about it:

> My hair has gone white
> My eyes are tired and sad
> So many tears have flowed
> In these past years.
> I live in the question:
> Will I see him some day?
> I wait so anxiously—
> It *must* happen.

It goes on from there. I have written a few other things. Somehow, I never thought that pain could be a source of inspiration. I only write popular poetry, because I don't have the training to write any other kind. It's folk poetry and says things very simply.

What I have done until now I will continue to do in the same way, because I think it's the only way I will be able to hold on. Sometimes I get so tired and would like not to do anything, but then I reproach myself for this attitude, take a deep breath, square my shoulders, and say to myself, "Jorge expects you to do what he was unable to do"—and I shall, I shall.

Irma Silva de Muller
Santiago de Chile, April 1985

CONCLUSION

Chile has traditionally been one of the Latin American countries with a profoundly democratic heritage. In approximately one hundred fifty years the country had only one very brief period of dictatorship, under the government of Carlos Ibañez (1927–32). Aside from that, Chile has always been characterized by an influential middle class, something that is unusual in many other Latin American countries.

When Salvador Allende Gossens assumed the presidency in 1970, many Western nations, especially the United States, reacted with a mixture of admiration and astonishment to the fact that a Marxist could have been democratically elected. The process whereby Allende triumphed was not something that emerged all of a sudden or was created solely during the last years of his candidacy; rather, it was a gradual evolution with origins in the intense social changes that were already evident in the country during the period of Eduardo Frei's Christian Democratic government (1964–70).

Just as Allende represented a new democratic spirit for Chile, so has Augusto Pinochet been another radical change that has left a profound mark on the constitutional spirit of the Chilean people. Three years after he assumed power, in 1976, Pinochet began to wreak havoc in the country: leaders of the opposition disappeared, some died, and others had to go into exile. Torture was converted into a sophisticated system in order to subjugate all opposition to Pinochet's policies. Pinochet also proved himself a master at fostering the myth of internal conflict within the country, and for long periods of time he has been successful in keeping political leaders and their respective parties isolated.

Housewife Irma Muller is a part of all these violent changes affecting Chile. Owing to a particular historical event, she has assumed a leading role in the Association of Relatives of Detained-Missing Persons, a role she has stamped with her personal drive and with her inventiveness in creating ever new methods to manifest her opposition to the dictatorship.

Through her, we see how what is political is also personal and how a country's policies affect the lives of all of its inhabitants, those who choose to be silent in order to survive and those who speak out in order not to die and not to forget. Irma Muller is one of those who refuses to be silent and who is a leader of the relatives' association. In her we can observe and come to understand the way a housewife in Chile becomes involved in politics. Even if her son never reappears, her search will not have been in vain.

15

Maria Ferreira dos Santos

Warren E. Hewitt

The rise of Roman Catholic lay and clerical reformers gained impetus from Vatican II, convened in Rome in 1962. Under the pope's direction, the prelates gave close attention to the need for social programs to improve daily life, especially in housing, food, potable water, and work as well as the need for political justice. This council of bishops resulted in two additional meetings specifically addressing Latin America at Medellín, Colombia, in 1968 and at Puebla, Mexico, in 1979. Priests and lay leaders were guiding forces in demanding reform and, in some cases, revolution. A few priests, such as Camilo Torres in Colombia, even became guerrilla leaders. The movement in general was given the label "liberation theology."

The new religious movements in Brazil are the subject of Warren Hewitt's research. He has concentrated especially on the Comunidades Eclesiais de Base (Christian base communities) in São Paulo's archdiocese and their local improvement strategies as the primary method to initiate social change. He finds that in the midst of the widely discussed revolutionary potential of these movements, there are certain limitations too often neglected by proponents of liberation theology.

In the vignette that follows, the author focuses on Maria dos Santos,* a resourceful and enthusiastic woman who demonstrates the potential for helpful social change through one Comunidade Eclesiais de Base. Her activities challenge age, gender, and class stereotypes that in the past would have eliminated her as a leader in her community. Yet she has succeeded, despite opposition from the local government, her neighbors, and conservative elements in the Church. Like many other women in this volume, Maria has overcome the limitations placed on her by a male-dominated society; and like Irma Muller of Chile, she has refused to let age prevent her from acting on her beliefs.

Before taking a professorship in sociology at the University of Western Ontario, Canada, Hewitt studied at McMaster University, Hamilton, Ontario, and the Universidade de São Paulo in Brazil and taught at the University of Lethbridge, Alberta. His research has emphasized sociological theory, industrialization and modernization, and

*Maria Ferreira dos Santos is a pseudonym.

religion, resulting in his publications on the Christian base communities in Brazil, including *Base Communities and Social Change in Brazil* (Lincoln, NE, 1991).

O nce or more per week in at least half the countries of Latin America, men and women Catholics meet together in small, informal lay circles known as Christian base communities or CEBs (*comunidades eclesiales* or *eclesiais de base*). Currently, there are well in excess of one hundred thousand of these groups in the region, some two-thirds of which are located in just one nation—Brazil.

In essence, the CEBs are religious associations, which engage in a range of devotional practices, but they also have profound sociopolitical implications for the societies in which they operate. This is because group members, most of whom belong to the least privileged social classes, often use their faith to guide them in an attempt to resolve the concrete social problems that affect them. In rural areas, for example, the CEBs actively promote the cause of land reform, while urban groups are frequently involved in neighborhood improvement projects designed to secure basic amenities such as running water, street lights, and garbage collection.

A number of studies have recently appeared that attempt to describe the organizational structure and orientation of the CEBs as they exist in Latin America today. This essay focuses instead upon the human content of the CEBs, to investigate the forces that create and sustain their vitality. To this end, we shall examine the role of one individual who, through her attempts to stimulate political awareness and action within her own group, demonstrates the power of the human spirit. This person is Maria Ferreira dos Santos, the leader of a Christian base community located in a working-class district in the Brazilian city of São Paulo.

The origins of the CEB phenomenon of which Maria dos Santos and her neighbors are a part can be traced to the early 1960s. According to most CEB analysts, the groups emerged in response to a host of both religious and political factors unique to this period. On the one hand, the rise of the phenomenon can be partially attributed to the influence of new and socially progressive Church teaching emerging from important sources such as the Second Vatican Council. The council, consisting of over two thousand Catholic bishops summoned to Rome by the pope in 1962, called for an enhancement of lay participation within the Church and greater attention to the problems of the least privileged social classes. This theme, broadened to include support for the CEBs directly, was reemphasized at subsequent meetings of the Latin American episcopate at Medellín, Colombia (1968), and Puebla, Mexico (1979). On the other hand, to a considerable extent the CEBs can be seen as the product of a desire for political expression on the part of the poor and oppressed themselves in Latin America. As the military took power in a series of countries after 1960, cutting off traditional avenues of protest, the lower classes increasingly turned to the Church for guidance and protection. In response, the Church offered the CEBs as secure spaces from which the poor could voice their dissatisfaction with repressive government policies.

Support for the CEBs has varied from country to country, but it has always been especially strong in Brazil, where the Church has wholeheartedly embraced the dictates of the "new" Catholicism that arose in the wake of Vatican II. Here, the bishops have taken full responsibility for the groups and have been on the front lines of CEB formation and development. Measures adopted by the episcopate to promote the CEBs over the past twenty years include the publication of official statements justifying the existence of the groups within religious and secular spheres and the creation of CEB Pastoral Commissions offering moral and material support to the phenomenon. Quite often, within individual dioceses, money has also been spent to acquire land for local CEB meeting places and to provide the CEBs with basic liturgical, discussion, and organizational materials.

Another extremely effective way the bishops have encouraged CEB information in Brazil is through the designation of priests and nuns to serve as pastoral agents. These individuals, who tend for the most part to be rather young and politically progressive, are dispatched to parishes in rural and semiurban areas where the poor and oppressed are concentrated. Their goal is not so much to stimulate the CEBs directly but to seek out potential lay leaders and encourage them to interest their neighbors in group activation.

In the Nossa Senhora das Dores parish of the São Miguel Episcopal Region on the eastern flank of the Archdiocese of São Paulo, one lay Catholic who has firmly taken up this call to action is Maria Ferreira dos Santos. Within a period of less than a year, Maria almost singlehandedly revitalized a fledgling group known as the Comunidade Santana, which was struggling to survive in a dusty, sprawling, working-class neighborhood with the exotic name of Jardim Copacabana.

Born in 1933 in the interior of São Paulo State, Maria is a *dona de casa* (housewife) who lives with her husband and two children in a small but comfortable home on one of the few paved streets in the area. In many ways, she is an ideal candidate for CEB leadership. Unlike most of her neighbors, who are semiliterate at best, Maria has acquired a primary-school education; and, although currently at home, she has gained valuable organizational experience in the working world as both a salesperson and a dressmaker. Maria's husband, she herself claims, has never worked steadily, yet between her own savings, and her son's income from a job at a local bank, the family maintains a higher-than-average income. This allows Maria the freedom to engage full-time in CEB promotion.

Like others in the vanguard of the CEB movement, Maria dos Santos is also an active supporter of the cause of social justice. Brazil, she claims, has been for too long in the grip of self-interested political leaders who have served only to perpetuate inequality. "In our country," she states, "the rich get richer and the poor get poorer. . . . Those in power don't want to leave; the people protest, but who eventually decides [things] are two or three men at the top, and everything remains the same."

To alter this seemingly intractable situation, Maria places her total faith in popular organizations such as labor unions, neighborhood groups, and other associations, which, she claims, serve to channel and intensify the inherent strength of the organized masses. Before becoming involved with the CEBs, Maria had long been an active supporter of the working-class Partido dos Trabalhadores (Workers' party) and was involved with the Unified Workers' Center, an organization that represents several local trade unions.

This commitment to the cause of justice through social action has been fortified through Maria's association with the Catholic Church. In some ways, it is true, she is very much a part of the "traditional" Church, attending Mass regularly and taking the sacraments. Nevertheless, she finds her principal inspiration in the teachings and actions of the "new" Church of the post-Vatican II era. As is the case for many of her fellow laypersons, and indeed many clergy, for example, she prefers to interpret the figure of Christ as "liberator of the poor and oppressed" and thus as the guiding light and principal impetus for the popular takeover of unjust social structures. Moreover, Maria strongly supports the efforts of the institutional Church in Brazil to bring about social transformation, through its attempts to resolve not only spiritual problems but also this-worldly concrete social issues such as unemployment, low wages, hunger, racial and gender discrimination, and abandoned youth. An especially significant development, in Maria's view, is the Church's role in promoting the CEBs. In a very fundamental way, she believes, the CEBs help awaken the poor to the reality of socioeconomic oppression and encourage them to participate actively in the secular world, thus making Brazil a more just and egalitarian society.

Although she may feel greatly inspired and encouraged by the Church's active role in the social transformation process, Maria is not entirely noncritical of the institution as it operates today. Just as she would like to see greater emphasis on justice and equality in society, so too would she like to see the Church open its own doors to the poor and oppressed. She is especially critical of the power of the hierarchy, which has been conducive to a continuing blind acceptance of clerical authority on the part of the laity. "The priest," Maria states, "is a man equal to all others. He is like us. He is nothing special. But there are a lot of people who think the opposite. And the heads of the Church, there in Rome, they want us to think that way."

Even those priests most active in the people's struggles have not escaped Maria's criticism. Unfortunately, she claims, their middle-class origins prevent them from a true appreciation of the plight of the poor. "The priest doesn't know poverty like we do," she asserts. "He is never hungry, never lacks comforts, such as a car and a telephone." Even women, she adds whimsically, are rarely lacking for the clergy. "I don't know why, but a priest is always one of the most sought-after men around here!"

As we shall see, Maria is also critical of the way that religious personnel involved directly with the CEBs in her own area attempt to control the groups without consulting the membership. Before discussing these and other CEB-related problems, however, let us first examine Maria's relationship with those members of the institutional hierarchy with whom she interacts on a daily basis.

One cleric for whom Maria does have a great deal of respect is Dom Angélico Sândalo Bernardino. Dom Angélico is bishop of the Episcopal Region of São Miguel, where Maria's neighborhood and CEB are located. Over the years, she has worked closely with the bishop not only as a representative of her own Comunidade Santana but also as CEB coordinator for her sector and as a member of the Regional Pastorate of Vocations (formed to bolster the local church's institutional ranks).

The area over which Dom Angélico presides is one of nine ecclesiastical subunits in São Paulo. It has a population of approximately 1.9 million and is territorially divided into seven subregional sectors and twenty-three parishes, some containing well over a quarter of a million people. The majority of the region's inhabitants are quite poor, earning at or slightly above the monthly minimum wage, and reside in self-constructed housing in sprawling dusty neighborhoods like Maria's, lacking even the most basic services such as running water, street lights, and sewers.

São Miguel Region is well known in São Paulo as an area of intense CEB activity. In 1983 about one hundred twenty CEBs, similar to Maria's Comunidade Santana, were officially reported to be operating here, more than in any other single region. The success of the CEBs is partly attributable to the youthful zeal of pastors working in the area (the mean age of the pastors is forty-three as compared to fifty-two for the archdiocese), and to the fact that most (63 percent) were ordained in the progressive wake of the Second Vatican Council.

According to Maria, though, the greatest impetus for CEB formation in the region has been the bishop himself, Dom Angélico. Born in the same year as Maria (1933), Dom Angélico has been in charge of São Miguel Region since its creation in 1975. Unlike many of his counterparts in other areas of São Paulo, he has embraced the Church's "preferential option for the poor" with extreme passion and, much to Maria's satisfaction, has moved to initiate CEB activity on a number of fronts. To begin with, he has encouraged decentralization of the region and of its parish system. This has been undertaken to allow the CEBs, and CEB leaders such as Maria, to have more say in the everyday internal workings of the Church. Second, he has called frequent CEB conferences to stimulate dialogue between the Church and the CEBs, and among the CEBs themselves. In Maria's view, this latter forum for communication and cooperation is extremely important to the development of effective political strategies within the groups. Finally, Dom Angélico has furthered CEB activities through the publication of highly politicized documents and statements. Material promoting the work of the CEBs is published by the region itself and is distributed both internally, to groups like the Comunidade Santana, and to other parts of the archdiocese.

The admiration that Maria shows for Dom Angélico and his accomplishments does not, however, extend to her local pastor, Pe. Franco, who ministers to the three hundred thousand residents of Maria's Nossa Senhora das Dores parish with the help of some ten religious and diocesan priests. On the surface, Pe. Franco appears to have a good deal in common with his immediate superior where the poor and oppressed are concerned. In Pe. Franco's view, for instance, the will of the people is inviolable, and he claims to approve of any and all means whatsoever that the poor might choose to overthrow their oppressors. In his interpretation of the CEBs, Pe. Franco is even somewhat more radical than his bishop and follows a strictly Marxist line. "The CEBs," he claims, "attempt to realize and confront their class position, their common situation. The aim is to perceive their common enemy [which is] American imperialism and capitalism, although not the American people per se."

In spite of Pe. Franco's rhetoric and apparent conviction, however, Maria is extremely wary of his motives. His concern, she believes, is political and self-serving, and he cares very little for the everyday problems of the people. Furthermore, in his dealings with parishioners, including herself, he is arrogant. One day, at lunch in her home with Pe. Patrick, an Irish priest who accompanies Maria's CEB, she explained her feelings this way: "He [Pe. Franco] wouldn't eat with us here, like Pe. Patrick is doing; not even go into a café to have a coffee with us. He talks a lot about the people, but is not of the people."

Maria is also bitter that, unlike Dom Angélico, Pe. Franco has done little to actually promote the CEBs in the area and rarely even stops to visit her Comunidade Santana. Nevertheless, her own contribution to the group would seem to more than compensate for the local pastor's lack of interest.

Maria dos Santos did not initiate the Comunidade Santana. In fact, she is a latecomer to the CEB, becoming involved some three years after it was formed in 1980. Originally, the CEB was designed to provide religious services to the local population (the nearest church is located several miles away), and over the years it has grown from five or six to about forty full-time members. Presently, about two-thirds of these are women, and about one-half are under thirty years of age. Like Maria, virtually all of them are poor.

In its relatively brief history prior to Maria's arrival, the Comunidade Santana was basically a CEB in name only. While the group did pursue a number of both devotional and political functions, these had traditionally been rather limited in scope. Its principal religious activities included the preparation of the local Mass (which is still said each Sunday by the local priest, Pe. Patrick), charity work, religious instruction, Bible study and reflection, and the planning of occasional religious festival days. Baptisms or weddings were not usually performed, nor were there training courses, as exist in some other groups, to prepare individuals to take these two sacraments.

The CEB's political involvement was essentially limited to consciousness-raising, where members would discuss matters pertaining to the reality of poverty and oppression at the local level and beyond. This was characteristically carried out during the Mass, or sometimes at special membership meetings. Though popular in many other CEBs, neighborhood improvement projects, designed to raise the quality of the local infrastructure by petitioning civic authorities, were rarely initiated.

In support of its functions, the Comunidade Santana had created a rather elementary organizational structure. Separate subgroups, for example, were established to help Pe. Patrick prepare the weekly Mass, for religious instruction, for charity work, and so forth. In addition, small nuclei known as *grupos de rua* (street groups) were formed to encourage reflection and political consciousness-raising in a more intimate setting. Some of these teams, especially the *grupos de rua*, met in the homes of individual members, while others met in the CEB's own community center. This building, initiated by the membership in 1982, is still under construction on land owned by the central curia.

The leadership of the Comunidade Santana was invested in a *conselho* (council) consisting of a small number of lay volunteers and the priest who accompanies the CEB, Pe. Patrick. This steering body was officially charged with coordinating the various subgroups as well as undertaking certain other special functions, such as fund-raising, and representing the CEB at the level of the institutional Church.

What had been a rather sleepy, almost inactive little CEB was, however, completely transformed with the arrival of Maria Ferreira dos Santos in 1983. She was originally invited to join the group by a friend and, in recognition of her experience with other popular movements, was elected almost immediately by group members to serve as president of the *conselho*. Since that time, she has come to be the principal driving force behind virtually all of the CEB's activities.

Initially, Maria attempted to convince the other *conselho* members to join her in her efforts to breathe desperately needed new life into the group. Her call for revitalization, however, very quickly fell upon deaf ears, leaving much of the responsibility for leadership on her shoulders alone. To this day she feels a certain bitterness toward the CEB's *conselho*. "This *conselho*," she rails,

> is weak, without a brain. They do whatever I suggest. "Let's launch a youth group," I say, for example, and they all think that's a great idea; but nobody actually participates, they leave all that up to me. "We need a person for catechism classes—Maria; a person for liturgy—Maria; a representative for the next sectoral conference—Maria."

Undaunted, Maria has moved unilaterally to push the Comunidade Santana to action. Her first step was to become personally involved with already established group activities, such as liturgy preparation, religious instruction, charity work, and Bible study, giving their respective teams new importance and impetus and encouraging them to meet regularly. Moreover, Maria has initiated two additional subgroups for the discussion of issues of importance to women and to young people. Admittedly, both of these do not yet meet regularly, and there is still a high degree of internal turnover. Nevertheless, they have proven extremely popular and do serve a definite need within the community.

Maria also has involved the CEB for the first time in neighborhood improvement projects, or *revindicações*. Such projects are especially important to her and, in her view, should be the principal concern of all CEB participants. "Our neighborhood," she explains, "lives in total abandonment by the public authorities." Remedial efforts to improve the basic infrastructure, she asserts, are not only desirable but also absolutely necessary to the betterment of the quality of life in the area. Yet, despite the obvious benefits to all, what successful attempts have been made to obtain better services in the area (for improved bus service, a health care post, road paving, and sewers) are largely a result of initiatives undertaken alone by Maria, who has taken the lead in circulating petitions and arranging seemingly endless meetings with civic officials. Not even the *conselho* of the Comunidade Santana has offered significant support to Maria in her efforts to improve local living standards. Recently, for instance, it met and agreed to lend material and moral support to a group of local *favelados* (slum dwellers) who wished to appropriate a publicly owned piece of land for the construction of new homes. When the time came for the invasion, however, not one *conselho* member showed up; not one, that is, except for Maria.

In addition, in accordance with the wishes of the local bishop, Dom Angélico, Maria was forced to move unilaterally to take over the local ratepayers' association, successfully having herself elected to its presidency and then integrating its functions with those of the Comunidade Santana. This ratepayers' group is one of dozens in São Paulo known collectively as SABs (Friends of the Neighborhood Societies). In essence, they are a type of citizens' complaint group but possess little autonomy, as they are funded and monitored by the São Paulo city hall. More often than not, the SABs are simply used by politicians and bureaucrats to neutralize, rather than stimulate, public involvement. Normally, this is accomplished by careful dispensation of favors to members considered influential in the community. In taking control of the SAB, Maria has sought primarily to use its established ties to local authorities to promote the Comunidade Santana's neighborhood improvement projects.

Another area of intense involvement for Maria has been the cause of the Comunidade Santana's community hall, which she hopes will someday become the true spiritual and organizational center of not only the CEB but also of the entire neighborhood. As previously mentioned, this structure was initiated in 1982 but remains largely unfinished. Upon entering the CEB, Maria had attempted to interest group members in pooling their labor to ensure a swift completion of the building. Offers of assistance, however, were never forthcoming, and, consequently, a local stonemason was hired to complete the structure by himself.

Finding money to keep the project alive, though, has not been easy. Having taxed the generosity of the membership (admittedly quite limited to begin with), Maria has been forced to solicit contributions from a variety of alternative sources. She has managed to convince Pe. Patrick, for example, to appeal to his friends in Ireland to send money. So far, the priest's old soccer team has made at least one generous donation. In addition, Maria has organized bazaars and bake sales and has made frequent trips to the pastors of more affluent parishes in central São Paulo in search of support. To date, however, little has been forthcoming from the local clergy, many of whom Maria describes as tightwads. More recently, she has even appealed to charitable sources outside Brazil, including Catholic Development and Peace in Canada.

These fund-raising activities, it might be mentioned, have landed her in considerable hot water with local authorities, including Dom Angélico. The bishop, rather paternalistically, has repeatedly stressed that efforts by the groups to secure funds from charitable sources should be discouraged and that the CEBs must operate within their own means. Ostensibly, this is to ensure that the groups do not simply become welfare recipients as opposed to self-sufficient popular organizations. For Maria, such suggestions are unfortunate and merely represent an effort by the Church to maintain its influence over the CEB movement. Adequate funding of the groups, from whatever source, Maria asserts, is absolutely crucial to their successful operation. "If we had the money," she states, "we could do good work, with youth and their families, with the women of our neighborhood, with the unemployed, and so many other things. . . . It's a real shame, when you have a desire to work for the conscientization of the people, but don't have the funds, only goodwill."

One more way Maria has contributed to the revitalization of the Comunidade Santana is through her efforts to reduce the often overbearing ecclesiastical control exercised by the group's *agente pastoral*, Pe. Patrick. In some respects, she is a great admirer of the priest and strongly praises his efforts at raising the political consciousness of group members at the weekly Mass. "As you noticed in the Mass," she related approvingly, "the priest really has to speak strongly to motivate the people here." Maria also defends him from frequent criticisms, often emanating from more elevated sources, about his national origin. "You know," she explains, "they want to remove him from the sector because he is a foreigner. There are even people around here who ask why we have a foreign priest among us. He must know this. He is so good, but everybody talks about him."

It is Pe. Patrick's rather authoritarian and paternalistic attitude with respect to the group and its activities, though, that profoundly disturbs Maria. By his own admission, Pe. Patrick attempts to shield the CEB from "undesirable" or "harmful" influences. "I don't allow the *comunidade* to be used," he warns, "for specific ends, be they political or personal." In the period leading up to the general elections of 1982, he claims to have demonstrated this intent by denying politicians from all political parties the right to speak to the congregation following Sunday Mass. The researcher himself was similarly denied access to the group until such time as he had thoroughly discussed with the priest the nature and purpose of this study. Even after Pe. Patrick's approval was granted, many CEB members remained reluctant to speak with the researcher and refused to cooperate until they had received Pe. Patrick's verbal permission. For Maria, such tendencies are both distasteful and inappropriate and have no place in a democratically formed association of the people. Liberty, she asserts, should not be limited to the secular sphere.

The priest's attitude also had had an effect on one of Maria's most cherished undertakings—the formation of a viable, active youth group. Young people, she claims, are difficult enough to organize, but as a representative of the Church, Pe. Patrick compounds this difficulty. Often, Maria explains, young people feel constrained and limited by Church teaching, especially that related to sexual behavior. Though they are attracted by the Church's call to political action, they are constantly reminded by Pe. Patrick that matters such as birth control, premarital sex, and abortion are not open for discussion or interpretation. As a consequence, she observes that "at first, they [young people] become involved with full force, but drop out just as quickly. Because they are young, they wish a certain degree of liberty, and feel constrained by the Church; the Church is holding them and they want freedom." This state of affairs, she adds, is truly a shame, since it is young people, with their zeal for justice and liberty, who represent the real hope for the future of Brazil.

One might assume, then, that Maria's rather solitary efforts on behalf of what is a rather apathetic membership would lead to a certain degree of bitterness and disillusionment. In fact, however, her work with the poor has been personally rewarding in a number of respects. In joining the CEB, she claims, her faith in God and in the Church (despite its faults) has been strengthened. She has become more aware of the poor's problems and has developed a strong interest in those problems. Such awareness, moreover, has given her a firm objective in life that had been formerly lacking: raising the consciousness of the people.

The only regret she has is with respect to her family life. Her active involvement with the Comunidade Santana has left her little time to devote to her own husband and children and to their problems. Sadly, as well, she was left with little time to grieve for her eldest child, a married daughter, who was violently murdered with her husband by men who Maria believes were drug dealers, who had become involved with her son-in-law. The fact, incidentally, that she learned of her own daughter's death not from the police but through word of mouth several days after the event greatly intensified both her disdain for local government officials and her commitment to the cause of social justice.

~

In the current cold war atmosphere of the developed world, with its narrow focus on East-West relations, there are many who would suggest that Maria Ferreira dos Santos is a Communist, rebel leader, or potential urban guerrilla. Indeed, there are those within the Brazilian Catholic Church who share this view. Contrarily, there are still others on the political left who would praise her as a saint, a visionary, or a great revolutionary figure. In actual fact, however, as Maria herself will readily tell you, she is none of these things. Rather, she is an ordinary person who is engaged in an extraordinary struggle to help the poor of Brazil to become full citizens in their own country. In effect, she seeks no more for herself and her neighbors than most North Americans take for granted—a chance to participate equally in all aspects of social, economic, and political life. Maria Ferreira dos Santos is the kind of person who, like countless others working in thousands of CEBs throughout Brazil and the rest of Latin America, will likely never be cited in history books but who, in their own way, will help in some measure to transform their societies.

SOURCES

The data for this biography of Maria Ferreira dos Santos were gathered as part of a larger research project conducted in Brazil in the spring of 1984. The purpose of the research was to investigate the organizational structure and orientation of a select sample of twenty-two CEBs located in the Archdiocese of São Paulo. Information was obtained over a five-month period from representatives of the institutional Church, CEB leaders like Maria dos Santos, and ordinary CEB participants using interviews, self-administered questionnaires, and participation observation.

With the exception of Dom Angélico Sândalo Bernardino, bishop of São Miguel Episcopal Region, the names of all persons and places in this report have been changed to protect those involved, especially Maria dos Santos, from possible recriminations by local authorities.

FOR FURTHER READING

Adriance, Madeleine. *Opting for the Poor: Brazilian Catholicism in Transition.* Kansas City, 1986.
Barreiro, Alvaro. *Basic Ecclesial Communities.* Translated by Barbara Campbell. Maryknoll, NY, 1982.
Bruneau, Thomas C. "Basic Christian Communities in Latin America: Their Nature and Significance." *Churches and Politics in Latin America,* edited by Daniel H. Levine, 225–37. Beverly Hills, 1980.
———. *The Church in Brazil.* Austin, TX, 1982.
Cox, Harvey. *Religion in the Secular City.* New York, 1984.
Deelen, Gottfried. "The Church on Its Way to the People: Basic Christian Communities in Brazil." *Cross Currents* 30 (1980): 385–408.
Hewitt, W. E. "Basic Christian Communities in Brazil." *The Ecumenist* 24 (September–October 1986): 81–84.
———. "Strategies for Social Change Employed by Comunidades Eclesiais de Base (CEBs) in the Archdiocese of

São Paulo." *Journal for the Scientific Study of Religion* 25 (March 1986): 16–30.

Mainwaring, Scott. *The Catholic Church and Politics in Brazil, 1916–1985*. Stanford, 1986.

Torres, Sergio, and John Eagleson. *The Challenge of Basic Christian Communities*. Translated by John Drury. Maryknoll, NY, 1981.

Welsh, John R. "Comunidades Eclesiais de Base." *America* (February 8, 1986): 85–88.

16

Leticia: A Nicaraguan Woman's Struggle

Dianne Walta Hart

The Nicaraguan people overthrew the forty-six-year-long dictatorship of the Somoza family in July 1979, and Daniel Ortega established in its place a revolutionary government named for an early martyr of the struggle for national autonomy, Augusto Sandino. The U.S. government opposed this regime; and, by 1981, the Reagan administration had created and funded a counterrevolutionary group, the Contras, to overthrow the Sandinistas. The Contras from bases in Honduras launched a war against the legitimate government of Nicaragua that continued for eleven years. During this time, despite the high cost of national defense, the Sandinistas attempted to implement revolutionary programs to bring social and economic justice to their people. The Contra invasions only halted with the election of Violeta Chamorro, favored in Washington, in 1990.

In the midst of the struggle, life for everyday Nicaraguans went on, complete with all the frustrations and the pleasures common to most people in contemporary society. Leticia had her own ambitions and problems: difficulties with her husband drove her to join others who were fleeing the incessant fighting between Sandinistas and Contras to enter the United States illegally. The lure of her family, however, eventually brought her back to Managua and the challenges of coping in a revolutionary society. The Sandinista success meant not only new opportunities for Leticia and others like her but also new hardships for them as they attempted to earn their living.

Leticia's story is told with warmth and humor by Dianne Walta Hart of the Spanish Department of Oregon State University. Besides serving as executive secretary of the Pacific Northwest Council on Foreign Languages, Hart has found the time to act as adviser to Oregon State's Japanese Traditional Karate Club. Spanish, linguistics, and adult education are Hart's teaching specialties, while her research since 1984 has concentrated on the oral history of Leticia and her family, whom she met in 1983. Continuing her interviews with members of the family, Hart has explored their experiences in *Undocumented in L.A.: An Immigrant's Story* (Wilmington, DE, 1997). Both this essay and the book examine daily challenges and dangers beyond the ken of most North Americans. Hart also has published articles on Nicaraguan women and Sandinista society.

The balance between personal needs and national goals that Leticia and others maintain in Nicaragua is revealed in this vignette. Her story adds a human dimension and female perspective to the Sandinista struggle for social justice. Leticia (a pseudonym) and her family have requested that their real names not be used and that minor details be changed because they fear retaliation even now from opponents of the Sandinistas.

> Nicaragua's crisis is so long, so long . . . we
> walk each day so near to hope and to despair.
> —Uriel Molina, *Barricada*, August 1986

> I would like to discuss with you
> how now I live in the catacombs
> and how determined I am to kill the hunger
> that is killing us
> when you discuss this
> discuss it long and hard
> when no one who sows hunger is around
> nor a spy for those who sow hunger
> nor a guard for those who sow hunger.
> —Leonel Rugama, Estelí poet killed at the age
> of twenty in 1970 by Somoza's Guards[1]

Leticia's story begins in Estelí, Nicaragua, capital of the province of the same name. It is a city of fifty thousand people that has been her home most of her life. In Estelí, she can chat with old friends on the street, describe the histories of families and buildings, go down to the river where her mother used to make her living washing clothes, and stop by the cemetery where a tall tree has grown from a seed the family planted to shade her brother's grave.

Estelí is two hours north of Managua in Nicaragua's hilly tobacco country. The Pan-American highway cuts through the town, bringing with it motorcycles and four-wheel drive vehicles that seem both to bounce and roar on the rough streets. Bordering the lively central park are government buildings, a run-down theater, and vendors selling vegetables. Sloths hang from the park trees and children chase each other around the swings. Sophisticated helicopters drone over the city by day and at night one can hear distant gunfire.

Leticia describes the people in Estelí as nicer, more hospitable, and less prejudiced than other Nicaraguans. They don't gossip and criticize each other, but, at the same time, they know where everyone lives, and they are concerned about their neighbors. They have few luxuries, but they like to dress well, even if only inexpensive fabric is available. The climate is cooler than Managua's, and the people are lighter skinned, not as burned by the sun. Many people have green or blue eyes, and it is said that the women of Estelí are beautiful.

There is another dimension to Estelí, though. Popular tee shirts proclaim Estelí as a *pueblo heroico* for several well-fought reasons. It is one of the towns that most openly defied the Somoza government, causing Estelí to be bombed more than any other city in Nicaragua. Many of the downtown buildings still show the scars of the battles that destroyed most of Estelí's businesses. Out of those battles has come a feeling that the city and its people will never give in, never be defeated. They view themselves as warriors. The young poet and early martyr, Leonel Rugama, came from Estelí, and his attitude represents the spirit of the city. His finest verse, some say, was his profane last words in defiance of Somoza's Guards just before they killed him: "Tell your mother to surrender!"

Leticia's story, and that of her mother, brother, and sister, started in Estelí in desperate hunger and poverty. Their mother, Dora, lived with five different men in her life. All but one beat her, and all of them abandoned her. Landlords often chased them out of shanty homes, their few possessions on their backs. At the age of six, the children began working fourteen hours a day. They shined shoes, picked tobacco, and sold food door-to-door in an attempt to add to the money Dora made as a laundress. As hard as they all worked, it often was not enough. "Some days," according to Leticia, "we would wake up in the morning and there was nothing to eat. Sometimes we didn't even have wood to start a fire. Sometimes we'd eat a piece of bread in the morning, with a cup of coffee; that was all until night, when—if my mother had washed and if the clothes had dried and if she had been able to deliver the clothes—we would eat again."

All of them fought, in different ways, to overthrow the Somoza dictatorship that had controlled Nicaragua since the early 1930s. As a teenager, Leticia's brother, Omar, fought for two years in the mountains. Her sister, Marta, was forced to stand for a month in a foot of water in a government prison because she refused to tell Somoza's guardsmen her brother's whereabouts. Leticia, born in 1948 and at least ten years older than her sister and brother, provided a safe house in Managua for Omar, burying his dirty clothes in the backyard, providing him with clean ones, and hiding him, although such actions endangered her three young daughters and husband. A second brother died in the struggle.

Today, Leticia, Marta, and Omar are still committed to the revolution. Leticia volunteers for AMNLAE (the national women's organization) and takes her turn watching over her barrio at night. Marta and Omar are Sandinistas; she works for AMNLAE, and he is still in the military.

Leticia and her family have been actively involved in the social changes that have taken place in Estelí and in all of Nicaragua since the revolution. As children in prerevolutionary Nicaragua, Leticia and her siblings went to school at night whenever they could find time, because they had to work during the day. Leticia remembers those years with sadness: "A child cannot study without food. When I would pick up a book to study a lesson, I wouldn't remember anything. My head would start to ache. It would feel heavy, and I would have to stop studying." Now, children like those of Leticia, Marta, and Omar go to school with full stomachs. They go to school during the day. At night the schools are attended by adults.

With a voice in their community, better access to medical care, and better education for their children, Leticia and her family, for the first time, share in the responsibility for their own lives and that of their community. They are proud of Estelí and proud of Nicaragua. They are also happy that the leadership and courage shown by many Nicaraguan women during the struggle has not been forgotten, as evidenced by the laws protecting women and their enforcement by the Sandinistas. Even though the legal status of women has been improved, many old attitudes persist.

The Sandinista government built subsidized housing in the years after Somoza's overthrow, and today Dora and Marta live together in a government-built duplex. It is the first time that either woman has lived in a house where the front door locks. It is also the first time that they do not have to worry that someone will come along and chase them out.

Leticia lives a block away. She is small, quick to cry, and an important member of the family. Within the family, her ninth-grade education is surpassed only by that of her university-educated husband. As a teenager, she took a correspondence course in cosmetology, worked in a Sony store, and met her first boyfriend, an intense young man named Antonio, nine years older than she. When they first met, she did not know that he was already working with the Frente Sandinista. Often he disappeared for days, and she believed that he had another girlfriend. He denied this and told her that he visited a family in Santa Clara. On her fifteenth birthday in 1963, he gave a party for her and presented her with fabric for a dress, white cloth with golden stripes. Although Antonio knew the law required permits for private parties, he did not get one, and Somoza's Guards broke up Leticia's only birthday party. "Soon after that, he asked me if we could have a civil marriage. I don't know why, but I became afraid and told him that at fifteen, I was too young. I was nervous; my teeth even chattered. It wasn't that I didn't love him because I did. He was my first boyfriend, and I loved him a lot. But he didn't think I loved him." Not long after, Antonio "went to the mountains," that is, he joined the guerrillas. She never saw him again. He became a *comandante*, a national hero, and, upon his death in 1979, an official martyr. In Estelí, there is a barrio named after him.

Leticia went on to a cosmetology school in Managua. She lived with the owner, a woman who fed her *gallo pinto* (beans and rice) three times a day in return for Leticia's working seven days a week. When she finished school, she moved to Matagalpa, not far from Estelí, took out a loan to buy a mirror and a dryer, hired someone to make a table, and placed a sign, *Centro de Belleza Leticia*, outside her apartment. She was twenty years old and in business.

"I felt good about it. I felt liberated. Whenever I had a slow day, I would come and see my mother. I would come to leave her a little money. Then I would leave. I liked Estelí, and I wanted to stay there because it was where I was born, but I don't know—[at that time in my life], Estelí brought back a lot of bad memories for me. I felt sad whenever I went to Estelí, probably due to my childhood, due to all the difficulties we went through with my mother. We suffered hunger because my mother was on her own. She has always been on her own. I have always admired her, maybe because I was the eldest and could understand the situation a bit better. She always had to wash and iron to support us; this would make me feel sorry for her. It would make me sad to think of all the things that we went through.

"And then I met Sergio. One day his sister came to my beauty parlor and invited me on an outing to a farm. She and her friends didn't know me and weren't even my friends, but I thought that maybe they liked me, and that's why they invited me. That was not so—there was more to it. Sergio's sister was jealous of her boyfriend. She thought her boyfriend was in love with me. But that was not true. He was a friend of mine because he worked with my roommate. They both worked at PROLASA, a dairy product factory. We were friends, and he would come to visit, but he wasn't in love. She thought he was in love with me, so she came to the beauty parlor. It was part of her plan. Sergio's sister and her friends invited me on the trip so that I could see that she was his girlfriend. I went, but took it very naturally because there wasn't any truth in the rest.

"When I was going to the farm, when I got into the truck that we used for the trip, Sergio was in it. He moved so that I could sit down. So I sat down beside him, and then we drove off. We started to talk about everything, but nothing related to falling in love and all those things. We went to the farm on the fourteenth of February 1970.

"We spent the day there; we walked and had a party and a *piñata*. The farm was very nice because it had a big river where we went swimming. Then I realized that he had fallen in love with me and I with him. We returned home that same day, at night. He went home to bathe and returned later that night to see me. The girls who had invited me to the party were very happy and became good friends of mine. They were happy because they no longer worried about the boyfriend.

"Sergio started to visit and soon, during the first week of March, they planned another trip to the farm for Holy Week. So we went back again and spent a whole week on the farm. It was during that week that we became engaged. He was just starting his first year at the university; he was twenty-one and I was twenty-two.

"When he told his mother that he wanted to marry me, she said, no, that if he married me, she wouldn't help him with his studies and that he would have to leave her house. He left, and we were married on the fourth of April. We married quietly, without his family knowing. I wrote to my mother and told her all about it—that I had found a man and was going to marry, that I was having only a civil wedding to see if it would work. I hadn't known him for too long, but I was sure that I was in love because I had had another boyfriend before for two years and had never felt so in love with someone as to get married."

During the next few years, Sergio attended the Universidad Autónoma de Nicaragua in Managua while Leticia continued her work as a hairdresser in Matagalpa. They saw each other on weekends. Her first daughter was born on May 22, 1971; three of her four daughters would be born before 1979. Leticia eventually moved to Managua to be with her husband.

After Sergio finished the university, he worked for Sears, Roebuck and Company and later for the Bank of America. Politics did not interest him. Leticia did not tell him that her brothers were working with the Sandinistas in the struggle to overthrow Somoza. Later, she learned that he knew all along but said nothing to her.

One night, when Leticia's brothers had sneaked into Managua and were sleeping at her house, she woke up after hearing a jeep go around the block several times. She worried about her innocent husband and children. She had not meant to endanger them. "The guards stopped in front of my door and got out of the jeep. They kept the jeep running. I could hear them get their guns ready to shoot. I got up quickly and, without turning on a light, I ran to my brothers. They slept with their clothes on, ready for what might happen. After I warned them, I went to the living room in the dark and knelt on the floor. I asked God to help us, to please not let the guards come to our house. I heard one guard say, as he came closer to us, that he thought people were there, but the other one said that there was no one. They got in their car and left."

In July 1979, after a month of fierce fighting, there was a moment of calm as troops withdrew. Leticia, along with her husband, children, and friends, took advantage of this time to scout for refuge from the battle—someplace outside of Managua. They stopped at a small farm owned by a friend of Sergio's. As they rested, they heard a helicopter above and then watched with horror as it landed next door, at a farm owned by a *comandante* in Somoza's Guard. When they realized that the helicopter was full of guardsmen, they hid under beds and in closets, certain that they would be killed. But instead of coming to look for them, the guardsmen waited for the *comandante,* who left his house with the few bags he had packed. The guardsmen loaded the suitcases into the helicopter, the *comandante* got in, and they flew away. At that moment, Leticia knew, without hearing it officially, that the revolution had been successful. Much earlier she had made a red-and-black flag for this victorious moment and had hidden it in her purse. Now she pulled out the flag, ran to their car, and tied it to the antenna. They laughed and cried and began the victory drive into Managua on roads full of people singing, shooting guns, and playing mariachi music to celebrate the triumph of the revolution.

In time, Sergio accepted a government position, so once again Leticia moved her table, dryer, and mirror to a new Centro de Belleza Leticia. This time their move was to Estelí, her hometown. Later, the Sandinista government sent Sergio to study in Cuba for a year. They both considered a divorce during his absence. Leticia thought they had gone their separate ways; her community involvement had become time-consuming. Sergio did not understand and occasionally beat her. She felt that he wanted her to be his slave, not his companion for life. In Cuba, Sergio watched men and women interact and was impressed with how different it was from Nicaragua, how men and women treated each other more as equals. He wrote that it changed his attitude and that he wanted a second chance. She agreed.

In 1981 the U.S.-backed Contras began their war against Nicaragua; the battle often touched the lives of Leticia and her family. Omar was usually in the battlefield and often suffered from nightmares and fears. The stress and war-related anxiety eventually debilitated him for a year, causing the Sandinistas to take away his rifle and relieve him from actual battle responsibilities until his emotional health improved. Marta's work, similar to a paramilitary position, placed her near the war zone where the Sandinista soldiers fought the Contras. She was in the border town of Santa Clara in 1984 when U.S. mercenaries from the Alabama-based Civilian-Military Assistance attacked by air and were shot down by the Sandinistas. It seemed never to end. The father of the family in the other side of their duplex was killed fighting the Contras. The rumors of children with slit necks, of dead bodies in the river, and of random and senseless Contra attacks on civilians added to the tension, as did the low car with a loudspeaker on the top, making its way through the barrio, announcing the latest death of someone from Estelí. They wondered if they would ever have peace.

The symbolic importance of Estelí was not lost on the Contras. They attacked it in August 1985, knowing how significant the defeat of Estelí would be. During the attack on the city, Marta was in charge of coordinating the civilian defense of the city's perimeters. Omar sat helplessly immobile in his tiny ramshackle hillside home with a cast on a broken leg, painfully reliving, in an emotional sense, his wartime horrors as he heard the Sandinista helicopters strafe the nearby hills in their attempt to repel the Contras. Leticia stood watch over her barrio at night, as she had done once a week since 1979, to protect the area. She made coffee and food for others, when she was not on watch, and worried as Estelí buried ten people in one day. Eight days later, the Contras retreated. The people of Estelí felt that once more they had been victorious.

By this time, Leticia had become the emotional center of the family. She had, by everyone's account, assumed the dominant role. She was the one in whom the family members traditionally confided; she, in turn, worried about them and advised them. That she struggled with this responsibility and their confidence in her was evident in her overall sadness.

Leticia and her four-year-old daughter left Nicaragua three months later, in November 1985, leaving behind not only her mother, brother, and sister but also three teenaged daughters and her husband. She had never before been outside Nicaragua and had only vague knowledge of the location of the cities and countries that lay ahead of her. She had never seen a map. She said that her reason for leaving was not Nicaragua: "I am convinced that the revolution is for us, for the poor, for those of us who were always marginalized." She added that, as a Nicaraguan, her duty was in her country.

If her duty was in Nicaragua and the reason she left was not Nicaragua, why then did she leave? She left to get away from Sergio. She could no longer tolerate having him come near her. A cousin in Nevada had invited her to the United States and offered to pay her way. A friend had advised her that maybe she would feel better about Sergio if she left for a couple of months. The invitation came at the perfect time.

However, in a way, the problem *was* Nicaragua. Danger from the Contras to family and friends is omnipresent in the towns far from Managua; it strains relationships like no other stress can. Every day Leticia heard of a sorrow unimagined the day before. And Leticia visibly suffers more than others; she has said, "I am one of those people who is always worrying about what is happening to others." She remembers as a child watching one of Somoza's Guards hit an old man with his rifle butt. She stood on the street corner screaming at the guard, telling him that the old man was a drunk. But the beating continued, and Leticia ran to her house, crying over her inability to help. When she was in Nicaragua, no orphaned child or abandoned mother went unhelped by Leticia. She volunteered for AMNLAE, went to two weekly meetings of her Christian base community where they discussed a practical approach to being Christians, and stood watch over her neighborhood. However, her marital problems, exacerbated by her family responsibilities and the anxieties caused by the last Contra attack on Estelí, had become too great.

Sergio and their daughters took her to the Nicaraguan-Honduran border where she joined eight other Nicaraguans, all with Mexican visas but with no intention of staying in Mexico. They rode in a van, mostly in silence, through Honduras, El Salvador, Guatemala, and Mexico. They missed, by a few minutes, a military confrontation in El Salvador. At night they stayed in small hotels or slept in the van.

When they reached the U.S.-Mexican border, they waited until 5 A.M. to begin their illegal entry into the United States. Carrying a small suitcase brought from Nicaragua, Leticia and her daughter climbed over a wall and walked through heavy rain, mud, and standing water for one and one-half hours until they reached an abandoned house. Later, they made the three-hour trip to Los Angeles in two cars, the men in the trunks and the women and children lying down in the back.

Then the confusion began. When her cousin invited her, he thought she was emigrating. He had no intention of paying for a mere visit. As for her child, Leticia had told someone to ask another person about the advisability of taking her daughter along but had interpreted the response—"No hay ningún problema"—to mean there would be no charge. As a result of these misunderstandings, Leticia was presented with a bill for $1,500. She had no money and no way of earning enough to repay this unexpected debt.

Leticia and her daughter moved to Nevada with her cousin where they shared an apartment with other Nicaraguans who had entered illegally. She worked for a few weeks in a factory. Later, they were invited to Oregon by friends and spoke with groups of university students about the Nicaraguan revolution. She said, "I think it was a bad decision [to leave Nicaragua] but it is done. I have analyzed all this and I think that God always has His plans; a leaf on a tree does not move except by His will." She added that maybe what God had wanted her to do was talk with students and tell them about Nicaragua.

Her responsibilities had followed her: "I know that my sister and brother feel that I am their second mother. My mother will be able to die peacefully because she knows she has me. I cannot make decisions about my life . . . because my life doesn't belong to me but to my family."

Leticia and her daughter made their way to Miami where they could easily drop unnoticed into a world of illegal aliens and where, she hoped, she could find employment, earn plane fare back to Nicaragua, and maybe even make a few extra dollars. Although she had friends from Estelí there, Miami was difficult. Everyone spoke Spanish, but, she said, most of them were Cubans who spoke too fast and all the time. Even the Nicaraguans in Miami were always agitated, in a hurry, and running to catch a bus. She got a job cleaning and cooking in the house of a *señora*. Next, she worked with a *señor* whom she accompanied to the docks, greeting incoming tourist ships from Latin American countries and selling perfume, clothes, and souvenirs in her struggle to make enough money for the return ticket. As time went on, she found work in the evenings as an Avon lady, using her stylish good looks to advertise her products and her cosmetology background to sell them. She could keep 50 percent of what she brought in; the first night out, she sold $300 in Avon products and made $150 for herself. Finally, the perfect job.

Leticia did not hear very often from Nicaragua, but she did know that Sergio had accepted a promotion and had moved, along with their three teenaged daughters, from Estelí to Managua. She also heard that a niece had been killed by the Contras and that a stepsister had died of a stroke. She sensed that even more was wrong. When she telephoned Sergio, he almost always was the first one to suggest that the call end. He seemed not to be very interested in talking to her, and she wondered if there was another woman. In May, on her thirty-ninth birthday, a friend in

Miami called to congratulate her and added that she had heard from a relative that Leticia's husband was going out with another woman, publicly, in front of everyone. No one had told her because they did not want her to worry.

A few weeks later, in June, Leticia called Sergio's Managua office and found out that he had quit his job. When she asked for him, the secretary said, "He no longer works here, but if you wish to leave a message for him, I can ask the driver to take it to him." Leticia asked if the secretary had the address. The answer was, "Not of his house, but I know the address of the woman he lives with." Leticia was stunned. She asked that he call her in Miami: "I wanted the secretary to think everything was normal, that it didn't matter, but that was a lie. I thought that I was dying."

Sergio did not return the call. Instead, his sister came to Miami and called Leticia, telling her that Sergio was leaving that week for Mexico. "It was another blow, because I still had the hope that it was a passing thing for him, and that when I returned, everything was going to be normal, as before. I was ready to forgive him because I thought he had done it because I wasn't with him. The majority of Latin men are *machistas*, and they say they cannot be without a woman. But when I heard he was leaving for Mexico, this meant it was serious. He hadn't even called me to tell me that he was going, or that I should come because the children would be alone. I knew I had to hurry and return before I had planned, even though I had hoped to stay a couple of months longer to make money. I called a relative to find out if he had actually left; she said he hadn't, so I asked her to tell him that he should wait for me."

Later that month, the U.S. House of Representatives voted to give $100 million to the Contras. That meant the war against Nicaragua would continue. Leticia, eight months after entering the United States, was finally on her way back to Nicaragua, spurred more by her husband's impending departure to Mexico than by political reasons. She had often worried about various aspects of her return. One was how she would be received after spending so much time in the country that was, in effect, at war with her country. The other problem was her lack of papers. Leticia had entered the United States illegally. If, on paper, she had not entered, how could she leave? No one seemed to know the answer to that question.

Entering Nicaragua and reestablishing her life there, from a political point of view, presented no problems. Oddly enough, neither did the lack of papers. No one asked for them when she left the United States and, in Nicaragua, the officials asked for no more than the form she filled out on the plane. She must have looked like most Nicaraguans who return from extensive shopping trips abroad because the fourteen boxes she brought back with her caused her no trouble at Customs.

The return itself turned out to be the easy part. It was her relationship with Sergio that presented the most difficulty. In his new position in Managua, he had been earning the maximum monthly wages (80,000 córdobas, equal to U.S. $57) that one could earn from a government job in Nicaragua, but it wasn't enough. In Leticia's absence, the córdoba had lost much of its value; in addition, living in Managua was more expensive than in Estelí.[2] Even if one could afford it, everything from meat to beans to beauty care products was difficult to find, more so than in the countryside, where the people were more affected by the war and where the government, as a consequence, maintained better food distribution and lower prices.

Nicaragua had changed in the eight months that Leticia had been in the United States. Nicaraguans had begun calling their country the land of "no hay" (there isn't any), so severe were the shortages of beans, corn, and spare parts. Basic goods were to have been available at low prices, but the impact on Nicaragua of the war with the U.S.-backed Contras and the effect of the U.S. government embargo, compounded by inefficiency and corruption in the Nicaraguan distribution system, had resulted in frequent shortages. Even one of Nicaragua's newspapers, *El Nuevo Diario*, called Managua's prices exorbitant. At the same time, an "increased flight of the technical-professional sector" was predicted, along with continued labor indiscipline and inflation, already at the astonishingly high level of more than 1,000 percent.[3] Nicaraguans lived in what was now being called a "survival economy."

The family met Leticia and her daughter at the airport. "We went to the house, talked a lot, and they asked me a lot of questions about what had happened in the United States. I began to tell them how hard life there really is because the majority of the people who go to the United States talk big—

how there is everything and how everything is pretty and how much money they make. That is the mistake, to not tell the truth. Because I believe that if all the world knew how it really is, very few people would want to go there. It is not for everyone."

Leticia and Sergio made love that first night but after that he became cool and distant. He accompanied her to Estelí where she went to see her mother and other family members, but he returned early to Managua. She struggled to find the answers. When she asked her daughters about the woman with whom her husband had had the affair, she learned that she was about the same age as Leticia but "shorter and not especially pretty." "Then why," she asked her children, "do you think that your dad went out with her?" "We don't know," they answered, "but you know how men are." The children told her that there were several nights that he did not come home while she was in the United States. Even some weekends. But they added that he checked on them often.

"Then one day," according to Leticia, "I went to Estelí again, to see my mother and that very day, he went with the woman, when I wasn't here. I had reached a limit; I couldn't stand it anymore—I couldn't bear the humiliation. I packed his bags and asked him to leave. I told him that even though I was a woman, I still had dignity."

She and Sergio argued. She accused him of leaving her for the other woman. He denied it, saying that he did not love the woman; he loved Leticia. Besides, the woman had two children and under no circumstances would he remake his life with a woman who had two children when he had four of his own whom he could no longer support on his salary. He was leaving to find work and to have time to think. And maybe, or so thought Leticia, to get even. She had left, and now he would.

Sergio planned to leave with his brother, starting out from Managua on an August evening. He was going to take his university diploma and other papers with him, hoping to get a position in Mexico for which his degree in business administration had prepared him. Other members of the family wondered if he intended to enter illegally the United States, much as Leticia did. She said no, that since she had told him how hard life is in the United States, his goal was to stay in Mexico. Since 1979 he had supported the revolution and worked for it; but he, unlike the others in Leticia's family, had not actually fought for it. Politics had never interested him and still did not.

Leticia had no definite plans. The children had to stay in Managua to finish the school year. Maybe she could leave them with Sergio's sister and return to Estelí. Certainly when the school year finished in early December, they would return. But how to support her family? The beauty shop that she left in Estelí had been poorly managed in her absence and no longer existed. Maybe she could set up a beauty shop in her house, but it would not be easy. In the years following 1979, the government purchased beauty products and distributed them to beauty salons. As the economic situation worsened, the government was unable to continue this, and salon owners had to find a way to purchase beauty products out of the country, a feat that was easier for owners of large salons than it was for Leticia. The products she had brought back with her would not last long. She knew life would improve if she could just get back to Estelí, if only for the ease with which she could get beans and rice.

Dora, Marta, and Omar still live in Estelí, and Leticia still considers it home. She is more comfortable there than she is in Managua or Miami. During her eight months in the United States, people in Estelí often asked about her and then commented that she would never return. Such remarks for a family committed to the revolution provided many awkward moments.

Estelí was also the home of the man who had driven Leticia and her daughter in his van to the United States and who supported himself by making such trips. She still owed him $1,500. He had called her in Miami, and she told him that she was working and would repay him when she could. A concern of hers had always been that he would damage her reputation by telling people in her hometown that she had not paid. Later, when she ran into him on a Nicaraguan street, she assured him that she had come back only to attend to family problems and that when she returned to the United States, even though she had no intention of doing so, she would earn the money to pay him. Repaying U.S. $1,500 when one makes córdobas would take a lifetime, and he understood that. A few weeks later, as he attempted to leave Nicaragua for Mexico by plane, this time taking several young draft evaders with him instead of people from Estelí, he was arrested and put in prison. As a result, the debt was not a problem, at least not for the moment, and Leticia's reputation and credit in Estelí remained intact.

In the month that she had been back, Leticia's visits to her mother's house had been brief. She appeared to be distracted when she did come to Estelí and often spent her time with other friends and relatives. She hadn't even had lunch with Dora, Marta, or Omar. To them, she seemed changed by her experience in the United States, and her absence had affected their attitude toward her. They knew that she was having trouble with her husband because he had not tried to keep his infidelity a secret. Such problems, though, did not make her family more sympathetic. Marta, commenting on Leticia's behavior of the past year, said that a woman can always get another man, but she has just one mother. Dora, who is slowly succumbing to heart failure, feels abandoned by the very daughter who earlier had shouldered the worries of the entire family.

Leticia's problems are not separate or isolated from those of her country. The inability of her husband to support his family on his managerial wage, the strains that long separations bring, and the fear of death and loss that come with war—while striving to retain the improvements they have made in Nicaragua and to ensure a better future for Nicaragua's children—have affected Leticia and all those around her. Each day, Leticia walks close to hope and to despair along with her country. The struggle continues. As the epitaph of Estelí's martyred poet, Leonel Rugama, reads:

Leonel Rugama
rejoiced in the promised land
in the hardest month of the planting
with no choice but the struggle
very near death
but nowhere near
the end.

NOTES

1. Leonel Rugama, *The Earth Is a Satellite of the Moon*, trans. Sara Miles, Richard Schaaf, and Nancy Weisberg (Willimantic, CT, 1984), 101.
2. In August 1983 the exchange rate was 25 córdobas to one U.S. dollar. In August 1984 it was 74 córdobas to a dollar; in August 1985 it was 600; and in August 1986 it was 1,400. The black market paid a thousand more than that.

In Leticia's absence (November 1985 to July 1986), a tortilla went from 10 córdobas to 50 córdobas in Managua. The price of five pounds of beans rose from 16 córdobas to 300. When beans were otherwise unavailable, they could be obtained on the black market at 1,100 córdobas for a 1 lb.-4 oz. bag.

3. "Slow Motion toward a Survival Economy," *Envío* (Managua, Instituto Histórico Centroamericano) 5, no. 63 (September 1986): 14.

Index

Latin American Silhouettes
Studies in History and Culture

William H. Beezley and
Judith Ewell
Editors

Volumes Published

William H. Beezley and Judith Ewell, eds., *The Human Tradition in Latin America: The Twentieth Century* (1987).
Cloth ISBN 0-8420-2283-X
Paper ISBN 0-8420-2284-8

Judith Ewell and William H. Beezley, eds., *The Human Tradition in Latin America: The Nineteenth Century* (1989).
Cloth ISBN 0-8420-2331-3
Paper ISBN 0-8420-2332-1

David G. LaFrance, *The Mexican Revolution in Puebla, 1908–1913: The Maderista Movement and the Failure of Liberal Reform* (1989).
ISBN 0-8420-2293-7

Mark A. Burkholder, *Politics of a Colonial Career: José Baquíjano and the Audiencia of Lima*, 2d ed. (1990).
Cloth ISBN 0-8420-2353-4
Paper ISBN 0-8420-2352-6

Carlos B. Gil, ed., *Hope and Frustration: Interviews with Leaders of Mexico's Political Opposition* (1992).
Cloth ISBN 0-8420-2395-X
Paper ISBN 0-8420-2396-8

Heidi Zogbaum, *B. Traven: A Vision of Mexico* (1992). ISBN 0-8420-2392-5

Jaime E. Rodríguez O., ed., *Patterns of Contention in Mexican History* (1992). ISBN 0-8420-2399-2

Louis A. Pérez, Jr., ed., *Slaves, Sugar, and Colonial Society: Travel Accounts of Cuba, 1801–1899* (1992).
Cloth ISBN 0-8420-2354-2
Paper ISBN 0-8420-2415-8

Peter Blanchard, *Slavery and Abolition in Early Republican Peru* (1992).
Cloth ISBN 0-8420-2400-X
Paper ISBN 0-8420-2429-8

Paul J. Vanderwood, *Disorder and Progress: Bandits, Police, and Mexican Development*. Revised and Enlarged Edition (1992).
Cloth ISBN 0-8420-2438-7
Paper ISBN 0-8420-2439-5

Sandra McGee Deutsch and Ronald H. Dolkart, eds., *The Argentine Right: Its History and Intellectual Origins, 1910 to the Present* (1993).
Cloth ISBN 0-8420-2418-2
Paper ISBN 0-8420-2419-0

Steve Ellner, *Organized Labor in Venezuela, 1958–1991: Behavior and Concerns in a Democratic Setting* (1993). ISBN 0-8420-2443-3

Paul J. Dosal, *Doing Business with the Dictators: A Political History of United Fruit in Guatemala, 1899–1944* (1993). Cloth ISBN 0-8420-2475-1   Paper ISBN 0-8420-2590-1

Marquis James, *Merchant Adventurer: The Story of W. R. Grace* (1993). ISBN 0-8420-2444-1

John Charles Chasteen and Joseph S. Tulchin, eds., *Problems in Modern Latin American History: A Reader* (1994). Cloth ISBN 0-8420-2327-5
Paper ISBN 0-8420-2328-3

Marguerite Guzmán Bouvard, *Revolutionizing Motherhood: The Mothers of the Plaza de Mayo* (1994).
Cloth ISBN 0-8420-2486-7
Paper ISBN 0-8420-2487-5

William H. Beezley, Cheryl English Martin, and William E. French, eds., *Rituals of Rule, Rituals of Resistance: Public Celebrations and Popular Culture in Mexico* (1994). Cloth ISBN 0-8420-2416-6 Paper ISBN 0-8420-2417-4

Stephen R. Niblo, *War, Diplomacy, and Development: The United States and Mexico, 1938–1954* (1995). ISBN 0-8420-2550-2

G. Harvey Summ, ed., *Brazilian Mosaic: Portraits of a Diverse People and Culture* (1995). Cloth ISBN 0-8420-2491-3   Paper ISBN 0-8420-2492-1

N. Patrick Peritore and Ana Karina Galve-Peritore, eds., *Biotechnology in Latin America: Politics, Impacts, and Risks* (1995). Cloth ISBN 0-8420-2556-1   Paper ISBN 0-8420-2557-X

Silvia Marina Arrom and Servando Ortoll, eds., *Riots in the Cities: Popular Politics and the Urban Poor in Latin America, 1765–1910* (1996). Cloth ISBN 0-8420-2580-4 Paper ISBN 0-8420-2581-2

Roderic Ai Camp, ed., *Polling for Democracy: Public Opinion and Political Liberalization in Mexico* (1996). ISBN 0-8420-2583-9

Brian Loveman and Thomas M. Davies, Jr., eds., *The Politics of Antipolitics: The Military in Latin America*, 3d ed., revised and updated (1996). Cloth ISBN 0-8420-2609-6 Paper ISBN 0-8420-2611-8

Joseph S. Tulchin, Andrés Serbín, and Rafael Hernández, eds., *Cuba and the Caribbean: Regional Issues and Trends in the Post-Cold War Era* (1997). ISBN 0-8420-2652-5

Thomas W. Walker, ed., *Nicaragua without Illusions: Regime Transition and Structural Adjustment in the 1990s* (1997). Cloth ISBN 0-8420-2578-2   Paper ISBN 0-8420-2579-0

Dianne Walta Hart, *Undocumented in L.A.: An Immigrant's Story* (1997). Cloth ISBN 0-8420-2648-7 Paper ISBN 0-8420-2649-5

Jaime E. Rodríguez O. and Kathryn Vincent, eds., *Myths, Misdeeds, and Misunderstandings: The Roots of Conflict in U.S.-Mexican Relations* (1997). ISBN 0-8420-2662-2

Jaime E. Rodríguez O. and Kathryn Vincent, eds., *Common Border, Uncommon Paths: Race, Culture, and National Identity in U.S.-Mexican Relations* (1997). ISBN 0-8420-2673-8

William H. Beezley and Judith Ewell, eds., *The Human Tradition in Modern Latin America* (1997). Cloth ISBN 0-8420-2612-6 Paper ISBN 0-8420-2613-4

Donald F. Stevens, ed., *Based on a True Story: Latin American History at the Movies* (1997). ISBN 0-8420-2582-0

Jaime E. Rodríguez O., ed., *The Origins of Mexican National Politics, 1808–1847* (1997). Paper ISBN 0-8420-2723-8

Che Guevara, *Guerrilla Warfare*, with revised and updated introduction and case studies by Brian Loveman and Thomas M. Davies, Jr., 3d ed. (1997). Cloth ISBN 0-8420-2677-0 Paper ISBN 0-8420-2678-9

Adrian A. Bantjes, *As If Jesus Walked on Earth: Cardenismo, Sonora, and the Mexican Revolution* (1998). ISBN 0-8420-2653-3

Henry A. Dietz and Gil Shidlo, eds., *Urban Elections in Democratic Latin America* (1998). Cloth ISBN 0-8420-2627-4   Paper ISBN 0-8420-2628-2

A. Kim Clark, *The Redemptive Work: Railway and Nation in Ecuador, 1895–1930* (1998). ISBN 0-8420-2674-6

Joseph S. Tulchin, ed., with Allison M. Garland, *Argentina: The Challenges of Modernization* (1998). ISBN 0-8420-2721-1

Louis A. Pérez, Jr., ed., *Impressions of Cuba in the Nineteenth Century: The Travel Diary of Joseph J. Dimock* (1998). Cloth ISBN 0-8420-2657-6 Paper ISBN 0-8420-2658-4